PERFORMANCE OF MUTUAL FUNDS IN INDIA

PERFORMANCE OF MUTUAL FUNDS IN INDIA

A Comparative Study of Public and Private Sector Mutual Funds

Ti.M. Swaaminathan

GYAN

The publication of this book was financially supported by ICSSR and the responsibility for the facts stated, opinions expressed or conclusions reached are entirely that of the author and ICSSR accepts no responsibility for them.

ICSSR Consultant

Dr. H.C. Gautam, Gauhati University, Guwahati

Performance of Mutual Funds in India—
A Comparative Study of Public and Private Sector Mutual Funds

ISBN: 978-81-212-1128-4

Published in 2011 in India by
Gyan Publishing House
23, Main Ansari Road
New Delhi-1100052
Phones : 23282060, 23261060
Fax : 011-23285914
E-mail: books@gyanbooks.com
Website: www.gyanbooks.com

Laser Typesetting : Quick Media, Delhi
Printed at : Chawla Offset Printers, Delhi

Dedicated to My Beloved Parents

Mr. T. Maikandanthan

Mrs. M. Gowri Ammal

Contents

Foreword

Mutual fund is a trust that pools the savings of a number of investors who share a common financial goal. The money thus collected is then invested in capital market instruments such as shares, debentures and other securities. The income earned through these investments and the capital appreciations realized are shared by its unit holders in proportion to the number of units owned by them. Thus, a mutual fund is the most suitable investment for the common man as it offers an opportunity to invest in a diversified professionally managed basket of securities at a relatively low cost.

The performance of mutual funds depends on the performance of securities that make up the portfolio of the mutual fund. Mutual funds pool the money of investors and then invest this pool in the designated securities. Once this is done, the investors must understand that the performance of a particular scheme will depend on the performance of the underlying portfolio. It may be noted that the performance of a scheme is restricted by the underlying portfolio and no scheme can rise faster than the rise in underlying portfolio. Even within a particular category or group of schemes, the performance of all mutual funds schemes under that category would not be the same. What is required on the part of investors is to look at each of the scheme and its underlying portfolio. This will help them to know how and where their money is being invested and about the risk indirectly taken by them.

Mutual funds have emerged as an important intermediary in all the capital markets of the world. The mutual funds play and will continue to play an important role in the growth of the capital market in India. One of the reasons for mutual funds becoming popular in such a short period is that they offer low risk coupled with stability of income and are ideally suited for average and small investors who, otherwise, probably cannot operate in capital market. Growth of mutual funds in India, as well as, in all the capital markets of the world is a testimony to the fact that mutual funds provided specialized financial securities to the investors. Mutual funds provide different services to investors for making investment. Making investment in a mutual fund is more convenient as compared to dealing in the capital market. So, a mutual fund is a suitable investment for a common man as it offers an opportunity to invest in a diversified and professionally managed basket of securities at a relatively low cost.

The mutual fund industry plays a significant role in the development of the economy as well. Its buoyant growth leads to lower intermediation costs, more efficient financial markets and increased vibrancy of the capital markets and higher local ownership of financial assets. If retail investment is directed through the mutual fund route, it will lead to greater wealth creation in the long run. Thus, the industry can be one of the causative factors for a healthy economy. It can be said that mutual funds are vital to the health and prosperity of every nation.

The relation between risk and return determines the performance of a mutual fund. As risk is commensurate with return, therefore, providing maximum return on the investment made within the acceptable associated risk level helps in demarcating the better performance from the laggards. So there is always a tradeoff between risk and return. Even though a lot has been said and written about mutual funds little has been written about their performance. The methods that can be used to analyze the performance of mutual funds are varied and different. This study helps practitioners and academicians understand the differences among different mutual fund schemes and the methods of evaluating these schemes to identify the best that suits them. In the present study the two attributes of an investment viz., risk and return have been considered for detailed analysis.

Professor Ti.M.Swaaminathan, Assistant Professor of Commerce at Pachaiyappa's College for Men, Kanchipuram has analyzed the performance of public sector and private sector mutual funds in India for a period of five years from 2003-04 to 2007-08. He has compared the risk and returns of 130 sample schemes from the public and private sector mutual funds across four different categories viz., income, balanced, growth and equity linked savings schemes and also evaluated their performance. The sample schemes have been evaluated on the basis of IRR, and the models developed by Sharpe, Treynor, Jensen, Fama, Treynor and Mazuy among others. The sample schemes have also been ranked based on their overall performance in order to identify the best scheme.

This study has brought out that the asset under management of both public and private sector mutual funds had a fluctuating growth during this period. However the private asset management companies were able to amass huge amount of investment in a very short span of time. The analysis of the total risk of the schemes suggests that in the private sector, income schemes and growth schemes are less risky, whereas balanced schemes and equity linked schemes were less risky in public sector. The mean IRR scores of the private sector schemes is considerably higher than that of public sector schemes across all categories. Applying Sharpe and Treynor measure it has been found that higher number of public sector schemes under-perform the sensex and it is relatively less in the case of private sector schemes. Under Jensen's measure also, the private sector schemes outperform the public sector schemes.

This study has also brought out the private sector fund managers' stock picking ability which outweigh their counterparts in public sector. Further the returns earned by the schemes due to the systematic risk and the diversification of the schemes are also analyzed. The public sector schemes exhibit marginally better diversification than the private sector. The Treynor and Mazuy model to study the market timing ability shows the private sector to have better market timing ability than the public sector. All the above analyses have also been done across all the four categories namely income, balanced, growth and equity linked savings schemes. The overall performance ranking of all the 130 schemes lead to top five schemes, all from private sector and belonging to growth category.

This information about the mutual funds is the key for right selection and successful investment across mutual funds. In summary this book helps the reader to understand the intricacies of mutual fund industry and guide him in the evaluation and selection of a mutual fund scheme for investment, thus making him a successful investor. It has every information for a mutual fund investor.

Associate Professor of commerce,
Pachaiyappa's College,
Chennai, India.

RAJARAJEN VANJEKO

Preface

Investors' continuous search to increase their returns opened up a wide range of financial opportunities and instruments. Equities, derivatives and other such assets have become more and more information oriented over the period of time. Price changes of these assets are decided by global events occurring at faraway places. An ordinary investor does not have adequate skill, knowledge, time and inclination to keep track of such events, understand the impact and act with speed to transact business in the stock market. Financial intermediation had come into being to assist the interested investors through their services. Mutual fund is one such institution, which is a collective investment vehicle, formed with the specific objective of raising money from a large number of individuals and investing it according to pre set and specified objectives.

With the increase in domestic savings and improvement in deployment of investment through markets, the need and scope of mutual funds' operations has increased tremendously. The innovative contents with which mutual funds have been offered make the investors confident that product differentiation will reach the various income segments, geographical segments and risk bearing segments of investors. Thus, mutual funds have emerged as important players in the capital market thus helping in stabilizing the Indian capital market particularly the secondary market.

Over the years, the introduction of privatisation and globalisation measures since 1991 has opened up plethora of opportunities not only for better earnings, but also and concomitantly for investment. In the mutual fund industry too, the arrival of private sector along with the foreign players has significantly increased the investment choices on the one hand, while making informed decision making difficult, on the other. Moreover, the Asset Management Companies which deal with the mutual funds is also not too transparent in providing necessary information to the investors. This requires a comprehensive analysis about the performance of the mutual fund industry by taking a larger sample size, longer period of study and against two benchmark indices. This is done in this book with the application of all the measures and methods of performance analysis in order to throw more light on the performance of the mutual fund industry.

1

INTRODUCTION

In any country, development of capital market is an important pre-requisite for industrial development and business growth which would thereby contribute to economic development. A well integrated financial system could hasten economic growth, through channelising productive resources towards industrial development. Hence, mobilization of finance takes a prime position in the list of priorities in the agenda of economic growth. A well defined financial system would comprise of three components viz., lending institutions, borrowing institutions and more importantly, the financial intermediaries. It is an accepted fact that the efficiency of the financial intermediaries would, to a great extent determine the efficiency of the financial system.

Past several decades have noticed a phenomenal growth in savings and canalization of these savings as capital for business and industry. The earlier route of savings going to banks and banks in turn, financing industries has slowly got transformed to savings directly getting into business and industry. This has been facilitated by the development of capital market. A slow but steady growth in disposable income of the people in the recent past, availability of information, and change in their attitude towards risk and its disposition, etc., have largely encouraged people to resort to investment in financial assets and securities. The percentage share of net bank deposits in total financial savings which was 29 per cent in 1991-92, started to increase and touched 40 per cent in 1997-98. But, it declined to 28.7 per cent in 2001-02 before moving marginally up to 30.6 per cent in 2006-07. On the other, the proportion of investment in shares and debentures was at 22.0 per cent in 1991-92, fell sharply to 3.4 per cent in 1997-98. It increased marginally to 4.1 per cent in 2000-01, and again to 10.7 per cent in 2006-07.[1] Thus, there is a trade-off between bank deposits and investment in shares and debentures. That is, whenever there is an up beat mood in the market, investment in shares and debentures has increased and *vice versa*.

Constant endeavour on the part of the investors to better their returns opened up a wide range of opportunities, which resulted in financial services being provided and recognized as separate activity in itself. Equities and other fixed income instruments, derivatives and other such assets, over the period of time, have become more and more highly information oriented. Price changes of these assets are decided by global events occurring at far away places. A typical individual does not have adequate skill, knowledge, time and inclination to keep track of such events, understand the impact and act with speed to transact business in the stock market. Financial intermediation had come into being to assist the interested investors through their services. Mutual fund is one such institution, which is a collective investment vehicle, formed with the specific objective of raising money from a large number of individuals and investing it according to pre set and specified objectives.

Meaning and Mutual Funds

The word "mutual" signifies a vehicle wherein the benefits of investment accrue pro rata to all the investors in proportion to their investment. A mutual fund is the ideal investment vehicle for today's complex modern world. It is an institutional device through which the investors pool their funds to invest in a diversified portfolio of securities thus spreading and reducing the risk quotient. Through this investment vehicle, small and medium investors put their funds under the direction of an investment manager. These funds are invested in a wide variety of securities in such a way as to minimize risk while ensuring steady return.

Mutual fund is a special type of institution, which acts as an investment conduit. It is essentially a mechanism of pooling together the savings of a large number of investors for collective investments with an avowed objective of providing attractive yields and appreciation in their value. The mutual fund concept which has been popular in western part of the world has gained popularity in developing countries including India, to bridge the gap between supply and demand of capital in the market.

Significance of Mutual Funds

With the increase in domestic savings and improvement in deployment of investment through markets, the need and scope of mutual funds' operations has increased tremendously. The innovative contents with which mutual funds have been offered make the investors confident that product differentiation will reach the various income segments, geographical segments and risk bearing segments of investors. The mutual funds have emerged as important players in the capital market thus helping in stabilizing the Indian capital market particularly the secondary market.

The most appropriate way of spreading the culture of equity would be through some form of professionally managed institutionalized risk pooling mechanism. Mutual funds appear to be the most suitable vehicle for this endeavour. It is mainly so because, they offer many advantages to investors. There are thousands of investors who can invest small amounts in mutual funds and become players in capital market securities, which may not be financially possible or viable for them to take up directly; investors get a blend of better returns, liquidity and safety; funds are invested in a balanced -portfolio of investment whereby the contributors derive the benefits of diversification, spreading and minimization of risk. Numerous options are provided so that the investors can choose schemes or a combination of schemes to specifically suit their investment objective. On some of the schemes, tax shelter is also available, which has been provided with a view to encourage participation in investment in financial assets on a larger scale, especially by the salaried class.

Risks Involved in Mutual Funds

Mutual funds also involve risk which the investors have to confront while investing in the industry.

1. The companies in which the fund has invested might perform poorly, suffer mismanagement or otherwise meet with misfortune.
2. Some economic, political or other development might cause the overall market to fall, dragging down with it the holdings of one's particular fund.
3. The fund management, for instance, may be doing things the investor does not know about or wouldn't like if he did. What one thinks is a plain domestic equity-income fund might, in order to boost returns, invest in derivatives, invest overseas, or invest in growth companies that pay little or no dividend. In a downturn, the investor could be in for an unpleasant surprise. There is also the risk that the fund will under-perform a benchmark index, which means that management fees aren't buying any added value.

Mutual Funds in India

In India, Unit Trust of India (UTI) was the first institution in the form of investment trust, which was established, by an Act of Parliament in 1963. The Trust has, over a period spanning more than 44 years, successfully launched a variety of schemes to meet the diverse needs of lakhs of investors. The first scheme launched by UTI was the Unit Scheme 1964 (US 64) which became immediately popular even among the lower middle income class people, as everyone started buying the units of US 64. The net resource mobilisation made through this scheme which was Rs. 18.73 crore in 1964-

65, went up to Rs. 117.98 crore in 1993-94.[2] With a view to provide a wide range of choice to small investors, the government also permitted the public sector banks and financial institutions to launch mutual funds in the country since 1987. The entry of these institutions in this field provided the much needed competition. This warranted improving customer services through widening the choice. Banks provided a wide range of products/services in mutual funds by introducing innovative schemes built around their regular services and attempted to use their base to reach the investors.

The Indian financial system in general and the mutual fund industry in particular have taken a turn-around during the first half of 1990s. The new government formed in 1991, declared a series of policy measures intending to make the financial sector more viable and efficient, and to bring it closer to international standards. As a first step, the government accorded statutory status to Securities and Exchange Board of India (SEBI) as an autonomous body through the enactment of SEBI Act in 1992 for the promotion and regulation of the capital market. Later, through an ordinance on January 25, 1995 the government amended the SEBI Act, 1992 so as to arm the SEBI with additional powers for ensuring the orderly development of the capital market and to enhance its ability to protect the interest of investors. Under SEBI's control and regulation, the financial sector was opened up for entry of private players, both domestic and foreign. To a greater extent, leaving the market forces to play, SEBI reformed the capital market and ensured fair and healthy competition in all segments of the capital market. A significant impact of such reforms was the entry of private sector institutions into the mutual fund industry in 1993. From the investors point of view, this brought in the much needed qualitative improvement in the services in the form of substantial reduction in the time involved in transactions with the funds, information provision, transparency etc. The phase of growth in the private sector has also been faster than that of the public sector.

Mutual Fund : Basic Concepts

Some of the basic concepts associated with the mutual fund industry are explained here.

Net Asset Value (NAV): The performance of a particular scheme of a mutual fund is denoted by NAV. Mutual funds invest the money collected from the investors in securities markets. In simple words, NAV is the market value of the securities held by the scheme. Since market value of securities changes every day, NAV of a scheme also varies on a day to day basis. The NAV per unit is the market value of securities of a scheme divided by the total number of units of the scheme on any particular date.

Sale Price: The price investors have to pay when they invest in a scheme is called the Sale Price. This is also called as Offer Price. It may include a sales load.

Repurchase Price: The price at which a close-ended scheme repurchases its units from the investor is the Repurchase Price and it may include a back-end load. This is also called Bid Price.

Redemption Price: The price at which open-ended schemes repurchase their units from the investors is known as the Redemption Price, and close-ended schemes redeem their units on maturity. Such prices are NAV related.

Sales Load: This is a charge collected by a scheme from the investor when it sells the units, which is also called as 'Front-end' load. Schemes that do not charge a load are called 'No Load' schemes.

Repurchase or 'Back-end' Load: It is the charge collected by a scheme when it buys back the units from the unit-holders.

Types of Mutual Funds Schemes in India

A wide variety of mutual fund schemes exists to cater to the needs such as financial position, risk tolerance and return expectations etc of various segments of the population.

- **By Maturity Period**
  - ➢ Open - Ended Funds
  - ➢ Close - Ended Funds
- **By Investment Objective**
  - ➢ Growth Funds
  - ➢ Income Funds
  - ➢ Balanced Funds
  - ➢ Money Market Funds
  - ➢ Gilt Funds
  - ➢ Index Funds
- **Other Funds**
  - ➢ Sector Specific Funds
  - ➢ Tax Saving Funds
  - ➢ Load Funds

A. Funds according to Maturity Period:

A mutual fund scheme can be classified into open-ended scheme or close-ended scheme depending on its maturity period.

(i) **Open-ended Funds:** An open-ended fund or scheme is one that available for subscription and repurchase on a continuous basis. These schemes do not have a fixed maturity period. Investors can conveniently buy and sell units at NAV related prices which are declared on a daily basis. The key feature of open-end schemes is liquidity.

(ii) **Close-ended Funds:** A close-ended fund or scheme has a stipulated maturity period e.g. 5-7 years. The fund is open for subscription only during a specified period at the time of launch of the scheme. Investors can invest in the scheme at the time of the initial public issue and thereafter they can buy or sell the units of the scheme on the stock exchanges where the units are listed. In order to provide an exit route to the investors, some close-ended funds give an option of selling back the units to the mutual fund through periodic repurchase at NAV related prices. SEBI regulations stipulate that at least one of the two exit routes is provided to the investor i.e. either repurchase facility or through listing on stock exchanges.

B. Funds according to Investment Objective:

A scheme can also be classified as growth scheme, income scheme, or balanced scheme considering its investment objective. Such schemes may be open-ended or close-ended schemes. Such schemes may be classified mainly as follows:

(i) **Growth / Equity Oriented Funds:** The aim of growth funds is to provide capital appreciation over the medium to long- term. Such schemes normally invest a major part of their corpus in equities. Such funds have comparatively high risk. These schemes provide different options to the investors like dividend option, capital appreciation, etc. and the investors may choose an option depending on their preferences. The investors must indicate the option in the application form. The mutual funds also allow the investors to change the options at a later date. Growth schemes are good for investors having a long-term outlook seeking appreciation over a period of time.

(ii) **Income / Debt Oriented Funds:** The aim of income funds is to provide regular and steady income to investors. Such schemes generally invest in fixed income securities such as bonds, corporate debentures, Government securities and money market instruments. Such funds are less risky compared to equity schemes. These funds are not affected by fluctuations in equity markets. However, opportunities of capital appreciation are also limited in such funds. The NAVs of such funds are affected because of change in interest rates in the country. If the interest rates fall, NAVs of such funds are likely to increase in the short run and *vice versa*. However, long term investors may not worry about these fluctuations.

(iii) **Balanced Funds:** The aim of balanced funds is to provide both growth and regular income as such schemes invest both in equities and fixed income securities in the proportion indicated in their offer documents. These are appropriate for investors looking for moderate growth. They generally invest 40 per cent in equity and 60 per cent in debt instruments. These funds are also affected by fluctuations in share prices in the stock markets. However, NAVs of such funds are likely to be less volatile compared to pure equity funds.

(iv) **Money Market or Liquid Funds:** These funds are also income funds and their aim is to provide easy liquidity, preservation of capital and moderate income. These schemes invest exclusively in safer short-term instruments such as treasury bills, certificates of deposit, commercial paper and inter-bank call money, government securities, etc. Returns on these schemes fluctuate much less compared to other funds. These funds are appropriate for corporate and individual investors as a means to park their surplus funds for short periods.

(v) **Gilt Funds:** These funds invest exclusively in government securities. Government securities have no default risk. NAVs of these schemes also fluctuate due to change in interest rates and other economic factors as is the case with income or debt oriented schemes.

(vi) **Index Funds:** Index Funds replicate the portfolio of a particular index such as the BSE Sensitive index, S&P NSE 50 index (Nifty), etc. These schemes invest in the securities in the same weightage comprising of an index. NAVs of such schemes would rise or fall in accordance with the rise or fall in the index, though not exactly by the same percentage due to some factors known as "tracking error" in technical terms. Necessary disclosures in this regard are made in the offer document of the mutual fund scheme.

There are also exchange traded index funds launched by the mutual funds which are traded on the stock exchanges.

C. Other Funds:

(i) **Sector specific Funds:** These are the funds which invest in the securities of only those sectors or industries as specified in the offer documents. e.g., Pharmaceuticals, Software, Fast Moving Consumer Goods, Petroleum stocks, infrastructure, etc. The returns in these funds are dependent on the performance of the respective sectors/ industries. While these funds may give higher returns, they are more risky compared to diversified funds. Investors need to keep a watch on the performance of the sectors / industries and must exit at an appropriate time.

(ii) **Tax Saving Funds:** These schemes offer tax rebates to the investors under specific provisions of the Income Tax Act, 1961 as the Government offers tax incentives for investment in specified avenues. e.g., Equity Linked Savings Schemes (ELSS). Pension schemes launched by the mutual funds also offer tax benefits. These schemes are growth oriented and invest predominantly in equities. Their growth opportunities and risks associated are like any equity-oriented scheme.

(iii) **Load Funds:** A Load Fund is one that charges a percentage of NAV for entry or exit. That is, each time one buys or sells units of the fund, a charge will be payable. This charge is used by the mutual fund towards marketing and distribution expenses. The investors should take the loads into consideration while making investment as these affect their yields / returns.

Organisational Structure of Indian Mutual Funds

There are four constituents of a mutual fund in India, viz.,

1. the sponsor,
2. the board of Trustees or Trustee company,
3. the asset management company and
4. the custodian.

The sponsor of the Trust holds the Trust property on behalf of investors who are the beneficiaries of the Trust. The sponsor is also required to contribute at least 40 per cent of the capital of the asset management company which is formed for managing the assets of the Trust. The assets of the Trust comprise of properties of the schemes which are floated by the asset management company with the approval of the Trustees. Schemes may have different characteristics - they may be open or closed ended or may have a particular investment focus or portfolio composition. Finally, the safe custody of assets of the Trust is entrusted to one or more custodians.

Performance Evaluation of Mutual Funds

The performance evaluation of mutual funds has been a widely discussed and researched issue in the area of finance. Harry Markowitz was the pioneer to stress the importance of portfolio, its construction and evaluation. Sharpe, Treynor, Jensen and Fama who developed and perfected the methods and measures, were all his followers. These contributions opened up new areas for research particularly regarding the relationship between risk and return.

It is normally considered that empirical evidence on mutual fund performance confirms the original version of the efficient market theory and that expenditure on research and analysis is wasted in such a market where prevailing stock prices contain the impact of all information. Taken as a whole, the results based on the empirical studies which analysed the performance of mutual funds were contradictory in the sense that some studies supported the efficient market theory while others were found to be inconsistent with that hypothesis. The performance evaluation of the mutual funds industry is relatively new which kick-started with the tools developed and introduced by Markowitz, Sharpe and others in the 1950s and 1960s. This opened the flood-gates for numerous empirical articles particularly in the Western countries, based mainly on the United States data.

In India also, many attempts have been made to analyse the performance of mutual funds using the data of the Indian MF industry. Some of them have studied the performance of open-ended funds including growth, income and balanced schemes, while some have analysed the performance of close-ended funds. Similarly, studies have also analysed the performance private sector and / or public sector funds. The time period of analysis obviously differs among them and so also the results. Most of the studies have applied the measures of Sharpe, Treynor, Jensen and Fama. The differing results basically imply that the nature of results depend on the benchmark index applied and also on the period of study.

Statement of Problem

Performance of the mutual funds depends on the performance of the stock market and also on the credit market. The integration of the Indian economy with the global economy has exposed the domestic market to the volatility of the global market. The entry of Foreign Institutional Investors has especially aggravated the degree of volatility of the stock market. Moreover, deregulation of the banking sector by the Government has given impetus to the individual banks to change the interest rates. Of late, interest rates on the Government securities are also fluctuating more often compared to the earlier periods. All these factors directly impinge upon the performance of the mutual funds, where the ability of the fund managers has now come under the scanner. On the other hand, there is no clear consensus on the suitability of the models developed by Sharpe, Treynor and the Capital Asset Pricing Model (CAPM) to study the performance of mutual funds in the Indian capital market conditions.

These diversified opinions emanates particularly due to the following reasons:

- Most of the studies are uni-dimensional as they have concentrated either on public sector funds or private sector funds:
- Most of the studies have taken only two or three categories of schemes for analysis;
- The number of schemes chosen or the sample size is normally less than 100;
- The length of the study period, which is an important factor in determining the outcome, is also short;
- In most of the studies, the number of observations available for each of the sample scheme is not uniform for all the selected schemes, which renders inter-sector and intra-sector comparison meaningless;[3]
- Most of the studies have used only one market index as benchmark (mostly Sensex).

All these point to a lack of comprehensiveness in the attempt to evaluate the performance of mutual funds in India. Hence, in order to arrive at an acceptable and meaningful result, a comprehensive attempt needs to be made by considering the mutual funds schemes from both public and private sectors, including various categories, with a long study period, with an identical number of observations for all the sample schemes and most of all by taking both Indian stock market indices, viz., Sensex of the Bombay Stock Exchange and Nifty of the National Stock Exchange as benchmark. The present study is an attempt in this direction.

Need for the Study

The small investors turn to mutual funds to reap the twin advantages of less risk and higher return. But, the advent of liberalisation measures through the 1991 economic reforms brought in by the Government has made the investors more vulnerable to the fluctuations of the international capital market. The deep spikes in the Indian stock market as well as credit market, particularly in the recent years have not only resulted in less return, but also negative returns. Moreover, the mushrooming growth of the asset management companies and also the plethora of new schemes introduced by them make the choice of investors next to impossible. The ordinary investors may not be aware of the challenges involved and the required tools to select the schemes for his investment. Hence, it is not only pertinent but also quite warranted to analyse the performance of the schemes of the asset management companies. In this backdrop, it is relevant to analyse the performance of Indian mutual fund industry especially by taking the recent years' data. Hence, the present study aims to examine the performance of the Indian mutual fund industry by taking the five years' data from 2003-04 to 2007-08 as the study period.

Objectives of the Study

The objectives of the present study are:

1. To analyse the growth of the Household sector savings in India and its components since 1993-94;
2. To study the growth trends in the Indian mutual fund industry since 1996-97 in terms of the number of asset management companies, number of schemes, amount mobilised, etc.;
3. To analyse the sample schemes in terms of their risk and returns, systematic risk (beta) and unique risk in terms of Sensex and Nifty separately;
4. To examine the performance of the sample schemes in terms of Sensex and Nifty separately

   A. based on risk and return (i.e.)

      (*a*) Internal Rate of Return (IRR)

      (*b*) Sharpe

      (*c*) Treynor and

      (*d*) Jensen

   B. measures based on stock selecting ability and diversification (i.e.)

      (*a*) Sharpe differential and

      (*b*) Fama's break up of returns in terms of beta, diversification and selectivity;

5. To evaluate the market timing ability of the sample schemes with the application of Treynor and Mazuy's model separately in terms of Sensex and Nifty;
6. To rank the sample schemes on the basis of their overall performance
7. To verify the normality of mutual funds' returns

8. To bring out the relationship between the investment size and performance of the schemes and
9. To suggest to investors suitable portfolio performance measures.

Period of the Study

This study analyses the performance of the Indian mutual fund industry for the period 2003-04 to 2007-08. This has been a very active period in the stock market, in the sense that the market enjoyed a long bull run, as the Sensex shot up from 2,997 in April 11, 2003 to 20,827 in January 11, 2008. This attracted not only huge number of investors but also new asset management companies. Hence, this period was chosen for the present analysis.

Methodology of the Study

This study is based on secondary data. To analyse the performance of the Indian MF industry, the NAVs of the selected sample schemes have been gathered for the study period, 2003-04 to 2007-08. The performance of the sample schemes is analysed by applying the following measures and methods that have been developed over the years by various researchers.

Return and Risk

Return of the mutual fund is calculated by taking the month-end NAV of the selected mutual funds. The NAVs of the sample schemes have been collected for the period April 2003 to March 2008. The NAVs are adjusted for dividends, assuming dividends are reinvested at the ex-dividend rate. The return is computed as follows:

$$R_{pt} = \ln (NAV_t / NAV_{t-1})$$

where, R_{pt} is the return of the scheme 'p' based on NAV in period 't', where 't' is the given month-end and ln is the natural logarithm.

The average return of the scheme is computed as follows:

$$AR_p = \sum_{t=1}^{n} R_{pt} / n$$

where AR_p is the average return of the scheme and 'n' is the total number of observations.

Mutual funds' returns involve huge degree of risk as they depend on the performance of the stock market. Hence, the performance of the mutual funds should be assessed only in the backdrop of risk. In investment, risk is defined as the degree of the probability of variations in the expected returns.

Variability of returns measured in terms of standard deviation is the most popular indicator which is the statistical measure of dispersion in returns. The smaller the deviation, the smaller the spread in the distribution and consequently, the lesser the risk involved. It is measured as:

$$\sigma_p = 1/n\left(\sum_{t=1}^{n}\{R_{pt} - AR_p\}^2\right)^{1/2}$$

where σ_p is the standard deviation of the sample scheme which indicates the scheme's total risk, R_{pt} is the return over a period of time and AR_p is the average return.

Return and Risk of Benchmark Indices

The return and risk of the mutual fund schemes, especially those of balanced and growth schemes depend to a great deal on the performance of the stock market. Hence, to explore the performance of the sample schemes further, it is pertinent to compare the return and risk of the sample schemes with that of the stock market. Here, the Sensitivity Index (Sensex) of the Bombay Stock Exchange (BSE) and Nifty of the National Stock Exchange (NSE) are taken as the benchmark indices. Though both these indices provide the market prices of more or less the same stocks, on any day, due to differences in trading volume, stock prices differ between these two indices. Morcovor, the weightage given to each of the stock in the basket also differs, which will impact the return and risk of the sample schemes. Hence, in this analysis, these two indices are used as benchmark indices. Monthly index data for both Sensex and Nifty that are provided by the Bombay Stock Exchange and National Stock Exchange are used here to compute their average return and total risk. The average return of the indices is computed as:

$$R_{mt} = \ln (I_t/I_{t-1})$$

where, R_{mt} is the return of the benchmark index in period 't', where 't' is the given month-end, I_t is the value of the index at time period 't' and 'ln' is the natural logarithm to the base 'e'.

The average return of the scheme is computed as follows:

$$AR_m = \sum_{t=1}^{n} R_{mt} / n$$

where AR_m is the average return of the index and 'n' is the total number of observations. Similarly, the total risk (standard deviation) of the market return is also computed:

$$\sigma_m = 1/n\left(\sum_{t=1}^{n}\{R_{mt} - AR_m\}^2\right)^{1/2}$$

where σ_m is the standard deviation of the index which indicates the market's total risk, R_{mt} is the return over a period of time. In order to understand the performance of the sample schemes in the backdrop of the return and risk of the market index, these are compared under the following four scenarios.

ONE: $AR_p > AR_m$; $\sigma_p < \sigma_m$

The schemes which come under this situation will be the best performing ones as their returns outperform the market, while they are less risky than the market.

TWO: $AR_p < AR_m$; $\sigma_p < \sigma_m$

This situation exhibits lower return of the schemes along with lower risk compared to the market index and thus comes second.

THREE: $AR_p > AR_m$; $\sigma_p > \sigma_m$

In this scenario, not only the schemes' returns are higher than the market, but also their risk. Thus, though investors can earn more under this situation, the greater risk quotient will make the investors wary.

FOUR: $AR_p < AR_m$; $\sigma_p > \sigma_m$

Situation four is the worst case where the sample schemes' returns are low compared to the market, while their risk is higher.

Systematic Risk

Systematic risk (beta – β) is that part of the total risk which is influenced by the changes in the overall market. It indicates the relationship between the scheme's return and the market return. This is caused by the external factors which are not under the control of the fund manager and hence, should be borne by all the fund managers. Beta is obtained by applying CAPM version of the market model. The estimable version of CAPM is:

$$R_{pt} = \alpha + \beta_p R_{mt} + e_{pt}$$

where α is the constant term, β is the systematic risk and 'e' is the error term. This explains the systematic component (β_p) of the total risk (β_p) of the scheme in terms of market return (R_{mt}). Beta can either be positive or negative and it indicates the impact on the risk of the scheme for a unit of change in the overall market.

Unique Risk and Diversification

The basic feature of mutual funds is the element of risk reduction through the process of diversification. Under efficient or optimal market conditions, a portfolio can be conditioned in such a way that the only risk involved is the risk of the market (systematic risk). However, the fund managers' efforts are constrained to the extent of imperfections in the capital market. This gives rise to what is known as unsystematic or unique risk. This risk is unique to the concerned fund, which arises mainly due to lack or inappropriate diversification. Diversification is a process of spreading the investment in more than one security. It irons out the spikes in the values of security prices. When one more security is added to an already existing portfolio, the return on the portfolio becomes the weighted average of the returns of the securities in the portfolio. As more and more securities are added to the portfolio, dispersion among the returns of the securities get reduced. This can be termed as the well diversified portfolio.

The R^2 is derived from the estimation of the market version of the CAPM, the linear regression model. The extent of diversification which is used to reduce the degree of unique risk is measured by R^2 of the portfolio. In a well-diversified portfolio, the unique risk is completely eliminated and only the market part of the risk (systematic risk) is retained. In such a case, the value of R^2 will be equal to one and on the other extreme, if R^2 value is equal to zero, it implies the complete absence of diversification or zero-diversified portfolio. Hence, R^2 ranges from 0 to 1 and cannot be negative.

Performance Evaluation of Mutual Funds

Performance of the mutual funds is evaluated in terms of its net asset value through different measures viz., Internal Rate of Return, the methods developed by Sharpe, Treynor, Jenson, Sharpe differential measure, Fama's measures, Treynor and Mazuy's market timing ability among others. These methods capture different aspects of the mutual fund like its superior returns in terms of total risk, systematic risk, stock selecting ability, impact of diversification and market timing ability of the fund managers.

Internal Rate of Return

The internal rate of return (IRR) is the rate which equates the present value of the cash inflow from the holding of mutual fund units to the acquisition cost. The cash inflow includes dividends and the terminal price. These are adjusted for bonus and rights issues. It is also comparable with other alternative investment measures. The IRR is calculated as follows :

$$P_0 = \frac{D_1}{(1+r)} + \frac{D_2}{(1+r)^2} + \frac{D_3}{(1+r)^3} + \dots + \frac{D_n}{(1+r)^n} + \frac{P_n}{(1+r)^n}$$

where, P_0 is the initial investment, which is the face value of the mutual fund unit;

$D_1, D_2 \ldots D_n$ represents the cash dividends received by the investor during the given period;

r is the rate of return and

P_n is the NAV at the end of the maturity period.

If no dividends are paid, IRR is calculated as:

$$P_0 = \frac{P_n}{(1+r)^n}$$

Sharpe Ratio

In assessing the performance of managed portfolios, a number of theories and models have been introduced, of which Sharpe's Ratio[4] is the pioneer. It is a ratio which indicates the relationship between the portfolio's additional return over the risk-free return and the total risk of the portfolio. This is also known as the reward to variability ratio ($RVAR_p$) and expressed as:

$$RVAR_p = \frac{AR_p - AR_f}{\sigma_p}$$

For purposes of analysis, the Sharpe's ratio is compared with the benchmark ratio, in which the total risk of the market ($ó_m$) is taken in the denominator. If the Sharpe ratio is higher than the benchmark ratio, it implies lesser variability of the portfolio compared to that of the market.

Treynor Ratio

Another measure of fund performance in terms of return and risk is that of Treynor.[5] It measures the relationship between fund's additional return over risk-free return and fund's volatility measured in terms of beta. This is called as reward to volatility (RVOL) and measured as:

$$RVOL = \frac{(AR_p - AR_f)}{\beta_p}$$

The benchmark for comparison with the measure of performance is calculated by taking the ratio of the additional return of the market over the risk-free return against the volatility of the overall market. But, as the volatility of the market is considered as unity, the benchmark comparison measure is taken the difference between the market return and the risk-free return.

Jensen Measure

A slight variation of the CAPM model was proposed by Jensen, in which a measure of market return, an important component of systematic risk is suggested by using beta. Jensen segregates the return due to market variations from that of risk premium; the alpha (á) value is identified as the risk-adjusted return of the scheme.[6] Symbolically the model is given as follows:

$$R_p - R_f = \alpha + \beta (R_m - R_f) \quad \text{OR}$$

$$\alpha = (R_p - R_f) - (\beta [R_m - R_f])$$

Higher the α value indicates better performance by the scheme.

Sharpe Differential Measure

In performance assessment, not only the extent of diversification, but also the quality of diversification needs to be analysed, which depends upon the nature of stocks that are added to the portfolio. Only by identifying the correct stocks, can the fund manager reduce the risk and / or increase return. This is indicated as the efficiency of fund managers in stock selection. This is termed as differential return by Sharpe, under his Differential Return Model.[7] This differential return is the risk adjusted return, net of risk-free return and systematic risk measures of return. This is calculated as follows:

$$\alpha = AR_p - \left[AR_f + \frac{(AR_m - AR_f)\sigma_p}{\sigma_m} \right]$$

where σ_m is the total risk of the market and α is Sharpe's differential measure, which suggests better stock selecting ability by the fund manager, if its value is higher and *vice versa*.

Fama's Break up of Return

The risk adjusted performance measures mentioned above analysed the overall performance of the sample funds. However, it is required to breakdown the performance into different components, which was done by Fama. According to Fama, portfolio return consists of four components viz., risk-free return, compensation for systematic risk (beta impact), compensation for inadequate diversification (diversification impact) and net superior returns due to selectivity (selectivity impact).[8]

Impact of Beta: It is the systematic risk explained by the â of the scheme. It explains the return due to change in the uncontrollable market value pertaining to the scheme. It is calculated as:

$$\beta (AR_m - AR_f)$$

Impact of Diversification: This explains the reward obtained for the extent of diversification of the scheme by the fund manager. Symbolically:

$$(AR_m - AR_f)\ [(\sigma_p / \sigma_m) - \beta]$$

Impact of Selectivity: It is meant to explain the reward for effectiveness of diversification of the fund manager. It is not only the degree of diversification, but also its quality, in the form of picking up the right stocks. It is calculated as:

$$(AR_p - AR_f) - [(\sigma_p / \sigma_m)(AR_m - AR_f)]$$

All the three measures need to be positive to indicate positive impact and return by that particular measure and a negative value suggests that fund manager is unable to earn anything positive. For instance, if the selectivity measure is negative, it implies that the fund manager's stock selection has resulted in negative return.

Treynor and Mazuy's Model of Market Timing Ability

This model attempts to analyse the timing ability of the funds with the help of a quadratic equation.[9] Market timing ability involves shifting of funds from one equity to another, based on the prediction of future direction of the market. This equation traces the relationship between the fund's return and market return. It is measure as follows :

$$(R_{pt} - R_{ft}) = \alpha + \beta (R_{mt} - R_{ft}) + \gamma (R_{mt} - R_{ft})^2 + e_{it}$$

α, β and γ are the constants, of which ã is the measure of the fund's timing ability. The ã value cannot be negative as the term is squared; if it is equal to zero, it implies the complete absence of timing ability, while a positively significant value suggests the existence of market timing ability on the part of the fund manager. Significant t-values imply better market timing ability of the concerned fund managers.

Overall Performance Ranking

When the performance of the mutual funds is evaluated under different methods in terms of both Sensex and Nifty, it cannot be expected that a single scheme will outperform others under all methods. When some schemes perform better under some methods and some other schemes perform better under some other methods, picking a single scheme as the best scheme will become difficult. To overcome this, the overall performance ranking of the schemes is done to identify the best scheme. The schemes are ranked under the measures that include IRR, average return, standard deviation, Sharpe, Treynor, Sharpe Differential measure, Jensen, Fama's impact of beta, diversification and selectivity and also market timing ability under both indices, and their final average ranks are arrived at. Schemes are ranked according to their performance, as the scheme with highest value under a measure is given the rank of 1, except under standard deviation, in which case the scheme with the least value is given the rank of 1. Finally, the scheme with the lowest average rank becomes the best scheme.

Normality of Returns

The stock market and the bond market jointly determine the returns of the mutual fund schemes and both these markets fluctuate considerably. Thus, the return of the schemes is also expected to fluctuate. Hence, it is important to verify the normality of the returns. This will help in ascertaining whether the returns produced by the schemes are normally distributed over the study period or not. The normality of the returns of both the sample schemes and market indices can be tested with the application of Kurtosis is measured as:

$$\text{Kurtosis} = \frac{\mu_4}{\mu_2^2} - 3$$

where, μ_4 is the 4th moment about the mean and μ_2 is the second moment. 'Minus 3' is used to make the kurtosis of the normal distribution equal to zero. If the kurtosis measure is positive, the curve is leptokurtic (more peaked) and if it is negative, the curve is platykurtic (more flat).[10]

Investment Size and Performance of the Scheme

The size of investment of the scheme and its performance in terms of net asset value are expected to have a direct and positive relationship, since the scheme with larger investment can afford more facilities and personnel and due to economies of scale, they can also reduce the average cost. This lower average cost will help it to lower expenses which will push up its net asset value. These two variables, viz., size of investment and net asset value are taken for all sample schemes for the concluding year of the study period, that is 2007-08, since year-wise data on the size of investment for all the sample schemes is not available. The monthly NAVs of the schemes are annualised for estimation purposes. This is tested with the application of an uni-variate regression model, which is specified as:

$$NAV_i = \alpha + \beta \, SIZE_i + e_i$$

where, NAV_i is the annualised NAV of the ith scheme pertaining to the year 2007-08 and $SIZE_i$ is the size of investment attracted by that scheme in the given year. á is the intercept term and â is the slope co-efficient, while 'e' is the normal error term. However, as both NAV and SIZE of the sample schemes are quite varying in their magnitude, both the variables are taken in their log form to reduce the impact of such magnitude. The equation to be estimated is:

$$\ln NAV_i = \alpha + \beta \ln SIZE_i + e_i$$

where 'ln' is the natural logarithm. A positive beta with a statistically significant t-value will prove the anticipated relationship between the two variables.

Sampling Design

The Indian mutual fund industry, which was evolved as a public sector industry, now includes private sector players as well. As on 31st March 2008, there were 33 asset management companies in India. Asset management companies from both the sectors were considered in sample selection. This sampling design is based on multi-stage purposive proportionate sampling technique.

In the first stage based on the availability of data for the study period, those asset management companies which had data for the whole five years (April 2003 to March 2008) were considered. Out of the 33 asset management companies which consisted of 28 private sector and 5 public sector companies, all those in the latter group were included, while 17 from the private sector were purposively included in the sample, since only those asset management companies had the sample schemes with the monthly data for the five year period, April 2003 to March 2008.

As open-ended funds portray the true spirit of open market and the de-regulated nature of the industry, only open-ended schemes were selected from the chosen asset management companies.

In the next stage of sampling, the categories of schemes were decided. Many categories like income, balanced, growth, ELSS, liquid, fund of fund, index, sector based funds, gilt funds, etc., exit in the market, though income, balanced, growth and ELS schemes are operated by all the asset management schemes. Also, these schemes are more popular among the investors and also they basically differ in their investment objectives and thus these four categories of schemes viz., income, balanced, growth and ELS schemes have been purposively chosen.

In the fourth stage of sampling, the sample schemes were selected. For this purpose, prime importance was attached to the availability of data with all 60 observations (monthly data for the five year period). Thus, between the two sectors and among the 22 sample asset management companies, within the open-ended schemes which included income, balanced, growth and ELS schemes, the total number of schemes available in the study period and the number of sample schemes chosen are shown below:

Category	Public Sector		Private Sector		**Total**	
	Available	Sample	Available	Sample	**Available**	**Sample**
Income	120	14	186	29	**306**	**43**
Balanced	22	12	102	28	**124**	**40**
Growth	13	8	41	20	**54**	**28**
ELSS	7	6	32	13	**39**	**19**
Total	**162**	**40**	**361**	**90**	**523**	**130**

Source: Accessed at www.amfi.com

In deciding the number of schemes in each category, equal weightage was given to both public and private sectors, as 25 per cent of the existing schemes (as on March 31, 2008) were selected. The final selection of schemes was again done purposively, as only those schemes which had 60 observations (monthly net asset value data from April 2003 to March 2008) were chosen. This was done in order to make the result comparable both inter-sector and intra-sector. Monthly data on the net asset value of the sample schemes are taken from the website www.amfiindia.com, the month-end Sensex and Nifty index values were collected from the web site: www.econstats.com, and the 91-day treasury bill rates for the study period have been gathered from various issues of Reserve Bank of India Bulletin.

Limitations of the Study

In both the sectors, both open-ended and closed-ended schemes are available. But, in the latter, in most of the asset management companies, there exist only income and growth schemes, which reduce the possibility of meaningful inter-sector comparison. Hence, closed-ended funds were not included in this study. Similarly, apart from the four selected categories of schemes, viz., income, balanced, growth and ELSS, others like gilt, liquid, fund of funds and floating rate schemes are also prevailing in the market. However, these schemes are not operated by all the asset management companies and also they are not available for the total study period. Hence, those schemes could not be included in the study.

The selected study period - April 2003 to March 2008 - might seem not too long. But, when the date was taken beyond 2003, like April 2001 or even April 2002, the number of schemes available for the whole study period came down drastically. Hence, to achieve a trade-off between the number of observations and number of sample schemes, this study period could not be extended beyond the selected one.

Plan of the Study

This study comprises of six chapters.

The First Chapter presents the general introduction to the Indian mutual fund industry, the basic concepts involved in mutual funds, the structure of the industry, the problem of the study, its need, objectives, methodology and limitations of the study.

The subject of performance evaluation of managed portfolio has attracted the interest of many scholars all over the world, as it directly deals with people's investment decisions. These scholars have developed and modified the measures of performance evaluation of managed portfolios. Some of the important studies are reviewed in Chapter Two.

In Chapter Three, origin of the mutual fund industry at the global level is traced along with the evolution of the industry in India under various phases. It also presents the growth of the industry in terms of number of mutual funds, number of schemes and amount mobilised.

Chapter Four begins with the analysis of the household sector savings in India since 1993-94. It analyses the sample schemes in terms of their risk and returns, systematic risk and unique risk.

In the Fifth Chapter, the performance of the sample schemes is evaluated in terms of IRR, and by using the measures developed by Sharpe, Treynor and Jensen, Sharpe's differential measure, Fama's break-up of return and the Treynor – Mazuy's model of market timing ability. The analysis of overall performance of the schemes is also included. Moreover, it also verifies the normality of returns of the sample schemes and also examines the relationship between the size of investment and performance of the scheme.

Chapter Six presents the summary of the study, the conclusion and suggestions to investors regarding the portfolio performance measures to adopt.

References

1. Report on Currency and Finance, RBI, various reports.
2. UTI, Annual Reports, various years.
3. Most of the studies which evaluated the performance of mutual funds have not paid much attention to the number of observations. Thus, the number of observations of the sample schemes was not uniform. That is, when some schemes had 60 observations, in a five year study period, some other and

schemes had less number of observations. In such a analysis, inter-sector and also intra-sector comparison of the results will not be possible and also meaningful.

4. Sharpe, William F., (1966), "Mutual Fund Performance". Journal of Business, 39, Supplement, pp. 119-138.
5. Treynor, Jack l., and Mazuy, Kay K., (1966), "Can Mutual Funds Outguess the Markets". Harvard Business Review, 44, pp. 131-136.
6. Jensen, Michael C., (1968), "The Performance of Mutual Funds, 1948-67", Journal of Finance, 23, pp.389-416.
7. Sharpe, William F, (1975), "Adjusting for Risk in Portfolio Performance Measurement." Journal of Portfolio Management, Winter, pp. 29-34.
8. Fama, Euegen F.,(1972), "Components of investment Performance", Journal of Finance, 27, pp. 551-567.
9. Treynor J.L., Mazuy K. (1966): "Can Mutual Funds Outguess the Market?", Harvard Business Review 44, p131-136.
10. Gupta, S.P., (2006), Statistical Methods, sultan Chand and sons, New Delhi, pp.350-351.

2

REVIEW OF LITERATURE

The performance evaluation of mutual funds has been a widely discussed and researched issue in the area of finance. Harry Markowitz was the pioneer to stress the importance of portfolio, its construction and evaluation. Sharpe, Treynor, Jensen and Fama who developed and perfected the methods and measures, were all his followers whose contributions are still being considered as path-breaking. These contributions opened up new areas for research particularly regarding the relationship between risk and return.

It is normally considered that empirical evidence on mutual fund performance confirms the original version of the efficient market theory and that expenditure on research and analysis is wasted in such a market where prevailing stock prices contain the impact of all information. Taken as a whole, the results based on the empirical studies which analysed the performance of mutual funds were contradictory in the sense that some studies supported the efficient market theory while others were found to be inconsistent with that hypothesis. The performance evaluation of the mutual funds industry is relatively new which kick-started with the tools developed and introduced by Markowitz, Sharpe and others in the 1950s and 1960s. This opened the flood-gates for numerous articles particularly in the Western countries, based mainly on the United States data.

In India, the mutual fund industry, to begin with was exclusively in the hands of the public sector, which was represented by the Unit Trust of India (UTI). Only in the 1990s private players and other public sector participants were allowed to enter the industry. Hence, analysis of mutual fund performance is of recent origin in India. In this chapter some of the important research studies which analysed the performance of mutual funds in India and abroad are reviewed.

International Studies

The evaluation of mutual funds' performance, especially in the Western countries, has attracted a lot of attention, as mentioned earlier, and thus, numerous studies are available in this area. Some of the important studies made in other countries are reviewed in this section.

Markowitz (1952)[1] proposed how rational investors will use diversification to optimize their portfolios, and how a risky asset should be priced. The Modern portfolio theory models an asset's return as a random variable, and models a portfolio as a weighted combination of assets; the return of a portfolio is thus the weighted combination of the assets' returns. He found that assets were affected differently by economic and other forces (interest rates, oil prices, weather, etc.). Risk can be reduced by investing in a diversified group of stocks, especially those whose individual movements help nullify the overall impact of the variability of the others. Stated another way, the important asset characteristic one refers to as risk (i.e. volatility, as measured by standard deviation) depended not upon individual volatility, but on how assets behave relative to each other. Markowitz's grand contribution was, therefore, in providing the formal conceptual framework to implement a rather simple idea. Because investors are concerned with the return on their entire portfolio of assets, the risk of any individual asset is relevant only in so far as it contributes to the risk of the overall portfolio.

Friend *et al* (1964)[2] had done an extensive and systematic study of mutual funds. The study considered 152 mutual funds with annual data from 1953 – 1958. Using their own benchmark, the authors found that mutual funds earned an (unweighted) average annual return of 12.4 percent, while their composite benchmark earned a return of 12.6 percent. On the whole, it was revealed that overall results did not suggest widespread inefficiency in the industry. The study also compared returns of the funds across turnover categories and expenses categories. The analysis did not reveal a strong relationship between turnover rates and performance. The same was found to be true in respect of expenses.

Friend *et al* (1965)[3] comprehensively examined investment policy and investment company performance, for the period 1952-58. Investment policy encompassed the structure of the portfolios, frequency, timing and methods of portfolios changes. Portfolio structure was influenced by the announced investment objectives. The common stocks accounted for a predominant share in growth funds (87.25 percent) and balanced funds (63.0 percent). The impact of funds' portfolio policies on activity in the capital market was determined by the distribution of their security holding by market place of listing. Invested funds, as they expanded in size, tended to change the percentage of their portfolio they held in securities other than those listed on particular exchange. As the size of individual transactions increased, it experienced a larger percentage of their portfolio sales in the over-the-counter markets by means of secondary offerings. The study confirmed that the validity of explanation of relatively higher portfolio turnover rates in the smaller funds could depend on the age of the fund and the expectation that a newly formed fund could record higher turnover rates as it shifted its assets from a temporary liquid position into permanent portfolio of securities. In view of a variety of investment objectives announced by the funds, a single measure of performance for all funds and for all investors were considered inadequate. During the period studied performance records varied considerably, both within and among the type of funds, but on the average it conformed rather closely to the behaviour of securities market as a whole. About half the funds performed better, and half worse, than unmanaged portfolios. These performance records were largely influenced by size, composition and portfolio structure.

Another study was conducted by **Sharpe** (1966)[4] to develop a composite measure that considered return and risk. He conducted an evaluation of performance of 34 open-ended mutual funds during the period 1954-63 by the measure so developed. He found the performance of 11 funds to be superior to that of Dow Jones Industrial Average (DJIA). His reward to variability ratio for each fund was significantly less than the same measure applied to the DJIA over the study period. Based on this evidence Sharpe concluded that on an average mutual fund performance was distinctly inferior to an investment in the DJIA. An analysis of relationship between fund performance and its expenses ratio indicated that good performance was associated with low expenses ratio. On the other hand, only a low relationship was discovered between sizes and performance. Notably, there was some consistency in the risk measure over time for alternative funds. His study concluded that out of 34 funds selected 19 had outperformed the benchmark in terms of total risk.

Treynor and **Mazuy** (1966)[5] found no statistical evidence to conclude that investment managers of the 57 funds had successfully outguessed the market. The results suggested that the returns for an investor in mutual fund completely depended on fluctuations in the general market. This is not to say that a skilful management cannot provide investors with a rate of return that is higher in both bad and good times than the one provided by market averages.

Jensen (1968)[6] developed a composite portfolio evaluation technique that considered returns adjusted for risk differences and used it for evaluating 115 open-end mutual funds during the period 1945-66. For the full period Jensen examined returns net of expenses and gross of expenses. The analysis of net returns indicated that 39 funds (34 per cent) had above average returns. Using gross returns, 48 funds (42 per cent) showed above average results and 67 (58 per cent) had below average results. He concluded that evidence on mutual fund performance indicated that not only these 115 mutual funds on the average were not able to predict security prices well enough to outperform buy and hold policy, but also that there was very little evidence to show that any individual fund was able to perform significantly better than that expected return.

Smith and **Tito** (1969)[7] reviewed three widely used composite measures of investment performance, examined their inter-relationships and put forward a fourth alternative measure. This measure was then compared conceptually and empirically, identifying some aspects of differentiation in the process. While ranking the funds on the basis of ex-post performance, alternative measures produced a little difference. In contrast, when performance comparisons were made with the market, conclusions differed widely as evidenced by earlier studies. In view of this, modified Jensen measure based on an estimating equation and slope co-efficient was recommended.

Carlson (1970)[8] examined the overall performance of mutual funds for the period 1948-67 with emphasis on analyzing the effect of market series used over different time periods. The analysis of performance relative to the market indicated that results were heavily dependent on the market series used, viz., S&P 500, NYSE composite or DJIA. For the total period, almost all fund groups outperformed DJIA but only a few had gross returns that were better than those for S&P 500 or New York Stock Exchange (NYSE) composite, although there was consistency in the risk adjusted performance measures. Carlson also analyzed performance relative to size, expense-ratio and a new-fund factor. The results indicated no relationship with size or expense ratio, although there was a relationship between performance and a measure of new cash into funds.

Arditti (1971)[9] attempted to add an important dimension to the Sharpe study and showed that when the third moment of fund annual rate of return was introduced, Sharpe's conclusion got altered. As a measure of direction and size of distribution tail, the third moment provided significant information. Thus, contrary to Sharpe's observation, it was found that average fund performance could no longer be judged inferior to the performance of DJIA. Yet another important fallout was that either fund managers were willing to forego return at a given level of risk or were tempted to opt more variability in exchange for larger annual returns.

Simonson (1972)[10] noted that mutual funds had shown consistent shift toward speculative investment policies over time. The concern over this shift in behaviour stemmed from the risk, which altered the new disposition of fund managers to strive for quick gains from short-term extrinsic increase in the price-earning ratios of securities. The study also identified the measure of systematic skewness explaining alleged shift among mutual funds towards more highly aggressive investment policies and apparent increase in the diversity of investment policies from fund to fund over times.

Williamson (1972)[11] made a comparative ranking of 180 funds over the period 1961-65 with their ranking over the subsequent five year time period 1966-70. The absence of correlation between rankings over the two time periods for the entire group of 180 funds was consistent with the identical investment ability of most of the fund managers. The study also highlighted the growing prominence of volatility in the measurement of investment risk.

Fama (1972)[12] suggested alternative method for evaluating investment performance with finer breakdowns of performance. He developed methods for distinguishing part of an observed return due to the ability to pick up the best securities at a given level of risk (selectivity) from the part that is due to the prediction of general market price movements (timing). He also suggested methods for measuring effects of foregone diversification in the event of an investment manager deciding to concentrate his holdings in what he considered as a few winners. The study also presented a multi period model that allowed evaluation both on return and portfolio that could be subdivided into two parts, viz., the return for security selection and return from risk bearing. Various finer subdivisions of both selectivity and risk were also presented. To a large extent, the suggested models were an attempt to combine concepts from modern theories of portfolio selection and capital market equilibrium with more traditional concepts of what constituted good portfolio management.

Klemosky (1973)[13] analyzed investment performance of mutual funds based on quarterly returns for 40 funds during 1966-71. The analysis identified bias in Sharpe, Treynor and Jensen measures, which could be removed by using mean absolute deviation and semi-standard deviation as risk surrogates. The resultant performance measure was claimed to be a better risk adjusted measure than composite measures derived from the CAPM.

John McDonald (1974)[14] examined performance of 123 mutual funds relating it to the stated objective of each fund. The results indicated a positive relationship between objectives and risk measures, that is, risk increasing with the objective becoming more aggressive. Rate of return generally increased with aggressiveness and as expected, there was a positive relationship between return and risk. The relationship between objective and risk-adjusted performance indicated that more aggressive funds experienced better results, although only one-third of the funds did better than aggregate market.

Meyer's (1977)[1515] findings based on stochastic dominance model re-validated Sharpe' s findings with the caution that these were relevant to the mutual fund performance in designated past period rather than implications for the future.

Malkiel (1977)[316] attempted to develop some theoretical principles concerning the valuation of shares of close-ended investment companies, with a sample of 24 major close-end stock funds over an eight year period 1967-74. The time series analysis showed an important additional attraction to close-end funds, their discounts narrowed when market fell and widened when market rose. The covariance of fund premium with market movements suggested that close-end funds were particularly attractive investments when it was less than one. The study concluded that pricing of close end investment company shares did provide an example of a market imperfection in the valuation of capital assets.

Thompson (1978)[17] investigated the extent to which discounts and premiums provided information about future expected rates of return on close-end investment company shares. It was found that discounted fund shares, adjusted for risk, outperformed the market during the period 1940-1975. Funds selling at a premium appeared to have been bad investment over the same period. It concluded that two-parameter CAPM failed to describe the return generating process of close-end funds.

Kon and **Jen** (1978)[18] empirically estimated the levels of systematic risk and performance of 49 mutual funds over the period 1960-71 based on monthly data by using Sharpe, Linter and Mossin and Blake model as benchmark equilibrium. The results indicated that a very substantial fraction of mutual funds had two levels of systematic risk during each of three sub periods. It also examined the performance bias and reproduced the same in favour of high risk mutual fund portfolios as found by Klemkosky and McDonald. In the process, it found switching regression estimates as unbiased risk-adjusted measures of performance. The study demonstrated that, if fund managers had no forecasting ability, then the findings of Blake, Jensen and Sharpe would appear inconsistent.

Guy (1978)[19] summarized general behaviour of forty-seven investment trusts by grouping them into equal-and-value weighted portfolios with monthly price and investment returns for the period 1960-70. By using traditional performance measures developed by Jensen, Treynor and Sharpe, it found that the results were significantly different from zero. The absence of superior performance validated market efficiency hypothesis. It also investigated two additional performance measures, viz., empirical estimates of security market line and the zero-beta form of CAPM and obtained significant measures of performance.

Cornell (1979)[20] contested Mayers and Rice methodology based on CAPM and pointed out that CAPM could not be resurrected as a practical tool for performance measurement, thus outlining a performance measure based only on returns. This measure was found robust as it was capable of correctly designating superior performance in the context of CAPM, arbitrage pricing theory (APT) and many other equilibrium models of security prices.

Ang and **Chua** (1979)[21] examined the mean-variance measures and found them unsatisfactory in evaluating investment performance in view of the systematic bias. The study attributed it to the asymmetry of return distributions at small intervals and failure to appropriate holding period influencing systematic bias. It showed the superiority of performance measures that considered asymmetry of distributions along with mean and variance.

Fabozzi *et al (*1980)[22] empirically identified a more general form of rate of return-generating model for 85 funds during 73 months period from December 1965 to December 1971. It was found that a significant number of funds exhibited a functional form, which differed significantly from traditional linear and logarithmic rates of return generating process. Such a departure resulted in a specification bias for the systematic risk estimate although the bias was not found material when monthly rates were estimated. The study also empirically investigated the relationship between functional form parameter and residual of the model.

Hendrickson and **Merton** (1981)[23] derived a statistical framework for both parametric (using models based on assumptions) and non-parametric tests (which do not make assumptions about the distribution of the variable) of market timing ability. If the manager's forecasts were observable, the parametric test could be used without further assumptions on distribution of security returns. If not, the parametric test under the assumption of either CAPM or multi-factor return structure could be used. This permitted identification and separation of gains from market timing skills and from stock selection skills.

Jobson and **Korkie** (1981)[24] derived asymptotic distribution of the estimates of Sharpe and Treynor performance measures and also developed multivariate performance comparison measures with corresponding asymptotic distributions. The behaviour of these new performance measures was evaluated in small samples. Sharpe's 'z' statistics was found to be well behaved in single comparison and also for multiple comparisons. Similarly, Sharpe's chi-square was also discovered to be reasonably behaved. The powers of the tests were also found to be quite sensitive to the population co-efficient of variation. However, multivariate test-statistics based upon Treynor measure was not very satisfactory.

Reilly (1982)[25] studied the performance of open-end mutual funds over 15 years period, 1966-80 and found that return of all the funds was quite close to that of the market. On the basis of return alone, 12 funds outperformed the market. The study noted large range of fund returns indicating inadequacy of portfolio diversification. Similarly, the two risk measures (standard deviation and beta) exhibited a wide range, but generally consistent with expectations. Specifically, 14 funds had a standard deviation larger than market, which was found consistent with the lack of complete diversification. The performance of individual funds was very consistent for alternative performance evaluation models. Sharpe's model indicated that 13 funds had a higher value than the market and the Jensen's model indicated 13 of the 20 having positive intercepts, with only one being statistically significant. These results indicated that, on average, sample funds out performed the market during the period of study.

Kon (1983)[26] proposed an empirical methodology for measuring the market-timing performance of an investment manager and provided evidence for a sample of mutual funds. The results indicated that at the individual fund level there was an evidence of significant superior timing ability and performance. The multivariate tests also produced results consistent with efficient market hypothesis. That is, fund managers as a group had no special information regarding expectations on returns of market portfolio.

Chang and **Lewellen** (1984)[27] employed the parametric statistical procedure developed by Hendrickson and Merton to empirically evaluate investment performance of mutual funds. This procedure and associated findings were compared with those of prior investment performance evaluations. The new procedure produced more favourable judgment about mutual fund security selection performance in aggregate and the performance evaluations of various individual funds in which fewer fund managers displayed more market skills than before. The study concluded that the fund managers were collectively unable to outperform a passive investment strategy, an endorsement of the market efficiency.

Hendrickson (1984)[28] empirically investigated market timing ability of 116 open-end mutual funds for the period 1968-80. The findings of the study did not support the hypothesis that mutual fund mangers were able to follow investment strategies that successfully time the return on market portfolio. It found no evidence to support that forecasters were more successful in their market timing activity with respect to predicting large changes in the value of market portfolio relative to smaller changes. The absolute magnitude of returns on the market portfolio did not have any influence on measures of performance evaluation.

Davanzo and Nesbit (1987)[29] pointed out that traditional compensation structure had hardly any relation with typical performance objectives like outperforming market averages. It found asset based fees more akin to the compensating corporate officers in relation to the size of their company or division and net profits. As a result money managers had an incentive to become large, a characteristic frequently cited as hampering otherwise good firms. Tying management compensation directly to the portfolio performance objective would prevent sponsors from paying high fees for mediocre results. Although any active stock or bond manager could be eligible for a performance fee, managers with high fees would be the best candidates from the sponsor's viewpoint, as the sponsor would not have to pay high fee unless the manager produced high returns.

Kane and **Marks** (1988)[30] developed exact conditions under which Sharpe's measure would correctly and completely order market timer according to ability. The derived conditions were necessary, sufficient and observable. The study compared these derived conditions to empirical estimates. The practice of using quarterly portfolio return data would frequently result in a failure of the Sharpe measure to order market timers according to their ability. However, such failures could be greatly reduced by more frequent sampling of managed portfolio returns.

Grinblatt and **Titman** (1989)[31] reported that superior performance existed particularly among the aggressive growth funds and in those funds with smallest net asset values. Incidentally, these funds also had the highest expenses. As a result, their actual returns net of expenses did not exhibit superior performance. It indicated that investors could not take advantage of the superior abilities of portfolio managers.

Ippollito (1989)[32] tested the efficiency of capital markets when information is costly to obtain. If formation is free, then market efficiency implies security prices incorporate all available information. This hypothesis was tested using 143 mutual funds for a 20 year period from 1965 to 1984, for the US market. The author applied the CAPM and concluded that net of all fees and expenses, except load charges, the selected mutual funds had outperformed the index funds on a risk-adjusted basis. The industry alpha, though significantly positive, was not sufficiently large to overcome the load charges that characterised the majority of funds in the sample. Thus, on balance, the evidence was consistent with the notion that expenses and charges affiliated with mutual funds were offset by superior results, a condition that characterised efficient markets, in the presence of costly information.

Cumby and **Glen** (1990)[33] examined the performance of 15 US-based internationally diversified mutual funds during the period 1982-88 by using

Jensen's measure and Grinblatt and Titman's positive period weighing method. The study did not notice any evidence that the funds, either individually or as a whole, provided investors with performance that surpassed that of a broad international equity index over the period under study.

Ankrim (1992)[34] calculated beta values for 25 small cap funds with minimum of four years standing in order to demonstrate attribution of investment manager's excess performance among allocation, selection, and interaction effects. The study produced evidence to suggest that the risk of the portfolios of at least some managers differed from that of benchmark. For many managers, the proposed risk adjustments were found near to zero. These were the mangers whose average portfolio beta was very close to the benchmark betas.

Coggin *et al* (1993)[35] empirically examined selectivity and market timing performance of US equity pension fund managers and found that, regardless of the choice of benchmark portfolio or estimation model, the average selectivity measure was positive and the average timing measure was negative to the choice of benchmark when managers were classified by investment style. Beta analysis revealed some real variation around the mean values for each measure. The 80 percent probability intervals for selectivity revealed that best mangers produced substantial risk-adjusted excess return.

Blake *et al* (1993)[36] examined two samples of bond funds using linear and non-linear models and found that bond funds have underperformed relevant indices – post expenses. The result was robust across choice of models. On average, the study noted that a percentage point increase in expenses led to a percentage point decrease in performance. It found no evidence of predictability of future performance based on past performance.

Grinblatt and **Titman** (1994)[37] concluded that mutual fund performance evaluation measures generally yield similar inferences with the same benchmark and that inferences vary even from the same measure, with different benchmarks. The analysis of determinants of fund performance revealed that test employing fund characteristics such as net asset value, load, expense, portfolio turnover and management fee reported better performance of the fund managers to earn abnormal returns.

Malkiel (1995)[38] examined fund performance and the extent of survivorship bias and found that in aggregate, funds had underperformed benchmark portfolios both before management expenses and net of expenses. The study noted, performance persisting during the 1970s was lacking during the 1980s. Survivorship bias had appeared to be more important than noted by the other studies. In short, this study failed to provide any reason to abandon the belief that securities markets were remarkably efficient. It also pointed out that investors would be considerably better off by purchasing a low expenses index fund, than by trying to select an active fund manager who appeared to possess a hot hand.

Ferron and **Wather** (1996)[39] attempted to modify classical performance measures, to take account of well-known market indicators and to remove some of the biases that plagued traditional measures through conditional performance evaluation, based on monthly data for 63 mutual funds and lagged dividend and treasury bill yields as market indicator. It also highlighted that traditional measure like Jensen's alpha had more often understated the performance. The same was reported about the market timing ability of fund mangers. On the whole, the result suggested that incorporating public information variables into the analysis of investment performance was important.

Gruber (1996)[40] attempted to resolve the puzzle relating to fast growth of mutual funds in spite of inferior performance of actively managed portfolios. The study reported that average mutual fund had negative performance compared to the market and provided evidence to support the persistence of performance. It resolved the puzzle that sophisticated clientele withdrew money from mutual funds in the event of poor performance, whereas these mutual funds found money from disadvantaged clientele under such circumstance.

Elton *et al* (1996)[41] examined predictability of mutual funds' performance based on risk adjusted returns and found past performance predicative of risk adjusted future performance. It also demonstrated application of modern portfolio techniques on past data to improve selection, which permitted construction of portfolio of funds that significantly outperformed a rule based on the past rank alone. The portfolio so selected was reported to have small, but statistically significant, positive risk-adjusted returns during a period when mutual funds in general had negative risk-adjusted returns.

Busse (1999)[42] had used daily mutual fund returns to shed new light on the question of whether or not mutual fund managers are successful market timers. Previous studies found that funds were unable to time the market return. He studied the funds' ability to time market volatility. He showed that volatility timing is an important factor in the return on mutual funds which led to higher risk-adjusted returns. The returns of surviving funds were especially sensitive to market volatility, whereas those of non-survivors were not.

Carhart (1997)[43], using a sample free of survivor bias, demonstrated that common factors in stock returns and investment expenses almost completely explained persistence in equity mutual funds' mean and risk-adjusted returns. On the basis of data collected from 1892 diversified equity funds for the period January 1962 to December 1993, the study found that the only significant persistence not explained by the study was concentrated in strong underperformance by the worst- return mutual funds. The results did not support the existence of skilled or informed mutual fund portfolio managers.

The study made by **Cai** and **Yamada** (1997)[44] analysed the performance of Japanese open-type mutual funds for the 1981-1992 period, taken from 1151 mutual funds. Using Jensen's measure, the study opined that regardless of the performance measures and benchmarks employed, most of the Japanese mutual funds underperformed the benchmarks by between 3.6 per cent and 10.8 per cent per year. The selected funds invested more in the large stocks with low book-to-market ratios. But this feature did not explain the underperformance. A possible explanation was the dilution effect caused by inflow of funds.

Detzler *et al* (1999)[45] in their paper studied the risk and return characteristics of global bond mutual funds during 1988-95. The actively managed funds did not demonstrate superior performance; net of expenses, against a wide range of benchmark the performance was negatively related to fund expenses. In the study period, returns on global bond funds were sensitive to exchange rate movements, even after controlling for local currency returns on country bond indices. The funds had high exposure to the European, the Canadian and the US bond markets and were least sensitive to the Japanese Bond index. The funds did not outperform the US Bond index, suggesting that expenses might have outweighed diversification benefits during the sample period.

Wermers (2000)[46] analysed the performance of US mutual funds by using the quarterly portfolio holdings for all the US equity mutual funds which existed during 1975 to 1994. The study applied the characteristic selectivity measure, characteristic timing measure and the average style measure to segregate the performance of the mutual funds. It had found that funds hold stocks that outperform the market by 1.3 per cent per year, but their net returns underperform by 1 per cent. Of the 2.3 per cent difference, 0.7 per cent was due to the underperformance of non-stock holdings, whereas 1.6 per cent was due to expenses and transaction costs. Thus, the study concluded that funds pick stocks well enough to cover their costs.

Dahlquist *et al* (2000)[47] studied the Swedish mutual funds from 1992 to 1997 for 210 funds. It analysed the relationship between fund performance and fund attributes through the alpha in a linear regression of fund returns on different benchmark assets, thereby allowing for time-varying betas. The estimated performance was then used in a cross-sectional analysis of the relationship between performance and fund attributes like past performance, flows, size, turnover and expenses. The results showed that good performance occurs among small equity funds, low fee funds, funds whose trading activity was high and in some cases funds with good past performance.

In his study, **Khorana** (2001)[48] examined the impact of mutual fund manager replacement on the subsequent fund performance with the help of 393 US equity and bond fund managers who were replaced over the 1979-1991 period. Using the regression analysis, the study had documented significant improvements in post-replacement performance relative to the past-performance of that fund. On the other hand, replacement of overperforming managers resulted in the deterioration in post-replacement performance. The author had found evidence supporting the presence of strategic risk-shifting in the fund portfolio prior to the replacement. Moreover, the level of portfolio turnover activity decreased significantly in the post-replacement period. And, the replacement of poor performance was preceded by significant decreases in net new inflows in the fund.

Pastor and **Stambaugh** (2002)[49] constructed optimal portfolios of equity funds by combining historical returns on funds and passive indices with prior views about asset pricing and skill. By including both benchmark and non-benchmark indices, they distinguished pricing-model inaccuracy from managerial skill. Investing in active mutual funds can be optimal even for investors who believe active managers cannot outperform passive indices. Optimal portfolios excluded hot-hand funds even for investors who believed momentum is priced. The large universe of funds offered no close substitutes for the Fama-French and momentum benchmarks.

The study conducted by **Prather** *et al* (2004)[50] provided a comprehensive examination of recent mutual fund performance in the US by analyzing a large set of both mutual funds and fund attributes in an effort to link performance to fund-specific characteristics. The results indicated that the hypothesized relationship between performance and the explanatory variables was generally upheld. After taking into consideration general market conditions and fund investment objective, the characteristic variables that related to fund popularity, growth, cost, and management also explained the performance. Finally, after controlling for survivorship and benchmark error as well as fund-specific factors, the results refuted the performance persistence phenomenon.

Using an international database containing 103 German, UK and US ethical mutual funds **Bauer** *et al* (2005)[51] reviewed and extended previous research on ethical mutual fund performance. By applying a multi-factor model they solved the benchmark problem most prior ethical studies suffered from. After controlling for investment style, they found little evidence of significant differences in risk-adjusted returns between ethical and conventional funds for the 1990-2001 period. Introducing time-variation in betas, however led to a significant under-performance of domestic US funds and a significant out-performance of UK ethical funds, relative to their conventional peers. Finally, they differentiated previous results by documenting a learning effect. After a period of strong under-performance, older ethical funds were finally catching up, while younger funds continued to underperform both the index and conventional peers.

Mutual fund mangers are the agents of investors and their efforts to improve their performance are influenced by either explicit or implicit incentive structures within fund organisations. An efficient fund evaluation should control for organisational elements that affect managerial incentives in evaluating their performance. The study made by **Choi** (2006)[52] proposed an incentive compatible to maximise investors gross returns net of managerial compensation. With the help of linear regression model this theoretical study provided not only an incentive compatible performance measure but also a tool for improving managerial efficiency by identifying the sources of inefficiency.

Huang *et al* (2007)[53] presented a simple rational model to highlight the effect of investors' participation costs on the response of mutual fund flows to past fund performance. By incorporating participation costs into a model in which investors learn about managers' ability from past returns, they showed that mutual funds with lower participation costs had a higher flow sensitivity to medium performance and a lower flow sensitivity to high performance than their higher-cost peers. Using various fund characteristics as proxies for the reduction in participation costs, they provided empirical evidence supporting the model's implications for the asymmetric flow-performance relationship.

Keswani and **Stolin** (2008)[54] employed a British data set of monthly fund inflows and outflows differentiated between individual and institutional investors. They documented a robust smart money effect in the United Kingdom. The effect was caused by buying (but not selling) decisions of both individuals and institutions. Using monthly data available post-1991 they showed that money was comparably smart in the United States.

The value of active investment management is traditionally measured by alpha, beta, tracking error, and the Sharpe and information ratios. These are essentially static characteristics of the marginal distributions of returns at a single point in time, and do not incorporate dynamic aspects of a manager's investment process. **Lo** (2008)[55] proposed a new measure of the value of active investment management that captures both static and dynamic contributions of a portfolio manager's decisions. The measure was based on a decomposition of a portfolio's expected return into two distinct components: a static weighted-average of the individual securities' expected returns, and the sum of covariances between returns and portfolio weights. The former component measured the portion of the manager's expected return due to static investments in the underlying securities, while the latter component captured the forecast power implicit in the manager's dynamic investment choices. This measure was computed for long-only investments, long/short portfolios, and asset allocation rules, and was particularly relevant for hedge-fund strategies where both components were significant contributors to their expected returns, but only one former garnered the high fees that hedge funds typically charge. Several analytical and empirical examples were provided to illustrate the practical relevance of these new measures.

Barras et al (2008)[56] developed a new technique to properly account for false discoveries, or funds which exhibit significant alphas by luck alone. They identified the proportion of funds with truly positive or negative performance in any segment of the cross-sectional alpha distribution, even with cross-fund dependencies in estimated alphas. They found that 26.6% of U.S. domestic-equity funds exhibited truly negative alphas (net of expenses and trading costs), while only 0.6% exhibit truly positive alphas over the 1975 to 2006 period. They also found a much higher proportion of skilled fund managers (9.6%) when they examined alphas before expenses (but after trading costs). Their findings suggested some important implications. First, the large growth in the number of actively managed funds resulted in a much lower proportion of truly skilled funds, and, second, the large number of actively managed funds did not result in a competitive level of fund fees and expenses.

Indian Studies

Despite the tremendous growth in the mutual funds industry in India, especially in the recent past and the abundant availability of literature on the tools and techniques required for the evaluation of their performance, the number of research studies on this subject is not too large. In India, some important studies pertaining to the mutual funds were made prior to 1998, which include Gupta (1974), Lee and Rahman (1990), Sarkar (1991), Obaidullah and Sridhar (1991), Barua *et al* (1991), Gangadhar (1992) and Shashikant (1993) among others. However, the studies conducted after 1998 have concentrated more on the evaluation of performance of the mutual funds industry.

Gupta (1974)[57] evaluated the performance of mutual fund industry by segmenting several subgroups by broad investment goals and objectives for the period 1962-71. The performance models devised by Sharpe, Treynor and Jensen were used. The study evaluated results by using both Dow Jones Industrial Averages (DJIA) and S&P500 of the US as market indices. The results obtained indicated that these performance models led to identical results. Also that almost all mutual fund subgroups outperformed the market using DJIA, except the income and balanced groups which based on S&P500. It also showed that return per unit of risk varied with the level of volatility assumed and that funds having higher volatility exhibited superior performance than the others. It also pointed out that all types of funds outperformed the market irrespective of choice of market index and performance measure.

Lee and **Rahman** (1990)[58] empirically examined market timings and selectivity performance of mutual funds by using simple regression technique to separate stock selection ability from market timing ability. The inputs to the model were return earned on fund and those earned on market portfolio. The results indicated some evidence of micro and macro forecasting ability of fund managers.

Sarkar (1991)[59] critically examined mutual fund performance evaluation methodology and pointed out that Sharpe and Treynor's performance measures rank mutual funds similarly on performance in spite of their differences in methodology.

Obaidullah and **Sridhar** (1991)[60] evaluated the performance of two major growth oriented mutual funds, viz., Mastershare and Canshare and concluded that these funds provided abnormal returns. Mastershare did it on a total risk adjusted basis and Canshare on a market risk-adjusted basis. The study provided contradictory evidence to the near strong efficient market hypothesis for these funds.

Barua *et al* (1991)[61] made a pioneering attempt to evaluate the performance of 'Master Share' scheme of UTI from the investor point of view. They employed the CAPM and computed the risk of the Master Share scheme for the period 1987-1991. The risk-adjusted performance was measured using Sharpe, Jensen and Treynor ratios. The benchmark selected was the 'Economic Times ordinary share price index'. The study concluded that Master Share had performed better in systematic risk, but not in terms of total risk.

Gangadhar (1992)[62] in his study pointed out that capital market was indeed undergoing a metamorphosis of unprecedented growth with the opening of the economy, enlargement of foreign investment, and disinvestments of government's holding in public sector undertakings. These booming conditions would, therefore, provide new avenues conducive for floating mutual funds.

Sarkar (1992)[63] examined the prospects of investment in mutual fund vis-à-vis other security alternatives and held the view that mutual funds are the best investment for those who had modest amount to invest.

Shashikant (1993)[64] critically examined the rationale and relevance of mutual fund operations in the Indian money market. It was pointed out that mutual funds would definitely be able to offer investors a reliable medium for short-term investment and therefore, could emerge as low-risk and low return investment avenue for conservative investors.

Shukla and **Singh** (1994)[65] tested the proposition whether portfolio manager's advance professional education resulted in superior performance and found that equity mutual funds managed by professionally qualified managers were riskier but better diversified than the others. It was also pointed out that these fund mangers outperformed others as a group, although performance difference was not considered statistically significant.

Saha and **Murty** (1994)[66] highlighted the relevance and importance of mutual funds and discussed an analytical framework for performance evaluation and justified the use of portfolio selection techniques in stock selection and portfolio composition. They emphasized that the performance evaluation models provided effective decision support system and thus facilitated informed judgment.

Jaideep and **Majumdar** (1994)[67] evaluated the performance of five growth-oriented schemes for the period from February 1991 to August 1993. They employed the CAPM to evaluate the performance. They also evaluated the boom period performance of the schemes during the first quarter of 1992 by employing the Jenson model. They concluded that the selected mutual fund schemes did not offer superior returns during the study period than the market in general. However, they also opined that in the boom periods the funds performed well.

Shah and **Thomas** (1994)[68] studied the performance of 11 mutual fund schemes, on the basis of market price data. The weekly returns were computed for these schemes since their commencement to April 1994. Jensen and Sharpe measures were used to evaluate the performance of the schemes. They concluded that except UGS 2000 of the UTI, none of the schemes earned superior returns than the market, in general. The risk of these schemes was found to be very high which implied that the funds might be inadequately diversified.

Kaura and **Jayadev** (1995)[69] evaluated the performance of five growth-oriented schemes in the year 1993-94, by employing the Sharpe, Treynor and Jensen measures. According to them, Master Gain 91, Can Bonus and Ind-Sagar had performed better than the market in terms of systematic risk but not in terms of total risk.

Khorana (1996)[70] found an inverse relationship between probability of managerial replacement and fund performance by taking growth rate in fund asset base and its portfolio returns as two separate measures of performance.

Chordia (1996)[71] provided an explanation for diversity in investment strategies and fees of open-end mutual funds. The empirical evidence was found consistent with model predictions that such fees dissuaded redemption in open-end funds and that fund held more cash when there was uncertainty about redemption.

Gupta and **Sehgal** (1998)[72] evaluated investment performance of 80 mutual fund schemes in the Indian market over a four-year period (1992-96). It tested the propositions relating to fund diversification, consistency of performance, parameter of performance and objective stationary in addition to examining risk-return relationship. The empirical results reported in the study indicated that mutual fund industry had performed reasonably well for the Indian market. However, it noticed lack of adequate portfolio diversification. The study produced evidence to support consistency of performance and non-stationary over time was noted in relation to risk- return parameters. Finally, a significant and positive risk-return relationship was documented by the study when standard deviation was used as a risk measure.

Chander (2002)[73] analysed the investment performance of 34 mutual funds schemes which included both public sector and private sector funds for the period 1997 to 2001, against the benchmark of Bombay Stock Exchange Sensex. The study made use of various measures like Sharpe, Treynor, and Jensen ratios. It concluded that the majority of the sample funds recorded higher average return as compared to the benchmark. The study also suggested that frequent buying and selling is the best investment strategy in view of greater element of volatility in the Indian capital market.

Ravindran and **Rao** (2003)[74] examined the performance of 269 open-ended Indian mutual funds consisting of growth, balanced and income funds from both public and private sectors for the period September 1998 to April 2002. The evaluation was carried out through Treynor ratio, Sharpe ratio, Jensen measure and Fama measures. It suggested that 58 schemes were able to satisfy the investors' expectations based on both premium for systematic risk and total risk.

The study made by **Sodhi** and **Jain** (2004)[75] analysed the performance of 26 equity mutual funds drawn from 22 Asset Management Companies belonging to both public and private sectors. They compared the rate of return generated by equity mutual funds against 364 days T-bills for the period 1993-2002. They concluded that the equity mutual funds had overall inferior performance in comparison to risk-free return.

Gupta and **Amitabh**'s (2004)[76] study assessed the investment performance of 57 growth schemes for the period April 1999 to March 2003. With the application of different evaluation measures like Sharpe, Treynor and Jensen apart from a regression analysis, the study found no conclusive evidence suggesting the point that the performance of sample mutual funds was superior to the market but some funds did perform better.

Muthappan and **Damodharan** (2006)[77] evaluated the performance of Indian mutual funds in the framework of risk and return during the period April 1995 to March 2000, for 40 mutual funds consisting of both public and private sector funds. It made use of Sharpe ratio, Treynor ratio, Jensen measure, Sharpe differential return measure and Fama's components of performance. The results indicated that the risk and return of mutual fund schemes were not in conformity with their stated investment objectives. Moreover, the sample schemes were found to be not adequately diversified. The funds were able to earn higher returns due to selectivity, though proper balance between selectivity and diversification was not maintained. It was also observed that the Indian mutual funds were not properly diversified.

Aggarwal and **Gupta** (2007)[78] analysed the performance of Indian mutual fund industry by using the quarterly returns performance of all the equity diversified funds during the period 2002 to 2006. The study employed the CAPM and the Fama-French models. The findings suggested that the mutual funds had actually added value and investing in them was worthwhile for the investors, which was opposed by the Fama-French model. The latter model predicated that returns on excess of market returns, size and value were actually due to exposure only to these factors and the fund managers did not add any value. The only factor that seemed to affect mutual fund returns was the excess market returns, while size and value factors when taken along with excess market returns did not hold any significance.

Bodla and **Garg** (2007)[79] tracked the performance of the Indian mutual fund industry for the period 1997 to 2004 by randomly selecting 24 growth funds. They made use of techniques of Sharpe, Treynor and Jensen and found out that most of the schemes have outperformed the market during the study period in terms of return. However, the difference in market return and funds' return is found insignificant. There existed a moderate positive correlation between risk and return of the sample schemes. The systematic risk beta of most of the schemes fell in the range of 0.7 to 1.3 and thus, they were not much risky. A large majority of the schemes had succeeded in earning a risk premium irrespective of the performance measurement model concerned. Moreover, most of the schemes had performed better than the market on the basis of risk-adjusted return, though the difference was not found significant.

Panwar and **Madhumathi** (2007)[80] examined the characteristics and the performance of the 269 open-end Indian mutual funds for the period May 2002 to May 2005, with the help of tools like average coefficient of variation and excess standard deviation adjusted returns. When residual variance was used as the measure of mutual fund portfolio diversification characteristic, there was a statistical difference between public sector sponsored and private sector sponsored mutual funds. Moreover, the mutual fund performance index measured in terms of excess standard deviation adjusted return has a statistically significant impact through diversification and residual variance.

Badrinath (2008)[81] took closer look at the concept of contrarian investment as an investment strategy and evaluated the performance of the various Contra Funds existing in India. Studying the performance of especially the State Bank of India (SBI) Contra Fund and comparing it with general equity diversified market the author concluded that the former had outperformed the latter. Moreover, the Contra Fund in general is considered as more suitable for those investors who have already invested in diversified equity stocks and large cap stocks and also who are willing to take more risks in anticipation of a higher return. These Contra funds typically have longer gestation period than the normal funds and time factor should be considered before making the decision.

Guha Deb's study (2008) focused on return-based style analysis of equity mutual funds in India using quadratic optimization of an asset class factor model proposed by William Sharpe. The study found that the Benchmarks of each of its sample of equity funds as optiinum exposure to 11 passive asset class indexes. The study also analyzed the relative performance of the funds with respect to their benchmarks. The results showed that the funds have not been able to beat their benchmarks on the average.[82]

It was also observed (***Mutual Fund Insight*, 2008**)[83] that the pension funds, like Templeton Indian Pension Fund and the UTI Retirement Benefit

Pension Plan were less risky than equity funds, though not totally risk free. The equity component does expose them to some amount of market risk, while the debt component holds the interest rate risk and the credit risk. But in the long run, these funds should manage to beat the returns offered by the other secured tax saving instruments.

The study made by **Tripathy** (2008) evaluated the market timing abilities of Indian fund managers of thirty-one tax planning schemes in India over the period December, 1995 to January, 2004 by using Jensen and Mazuy model and Henriksson and Merton model. The study indicated that the fund managers have not been successful in reaping returns in excess of the market, rather they are timing the market in the wrong direction.[84]

Conclusion

The review of the related literature in the area of performance evaluation of mutual funds indicates that most of the studies made use of the CAPM, Sharpe, Treynor, Jensen and Fama models. Though some of the studies suggested changes to these models in order to be more effective, they were found to be situation specific and hence, generalization may not be appropriate. Almost all studies had adopted variance in the returns as a measure of risk.

Factors considered as relevant in performance evaluation of mutual funds were; returns, risk, market returns, market risk, diversification, selectivity, timing, managerial compensation and the method of its computation, expenses of management and load factors. Risk measures were more appropriate when the interval in which the calculated return was shorter than those for which it was longer. In other words, monthly returns would be a better indicator than quarterly or annual returns.

Most of the studies relating to mutual fund schemes in India attempted to evaluate the performance of a small number of growth or equity oriented schemes or for a short period of time or not considering only a few factors. Moreover, there is lack of consensus not only regarding the outcome of the application of CAPM, but also the benchmark to be used, since outcome of the funds' performance evaluation is normally done vis-à-vis the benchmark index. The implication is that the CAPM is the most important model and as far as the benchmark index is concerned, it needs to be as much representative as possible. In the recent past, the Indian mutual fund industry has grown tremendously through the entry of both public and private sector players. But, no study has yet been made involving a large number of sample funds taking both sectors, comprising of growth, income and balanced schemes and especially making use of the recent data. The present study is an attempt to fill this void, albeit to some extent.

References

1. Markowitz, Harry, "Portfolio Selection", Journal of Finance, 7 (1), March, (1952), pp.77-91.
2. Friend I., Brown F., Herman E. and Vickers D., "A study of Mutual Funds", The American Economic Review, 54 (2), March, (1964), PP.198-203.
3. Friend, Irwin, Brown, E. Herman Edward, C., and Vickers Douglas, "A Study of Mutual Funds: Investment Policy and Investment Company Performance" in Hsiu-Kwang Wu, Alan J. Zaskon, ed. "Element of Investments: Selected Readings", Holt, Rinehart and Winston. Inc. (1965), pp. 371-385.
4. Sharpe, William F. "Mutual Fund Performance". Journal of Business, 39(1966), Supplement, pp. 119-138.
5. Treynor, Jack l., and Mazuy, Kay K., "Can Mutual Funds Outguess the Markets". Harvard Business Review, 44(1966), pp. 131-136.
6. Jensen, Michael C., "The Performance of Mutual Funds, 1948-67", Journal of Finance, 23 (1968), pp. 389-416.
7. Smith, Keith V. and Tito, Dennis A., "Risk-return Measures of Post-Portfolio Performance", Journal of Financial and Qualitative Analysis, 4 (1969), pp. 449-471.
8. Carlson, Robert S., "Aggregate Performance of Mutual Funds, 1960-69", Journal of Financial and Quantitative Analysis, 5 (1970), pp. 1-32.
9. Arditti, Fred D, "Another look at Mutual Fund Performance", Journal of Financial and Quantitative Analysis, 3 (1971), pp. 909-912.
10. Simonson, Donald G., "The Speculative Behaviour of Mutual Funds," Journal of Finance, 2 (1972), pp. 381-391.
11. Williamson, Peter J., "Measurement and Forecasting of Mutual Fund Performance: Choosing an Investment Strategy", Financial Analysis Journal, 28(1972), pp. 78-84.
12. Fama, Euegen F., "Components of investment Performance", Journal of Finance, 27(1972), pp. 551-567.
13. Klemosky, Robert C., "he Bias in Composite Performance Measures", Journal of Financial and Quantitative Analysis, 8 (1973), pp. 505-514.
14. McDonald, John G., "Objectives and Performance of Mutual Funds, 1960-69", Journal of Financial and Quantitative Analysis, 9 (1974), pp. 311-333.
15. Meyer Jack, "Further Applications oaf Stochastic Dominance to Mutual Fund Performance", Journal of Financial of Quantitative Analysis, 12 (1977) , pp. 917-924.
16. Malkiel, Burton G., "The Valuation of Closed– end Investment Company Shares", Journal of Finance, 3 (1977), pp. 847-859.

17. Thomson, Rex, "The Information Contents of Discounts Manage and Premiums on Closed – End Funds Shares", Journal of Financial Economics, 2-3 (1978), pp. 151-185.

18. Kon, Stanley J., and Jen, Frank C., "Estimation of Time-Varying Systematic Risk and Performance of Mutual Fund Portfolios: An application of Switching Regression", The Journal of Finance, 3 (1978), pp. 457-475.

19. Guy, James R F., "The Performance of British Investment Trust Industry", Journal of Finance, 33 (1978), pp. 443-455.

20. Cornell, Bradford, "Asymmetric Information and Portfolio Performance Measurement", Journal of Financial Economics, 3 (1979), pp. 381-390.

21. Ang, James S. and Chua, Jess H, "Composite Measures for the Evaluation of Investment Performance", Journal of Financial and Qualitative Analysis, 2 (1979), pp. 361-381.

22. Fabozzi, Frank J., Francis, Jack C. and Lee, Chang F., "Generalized Functional Form for Mutual Fund Returns", Journal of Financial and Qualitative Analysis, 2(1980), pp. 361-381.

23. Hendrickson, Roy D and Merton, Robert C., "On Market Timing and Investment Performance II: Statistical Procedures for Evaluating Forecasting Skills", Journal of Business, 4 (1981), pp. 513-533.

24. Jobson, J.D. and Korkie, Bob M. "Performance Hypothesis Testing With the Sharpe and Treynor Measure", Journal of Finance, 4 (1981), pp. 889-908.

25. Reilly, Frank K., "Investments", Dryden Press, (1982), pp. 643-648.

26. Kon, Stanley J., "The Market-Timing Performance of Mutual Funds Mangers" Journal of Business, 3 (1983), pp. 323-347.

27. Chang, Eic C. and Lewellen, Wilbur G., "Market – Timing and Mutual Fund Investment Performance", Journal of Business, 1 (1984), pp. 57-71.

28. Hendrickson, Roy D., "Market Timing and Mutual Fund Performance: An Empirical Investigation: Journal of Business, 1 (1984), pp. 73-96.

29. Davanzo, Lawrence E., and Nesbit, Stephen L., "Performance Fees for Investment Management"' Financial Analysts Journal, (1987), pp. 14-20.

30. Kane, Alex and Marks Gray, "Performance Evaluation of Market-Timers: Theory and Evidence", Journal of Financial and Quantitative Analysis, 4 (1988), pp. 425-435.

31. Grinblatt, Mark and Titaman, Sherdin, "Mutual Fund Performance: An Analysis of Quarterly Portfolio Holdings "Journal of Business, 3 (1989), pp. 393-416.

32. Ippolito, Richard a., "Efficiency with Costly Information: A Study of Mutual Fund Performance, 1965-1984", The Quarterly Journal of Economics, February, (1989), pp.1123.

33. Cumby, Robert E. and Glen, Jack D., "Evaluating the Performance of International Mutual Funds", Journal of Finance, 2 (1990), pp. 496-526.

34. Ankrim, Ernest M., "Risk Adjusted Performance Attribution", Financial Analysis Journal, 2 (1992), pp. 75-82.

35. Coggin, Daniel T., Fabozzi, Frank J. and Rahman Shafiqur, "The Investment Performance of U.S.Equity Pension Fund Managers". An Empirical Investigation", Journal of Business, 3, (1993), pp. 1039-1055.

36. Blake, Christopher R., Elton. Edwin J, and Gruber, martin J., "The Performance of Bond Mutual Funds", Journal of Business, 3 (1993), pp. 371-403.

37. Grinblatt, Mark and Titman Sheridan, "A Study of Mutual Fund Return and Performance Evaluation Techniques", Journal of Financial and Quantitative Analysis, 3, (1994), pp. 419-444.

38. Malkiel, Burton G., "Returns from Investing in Equity Mutual Funds. 1971 to 1991", Journal of Finance, 2 (1995), pp. 550-572.

39. Ferron, Wayne E, and Warther, Vincent A., "Evaluating Funds Performance in a Dynamic Market", Financial Analysts Journal, 52, (6), (1996), pp. 20-28.

40. Gruber, Martin, J., "Another Puzzle: The Growth of Activity Managed Mutual Funds", Journal of Financial Review, 3 (1996), pp. 783-810.

41. Elton, Edwin, J., Gruber, Martin J. and Blake, Christopher R., "The Persistence of Risk-Adjusted Mutual Fund Performance", Journal of Business, 2 (1996), pp. 133-157.

42. Busse, - Jeffrey. A., "Volatility Timing in Mutual Funds; Evidence from Daily Returns" Review of Financial Studies: 12(5), Winter (1999), pp. 1009-41.

43. Carhart, Mark M., "On Persistence in Mutual Fund Performance", The Journal of Finance, March, (1997), pp. 57-82.

44. Cai, Jun and Yamada, K.C.Chan Takeshi, "The Performance of Japanese Mutual Funds", The Review of Financial Studies, 10 (2), (1997), pp. 237-273.

45. Detzler, Miranda – Lam, "The Performance of Global Bond Mutual Funds", Journal of Banking and Finance; 123(8), August (1999), pp. 1195-1297.

46. Wermers, Rus, "Mutual Fund Performance: An Empirical Decomposition into Stock-picking Talent, Style, Transaction Costs and Expenses", The Journal of Finance, August, (2000), pp.1655-1695.

47. Dahlquist, Magnus, Engstorm, Stefan and Soderhind, Paul, "Performance and Characteristics of Swedish Mutual Funds", Journal of Financial and Quantitative Analysis, 35 (3), September, (2000)), pp. 409-423.

48. Khorana, Ajay, "Performance Changes Following Top Management Turnover: Evidence from Open-end Mutual Funds", Journal of Financial Quantitative Analysis, 36 (3), September, (2001), pp. 371-393.

49. Pastor, Lubos and Stambaugh, Robert F., "Investing in Equity Mutual Funds", Journal of Financial Economics, 63 (3), (2002), pp.351-380.

50. Prther, Laurie, Bewrtin, William J., and Henker, Thomas," Mutual Funds characteristics, Managerial Attributes and Fund Performance", review of Financial; Economics, 13 (4), (2004), pp.305-36.

51. Bauer, Rob, Otten, Roger and Koedijk, Kess C.G., "International Evidence on Ethical Mutual Fund Performance an Investment Style" Journal Banking and Finance, Vol.29, (2005), pp.1751-1767.

52. Choi, Yoon K., "Relative Performance Evaluation and Incentive Structure", Journal of Business, 79 (2), (2006), pp.903-921.

53. Huang, Jenniffer, Wei, Kelsey D., and Yan, Hong< "Participation costs and the Sensitivity of Fund flows to Past performance", Journal of Finance, May, 62, (3), (2007), pp.1273-1311.

54. Keswan I Abnel and Stolin, David, "Which money is Smart? Mutual Fund Buys and Sells of Individual and Institutional Investors", Journal of Finance, February, 63, (1), (2008), pp.85-118.

55. Lo, Andrew W., "Where Do Alphas Come From?: A New Measure of the Value of Active Investment Management", May, (2008). Available at http://ssrn.com/abstract=985127.

56. Barras, Laurent, Scaillet , O. and Wermers, Russ R., "False Discoveries in Mutual Fund Performance: Measuring Luck in Estimated Alphas", September (2008). Robert H. Smith School Research Paper No. RHS 06-043, Available at http://ssrn.com/abstract=869748.

57. Gupta, Manak C., "The Mutual Fund Industry and its Comparative Performance", Journal of Financial and Quantitative Analysis, 6 (1974), p. 894.

58. Lee, Cheng – Few and Rahman Shafiqur, "Market Timing, Selectivity and Mutual Fund Performance: An Empirical Investigation" Journal of Business, 21, (1990), pp. 261-278.

59. Sarkar, A.K., "Performance Evaluation of Mutual Funds" Management Accountant, 9 (1991), pp. 691-693.

60. Obaidullah, M., and Ganesan, Sridhar, "Do Mutual Funds in India provide abnormal returns: Chartered Financial Analysts, 5 (1991), pp. 3-6.

61. Barua, Samir K., Raghnathan V. and Jayant R., "Portfolio Management", Tata McGraw Hill, New Delhi, (1991), P.162.

62. Gangadhar, V., "The changing Pattern of Mutual Funds in India", Management Accountant, 12 (1992), pp. 924-928.

63. Sarkar, A.K. "Should We Invest In Mutual Funds", Management Accountant, 10 (1992), pp. 738-739.

64. Shashikant Uma, "Money Market Mutual Funds: Scope and Opportunities", Chartered Financial Analyst, 4 (1993), pp. 3-9.

65. Shukla, Ravi and Singh, Sandeep, "Are CFA Charter – holders Better Equity Fund Mangers", Financial Analysts Journal, 2 (1994), pp. 68-74.

66. Saha, Ashish and Murthy, Y. Shree Rama, "Managing Mutual Funds: Some Critical Issues", Pranjan, 1 (1994), pp.45-52.

67. Jaideep Sarkar, and Majumdar, Sudipata, "Performance Evaluation of Mutual Funds in India", NMIS Management Review Vol. VI No. 2, (July – Dec, 1994), pp. 64-78.

68. Shah Ajay, Thomas, Susan, "Performance Evaluation of Professional Portfolio Management in India". A paper prepared by CMIE, 10, April, 1994.

69. Kaura, Mohinder N. and Jayadev, M., "Performance of Growth Oriented Mutual Funds: An Evaluation". The ICFAI Journal of Applied Finance, I (1), January, (1995), pp. 1-14.

70. Khorana Ajay, "Top Management Turnover – An Empirical Investigation of Mutual Fund Mangers", Journal of Financial Economics, 3 (1996).

71. Chordia Tarun, "The Structure of Mutual Fund Changes". Journal of Financial Economics, 1 (1996), pp.3-39.

72. Gupta O.P., and Sehgal, Sanjay, "Investment Performances of Mutual Funds", Journal of Financial Reivew, 39(1998), pp.783-810.

73. Chander, Ramesh, "Performance appraisal of Mutual Funds in India", Finance India, 14 (4), December, (2002), pp.47-56.

74. Ravindran M., and Rao, Narayan S., "Performance Evaluation of Indian Mutual Funds", SSRN.com Article No.107, (2003).

75. Sodhi H.J., and Jain P.K., "Financial Performance of Equity Mutual Funds: Empirical Evidence from India", Dias Technology Review, 1 (2), (2004), pp. 69-78.

76. Gupta O.P., Gupta, Amitabh, "Performance Evaluation of Selected Indian Mutual Fund Schemes: Empirical Study", The Icfai Journal of Applied Finance, 10 (3), (2004), pp. 81-98.

77. Muthappan, P.K., and Damodharan E., "Risk-adjusted Performance Evaluation of Indian Mutual Fund Schemes", Finance India, 20, (3), September, (2006), pp. 965-983.

78. Aggarwal, Navdeep and Gupta, Mohit, "Performance of Mutuakl Funds in India", Icfai Journal of Applied Finance, 13 (9), (2007), pp.5-16.

79. Bodla, B.S., and Garg, Ashish, "Performance of Mutual Funds in India– Empirical Study of Growth Schemes", GITAM Journa lf Management 5 (4), October-December, (2007), pp. 29-43.

80. Panwar, Sharad and Madhumathi, R., "Characteristics and Performance Evaluation of Selected Mutual Funds in India", accessed from http://papers.ssrn.com/sol3/papers.cfm, on 11.03.2008.

81. Badrinath, Radha, "Contra Fund in India : A Quick Look", Portfolio Organiser, January, (2008), pp.31-34.

82. Guha Deb, Soumya, "Performance of Indian Equity Mutual Funds vis-a-vis their Style Benchmarks", The Icfai Journal of Applied Finance, Vol. 14, No. 1, January, (2008), pp.49-81.

83. Cover Story, Mutual Fund Insight, "Low Gain but Low Risk", February 15-March 14, (2008), pp.34-35.

84. Tripathy, Nalini Prava, "Market Timing Abilities and Mutual Fund Performance- An Empirical Investigation into Equity Linked Saving Schemes", Vilakshan, XIMB Journal of Management, June, (2008), pp.127-138.

3

GROWTH AND DEVELOPMENT OF MUTUAL FUND INDUSTRY IN INDIA

Introduction

Mutual fund is a kind of institution that works as an investment vehicle. It pools the savings of large number of investors together for collective investments purposes with a basic aim of distributing attractive returns through diversification of risk. Mutual fund attracts even those kinds of investors who otherwise will be vary of entering the stock market for the degree of risk involved and thus the level of expertise it demands on the part of the investors. The mutual fund industry throws open the flood gates for the small investors and the rural investors as it provides the twin advantages, viz., lower risk (compared to the stock market) and higher returns (compared to conventional investment products like post office / bank savings, etc.,). Moreover, increasing level of personal income in the economy increases the demand for newer investment products and vehicle like mutual fund is quite apt to the prevailing socio-economic conditions in India.

History of Mutual Fund

The first mutual fund originated in the capital market of Amsterdam that was in many ways well developed and transparent. More than one hundred different securities were regularly traded on the Amsterdam exchange even during the 1770s.

In 1774 the Dutch merchant and broker Abraham van Ketwich invited subscriptions from investors to form a trust named *Eendragt Maakt Magt*—the maxim of the Dutch Republic, "Unity Creates Strength." The founding of the trust followed the financial crisis of 1772–1773, and Van Ketwich's aim was to provide small investors with limited means an opportunity to diversify. Risk spreading was achieved by investing in Austria, Denmark, Germany, Spain, Sweden, Russia, and a variety of colonial plantations in Central and South America.[1]

The bulk of trade took place in bonds issued by the Dutch central and provincial governments and bonds issued by foreign governments that tapped the Dutch market. The governments of Austria, France, England, Russia, Sweden, and Spain all came to Amsterdam to take advantage of the relatively low interest rates. The other major category of securities consisted of plantation loans—or *negotiaties* as they were known in the Netherlands. Mutual funds emerged gradually, as merchants and brokers learned how to expand the range of investment opportunities to the general public during the 18th century. This broadening of the Dutch capital market eventually led to the introduction of the forerunners of today's closed-end mutual funds and depository receipts.[2]

Predecessors of Mutual Funds

Prior to 18th century, a number of investment vehicles emerged in Netherlands that created a joint interest in a pool of financial and non-financial assets. While these securities were not identical to modern mutual funds, they manifested many of the same characteristics. The first major type is a contract of survival. These included life annuities and, in particular, tontines.[3]

In a tontine, a borrower promises to pay to a group of individuals an annuity which will be divided among the surviving members. As members die, the payout to the survivors increases.

Life annuities are financial contracts whereby borrowers pay interest to the lender for the remainder of the lender's life, or that of a third person named in the contract.

Many early tontines were organized by governments, but examples of private tontines are known to date back to the 17th century. If the investment portfolio of a private tontine consisted of company shares, no fixed payments could be guaranteed, and the best participants could only hope the company would continue its dividend policy. This was the case with a 1670 private tontine organized in Amsterdam among thirty participants who jointly invested in a share of the Middelburg chamber of the Dutch East India Company. Private tontines resemble investment trusts in the joint ownership of financial securities. The difference from mutual funds becomes increasingly fine over time, as private tontine societies invested in diversified portfolios.[4]

However, the fortunes of the early mutual funds are closely linked to the fortunes of their predominant investments—plantation loans in the West Indies. The outbreak of the Fourth English War in 1780 hampered colonial shipments to their Dutch commission agents, affecting the proceeds that were pledged as the security for holders of the plantation loans.

Nineteenth Century Mutual Funds

In early 19th century in the commercial history of Egyptians, it was stated that the shares were sold in order to spread the risk of business ventures. In 1822, an investment trust called 'Societe Genral de Belgique' was formed in Belgium. The institution was formed by the royal family of Holland before the separation of Belgium and Holland. The institution has acquired securities in a wide range of companies and practised the precept of diversification. Later, the investment trust concept attracted many countries and considerable progress was made in Switzerland, France, Germany and rest of the Europe.[55]

The first investment trust outside of the Netherlands is the *Foreign and Colonial Government Trust*, founded in 1868 in London. Like *Eendragt Maakt Magt*, it invested in foreign government bonds. It was modelled after the Dutch trusts in the sense that investment income was projected to exceed dividends, and excess income would be used to liquidate shares over its projected twenty-four-year life. By 1875, eighteen trusts had been formed in London. It was during this period that the Scotsman Robert Fleming started his famous first trust, investing in U.S. railroad bonds, later named the First Scottish American Investment Trust. During the 1890s, investment trusts were introduced into the United States. Most of the early U.S. investment trusts were close-ended funds, like *Eendragt Maakt Magt*, issuing a fixed number of shares. The issue of new shares, or repurchases, were not precluded but were infrequent. Moreover, the repurchase or issue price was not necessarily proportional to the intrinsic value of the underlying portfolio.

This changed in 1924, when the Massachusetts Investors Trust became the first U.S. mutual fund with an open-ended capitalization, allowing for the continuous issue and redemption of shares by the investment company at a price that is proportional to the value of the underlying investment portfolio. Open-ended capitalization has become the dominant model for mutual fund organization, suggesting that it has been an important innovation contributing to its modern success.[6]

The period 1925-29 witnessed a substantial expansion of investment trust movement in the US. The banking houses promoted investment trusts to unload the unsaleable securities and to control the companies without investing substantial amount of their own money. Every financial group started forming some sort of investment trusts. As there were hardly any rules and regulations, mismanagement in these institutions was wide spread. During the great depression of 1930s, the investors had staggering losses from these trusts.[7]

In 1933, the US Congress directed the Securities and Exchange Commission to investigate the operations of the American Investment

Trusts. The Commission recommended the passage of a legislation which materialised in 1940. The Investment Companies Act of 1940 provided rules and regulations for the establishment and management of mutual funds.[8]

The mutual fund industry continued to expand. At the beginning of the 1950s in the US, the number of open-end funds topped 100. In 1954, the financial markets overcame their 1929 peak, and the mutual fund industry began to grow in earnest, adding some 50 new funds over the course of the decade. The 1960s saw the rise of aggressive growth funds, with more than 100 new funds established and billions of dollars in new asset inflows. Hundreds of new funds were launched throughout the 1960s until the bear market of 1969 cooled the public appetite for mutual funds. Money flowed out of mutual funds as quickly as investors could redeem their shares, but the industry's growth later resumed.

With the 1980s and '90s came bull market mania and previously obscure fund managers became superstars; Max Heine, Michael Price and Peter Lynch, the mutual fund industry's top managers, became household names and money poured into the retail investment industry at a stunning pace. With $12 trillion in assets in 2008, the U.S. mutual fund industry remains the largest in the world. In 2007, investor demand for mutual funds increased significantly, with net new cash flow to all types of mutual funds reaching $883 billion, a record high.[9]

Evolution and Growth of Mutual Funds in India

Mutual Fund's history in India can be traced back to the second half of the 19th century. Financial Association of India and China was the first investment trust formed in India in 1869. However, the growth of investment trust business started only after 1930. The need for the establishment of Unit Trust type of institution was felt in 1931 by the Indian Central Banking Enquiry committee. The Committee observed in its report that an immeasurable benefit to India is bound to grow from the establishment and proper working of unit trusts, and the assistance which they will give to the investor in the creation of intermediate securities which do not exist now, in providing a channel for investment in industrial and other fields, where the primary investor would be too scared or too ignorant.[10]

As opined by the Committee, unit trusts have not been formed, but the investment trusts have been established. In 1933, Industrial Investment Trust was established by Premchand Roychand at Bombay.[11] Almost all the large industrial concerns established investment trusts and transferred their surplus funds to them. During World War II and afterwards, the growth of investment trusts or companies gained greater momentum. These trusts were formed under the Companies Act.

The Committee on finance for private sector in India (1954) popularly called as the Shroff committee, reiterated the desirability of introducing unit trusts in the Indian capital market. The Committee had observed that in order to increase the capital available for industries, small savings have to be drawn into the investment market. For mobilisation of such small savings it felt, unit trusts are suitable. Therefore, the Committee suggested the introduction of unit trusts in both public and private sectors.[12]

In 1963, the then Finance Minister T.T.Krishnamachari had moved the Bill on the Unit Trust of India (UTI) in the Parliament. He stated that the establishment of UTI is an adventure in small savings. The objective of UTI was to provide an opportunity for middle and lower income groups to participate in the capital market. As an incentive to the investors, the government also announced certain exemptions under the provisions of Income Tax Act. The UTI was formed according to UTI Act 1963, and launched its first open-ended scheme, Unit Scheme 1964 in June 1964.[13]

Though the growth of the mutual fund industry in India was slow initially, it accelerated from the year 1987 when non-UTI players entered the industry. In the past decade, Indian mutual fund industry has seen a dramatic improvement, both quality-wise and quantity-wise. The private sector entry to the fund family increased the asset under management from Rs. 47,000 crore in March 1993 to Rs. 5,28,936 crore in March, 2008.[14]

Different Phases of Growth of Indian Mutual Fund Industry

The growth of Indian mutual fund industry is segmented into four different phases depending on the structural changes which have taken place in the industry. Initially, the Indian mutual fund industry was characterised exclusively by the UTI during 1964-87 and this is termed as the first stage. In 1987, other mutual funds were also permitted to enter, but only from the public sector and this phase existed for six years that is from 1987-1993. In 1993, the private players were allowed into the Indian mutual fund industry. This phase – the third phase – started in 1993 and went till 2003 (till October 2002, to be precise). In the end of 2002, the UTI which was formed by an Act of Parliament, was repealed and made into an asset management company, just like any other mutual fund. Thus, the fourth phase which put all mutual fund players in a level playing field began in 2003. These four phases are detailed below.

First Phase: 1964-87

Unit Trust of India was established in 1963 by the Reserve Bank of India (RBI) and functioned under its regulatory and administrative control. In 1978 UTI was de-linked from the RBI and the Industrial Development Bank of

India (IDBI) took over the regulatory and administrative control in place of RBI. The first scheme launched by UTI was Unit Scheme 1964 (US-64). At the end of 1988 UTI had Rs.6,700 crore of asset under management. Table – 3.1 provides the details regarding the resource mobilisation under US-64, the flagship scheme of the UTI and Chart – 3.1 presents its graphical view.

Table – 3.1 Resource Mobilisation under Unit Scheme 1964

(Rupees in Lakhs)

Year	*Sold*		*Repurchased*	*Outstanding*
	No. of applications	*Amount*		*(at the year end)*
1964-65	135000	1914	41	1873
1970-71	61713	1800	319	9225
1975-76	656748	2077	1095	15764
1980-81	99740	3966	1536	38978
1985-86	145945	31935	5077	128489
1990-91	1043562	69980	46078	726366
1993-94	4671097	4647	254	11798

Source: Report on Currency and Finance, Reserve Bank of India, various years.

US-64 helped fulfil the twin objectives of mobilizing retail savings and investing those savings in the capital market and passing on the benefits so accrued to the small investors.

Chart – 3.1 Resource Mobilisation under Unit Scheme - 64

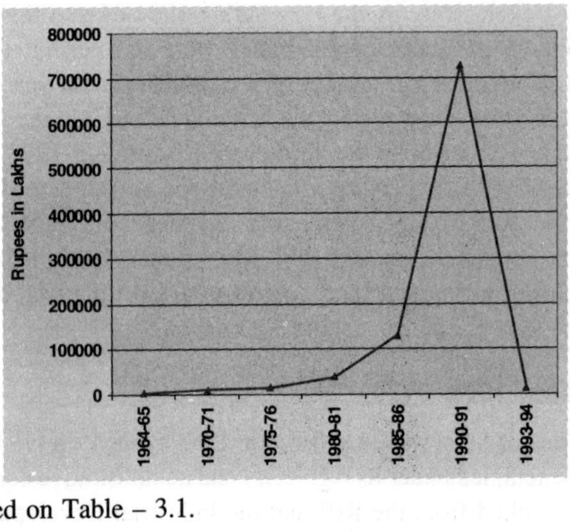

Source: Based on Table – 3.1.

Compared to other instruments of investment, the US-64 offered several benefits to investors. The small investors found investing in US-64 units far more lucrative in terms of interest amount than putting their money in a bank. Compared to some other instruments like Kisan Vikas Patras or National Saving Certificates, the US-64 offered its investors the benefit of a very high degree of liquidity. While one's money was locked in the above instruments for five to six years, a US-64 unit holder could sell his units back to the UTI any time in the year, except in the month of June, at the previously declared repurchase price. In any month, the repurchase price used to be only 15 to 25 paise less than the sale price, and did not mean any loss to the investor. After surrendering his units to the UTI, the investor got a cheque for his money in a week or so.

The US-64 was considered to be totally free from the risks of volatility that are associated with speculative investments. For about three decades since its inception, the investor's money was perfectly safe from the ups and downs (mostly downs) of the stock market. The investor had full faith in the US-64 units and thought that his money was safe in the custody of the "Government of India." Contrary to the monthly deposit schemes run by the post office, some banks and even private organisations like the Peerless or Sahara, the US-64 investors faced no risk of forfeiting any part of their principal or dividend or both, in case of default in payment for a couple of months. This was particularly to the liking of those who had no regular or fixed income.

Further, under the US-64, an investor was required to purchase a minimum of only 100 units; that meant an investment of only Rs. 1500 or so. Thus, even those with modest incomes and savings could become members of the scheme. Also, a US-64 investor had two options before him, of getting a cheque for the dividend earned by him or of reinvesting the same into more units, the conversion from one option to the other was not difficult and could be effected through simple correspondence. This offered another attraction for the investors.

It was these factors that made the US-64 investments highly attractive for the investor community as a whole. The scheme, on the whole, was a haven for small investors, particularly those working in the private or unorganised sector, who did not have any security of post-retirement or post-retrenchment benefits. Factory workers, peasants of all hues, artisans, middle class employees, pensioners, hawkers, small shopkeepers and vendors, head-load workers and even rickshaw-pullers - all used to confide in the US-64 units, taking this form of investment as their best security in bad days. This explains the tremendous success of the scheme and the very high number of investors it attracted - more than 20 million. This also explains how at the end of June 2001, the US-64 alone accounted for about 22 per cent of the Rs. 60,000 crore plus corpus of the UTI that ran a number of other schemes such as Monthly Investment Plan – 98, Children Gift Growth Fund, Market Index Fund and Petro Fund, etc. In fact, no scheme of the UTI achieved such tremendous success as the US-64 did, making the UTI the biggest mutual fund of the country and one of the biggest in the world.[15]

Second Phase: 1987-1993 (Entry of Public Sector Funds)

The 1980s witnessed the beginning of the process of liberalisation of the industrial sector by the Government of India, in pursuit of faster industrial and economic development. This not only brought in changes in the environment for Indian industries, corporate sector and the capital market, but also led to the emergence of demand for newer financial services such as issue management, corporate counselling, etc. Once it became apparent that its development objectives could not be met solely by using financial institutions and commercial banks, the Government removed the monopoly in the mutual fund industry in 1987 by permitting a large number of companies to raise funds through equity market and encouraging equity ownership through tax incentives. Table – 3.2 provides the data pertaining to resource mobilisation by the UTI and other public sector mutual funds during the period 1987-1993 and Chart – 3.2 presents the data pictorially.

Table – 3.2 Net Resource Mobilisation by UTI and Other Public Sector Mutual Funds, from 1987-88 to 1992-93

(Rupees in Crore)

Year	*UTI*	*Other Public Sector*	*Total*
1987-88	1768	250	2018
1988-89	3464	320	3784
1989-90	5491	1203	6694
1990-91	3199	2955	6154
1991-92	8685	1568	11253
1992-93	11057	1964	13021

Source: Report on Currency and Finance, Reserve Bank of India, various years.

Thus, after two decades of UTI monopoly, the mutual fund industry began to include some more players, though all of them from the public sector. State Bank of India Mutual Fund was the first followed by Canara Bank Mutual Fund (December 1987), Punjab National Bank Mutual Fund

Chart – 3.2 Net Resource Mobilisation by the Indian MF Industry, 1987-88 to 1992-93

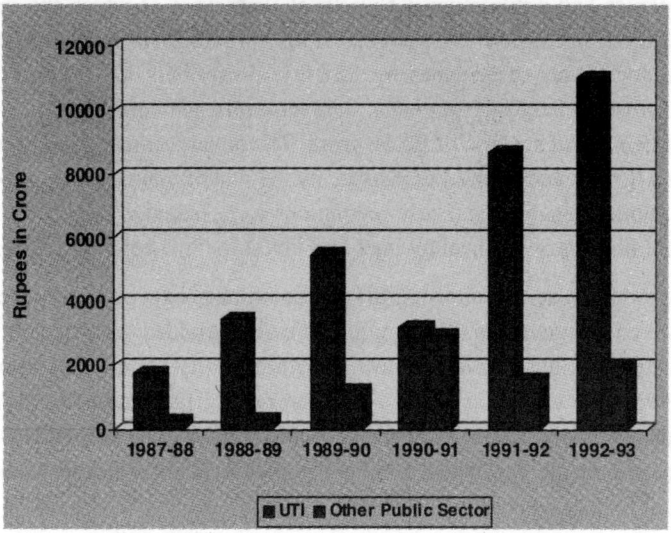

Source: Based on Table – 3.2.

(August 1989), Indian Bank Mutual Fund (November 1989), Bank of India (June 1990), Bank of Baroda Mutual Fund (October 1992), Life Insurance Corporation of India in 1989 and General Insurance Company in 1990. The end of 1993 marked Rs. 47,000 crore as asset under management of the mutual fund industry.

Third Phase: 1993-2003 (Entry of Private Sector Funds)

In 1993, private sector was permitted to enter the mutual fund industry, which till then was occupied exclusively by the public sector funds. The entry of private sector mutual funds was aimed at providing more choice to the investors in terms of innovative new products, through increased competition in the industry. Thus, the Indian mutual fund industry evolved in its entirety in 1993, which obviously warranted a thorough regulation, for which the SEBI was nominated as the regulator. Thus, the SEBI, for the first time in India, notified regulations for the mutual fund industry. Through these regulations, mutual funds were governed by a uniform set of regulations which required them to be formed as trusts and managed by a separate asset management companies and supervised by a Board of Trustees or Trustee Company. SEBI (Mutual Fund) regulations provided for arms length relationship between the various constituents of the mutual fund and thus brought about a structural change which ensured qualitative improvement in the functioning of the mutual funds.

The SEBI (Mutual Fund) regulations laid down certain eligibility criteria for the sponsors of mutual funds and required that the asset management companies had a minimum net worth of Rs.6 crore of which the sponsors must contribute at least 40 per cent. It also provided for an approval of the offer documents of schemes by SEBI. It prescribed that a closed ended scheme with a fixed size of mutual fund must raise a minimum of Rs. 20 crore and open ended scheme of Rs.50 crore. The advertisement code prescribed norms for fair and truthful disclosure by the mutual funds in advertisements and publicity materials. These regulations were intended to ensure that the mutual funds grow on healthy lines and investors' interests were protected.[16]

Under these regulations, all mutual funds, except UTI were to be registered and governed. These regulations also heralded the arrival of private sector players into the MF industry. With the entry of private sector funds in 1993, a new era started in the Indian mutual fund industry, giving the Indian investors a wider choice of fund families. The erstwhile Kothari Pioneer (now merged with Franklin Templeton) was the first private sector mutual fund registered in July 1993.

The 1993 SEBI (Mutual Fund) Regulations were revised on the basis of the recommendations of the Mutual Funds 2000 Report prepared by SEBI. The revision had been carried out with the objective of improving investor protection, facilitating competition, imparting a greater degree of flexibility and promoting innovation. The revised regulations also provided for portfolio disclosure, standardisation of accounting policies, valuation norms for net asset value and pricing.

In all 31 mutual funds (excluding the UTI) were registered with SEBI as of December 1996, under the SEBI (Mutual Funds) Regulations, 1993. Of these, 10 belonged to the public sector and 21 were in the private sector. 16 private sector mutual funds and 1 public sector mutual fund had foreign participation in their asset management companies. [17]

The UTI had around Rs. 60,000 crore under its management as on June 30, 2001 which was about 57 per cent of the total mutual fund industry in India. The flagship fund of the UTI, the US-64 alone had accounted for Rs. 12778 crore on June 30, 2001. The fund had a phenomenal success in the first three decades of its existence, as during the period 1965-95, the number of units held by the investors grew from 1.87 lakh units in 1965 to 15,277 million units in 1995.[18] However, the liberalisation of 1991 brought about a fundamental transformation in the investment scenario of the UTI. Attracted by the upswing of the stock market during 1991, fund managers of the UTI reduced the debt component of UTI from 64 per cent in June 1987 to 26 per cent in June 2000 without the knowledge of the investors and thereby increased its exposure to stock market. Moreover, the UTI invested heavily in the loss-making companies like Pritish Nandy communications, Business India, etc., due to political pressures. On the other hand, to meet its dividend commitment, US-64 kept selling its high yielding long term debt which reduced the interest income.

The net resource (Total sales – Redemption) mobilisation by the UTI, public sector and private sector mutual funds during the period 1993-2003 is presented in Table – 3.3. Chart – 3.3 provides the graphical view of the net resource mobilisation by the mutual fund industry.

Due to these pressures, the sale price of US-64 constantly decreased and became negative in 1998, which created panic among the investors who started to redeem the units. By June 2001, the scale of redemption reached such a proportion that on July 2, 2001 a six-month freeze was announced by the UTI on all transactions in US-64. As it directly affected the savings and

Table – 3.3 Net Resource Mobilisation by the Indian Mutual Fund Industry, 1993-94 to 2002-03

(Rupees in Crore)

Year	*UTI*	*Other Public Sector*	*Private Sector*	*Total*
1993-94	9297	387	1560	**11244**
1994-95	8611	1342	1322	**11275**
1995-96	-6314	348	182	**-5748**
1996-97	-3043	174	559	**-2310**
1997-98	2875	449	678	**4002**
1998-99	-2738	335	1453	**-950**
1999-2000	4548	-744	15166	**18969**
2000-01	323	-1045	9849	**9128**
2002-03	-7362	2586	21145	**16369**

Source: Report on Currency and Finance, Reserve Bank of India, various years.

investment of millions of investors, a huge political furore erupted in the country. This not only warranted a huge bail out package from the Government, but also restructuring of the UTI.

Chart – 3.3 Net Resource Mobilisation by the Indian Mutual Fund Industry, 1993-94 to 2002-03

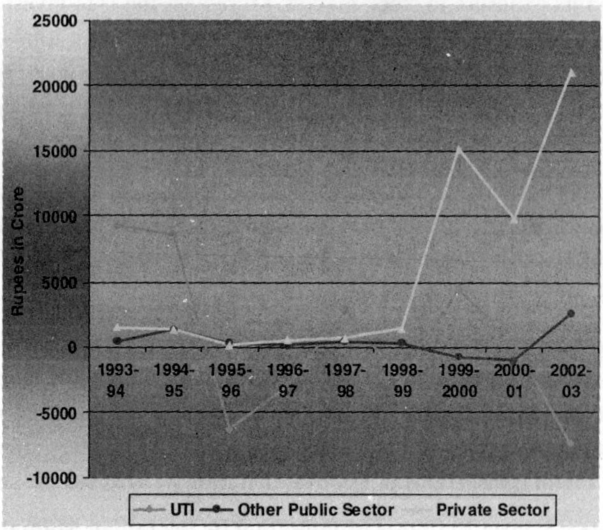

Source: Based on Table – 3.3.

Fourth Phase - since February 2003

Hence, in October 2002, an ordinance was promulgated which repealed the UTI Act and UTI was stripped of its special legal status as a trust formed by an Act of Parliament. The primary objective behind this was to bring all mutual fund players on a level playing field. Through this ordinance, the UTI was re-organised into two: UTI-1 (The Specified Undertaking of UTI – SUUTI) and UTI-2 (The UTI Mutual Fund). The UTI-2 is an unencumbered mutual fund, with only net asset value-based schemes. The UTI-1 has US-64 and the assured returns schemes. In January 2003, the UTI-2 was handed over to a new set of owners which included State Bank of India, Bank of Baroda, Punjab National Bank and Life Insurance Corporation of India.

The UTI-1 (SUUTI) was created with asset under management of Rs. 29,835 crore, which functions under an administrator and under the rules framed by Government of India and thus, does not come under the purview of the Mutual Fund Regulations. Table – 3.4 presents the data regarding the growth of Indian mutual fund industry in terms of asset under the management of the UTI, other public sector mutual funds and the private sector mutual funds during 2003-04 to 2007-08. Chart – 3.4 provides the graphical view of Table – 3.4.

Table – 3.4 Asset Under Management in the Indian Mutual Fund Industry during 2003-04 to 2007-08

(Rupees in Crore)

Year	*UTI*	*Other Public Sector*	*Private Sector*	***Total***
2003-04	20617	10345	98702	**134279**
2004-05	20740	11190	115938	**149189**
2005-06	29519	20683	180431	**230632**
2006-07	37613	32066	287158	**356835**
2007-08	48983	46192	432652	**528936**

Source: Accessed at www.amfi.com

The UTI-2 (UTI Mutual Fund Ltd,) which is sponsored by State Bank of India, Punjab National Bank, Bank of Baroda and Life Insurance Corporation of India, is registered with SEBI and functions under the Mutual Fund Regulations. With the bifurcation of the erstwhile UTI, the UTI-2 had an asset under management of Rs. 17,045 crore in October 2003.[19] With the setting up of a UTI Mutual Fund, conforming to the SEBI Mutual Fund Regulations, and with recent mergers taking place among different private

Chart – 3.4 Asset Under Management in the Indian Mutual Fund Industry during 2003-04 to 2007-08

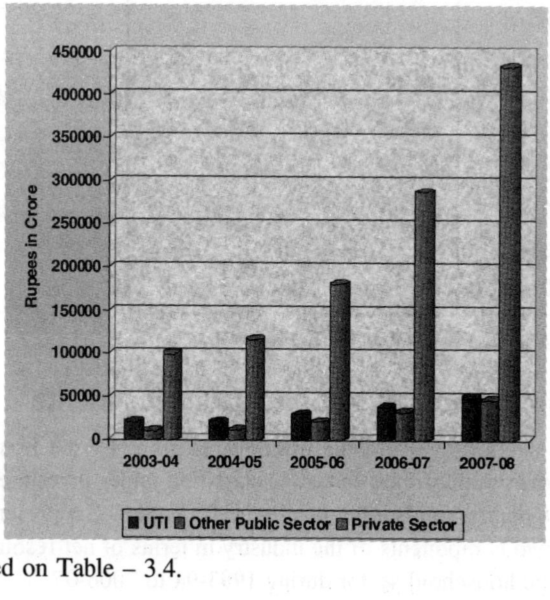

Source: Based on Table – 3.4.

sector funds, the mutual fund industry has entered its current phase of consolidation and growth. The number of mutual fund houses kept on increasing, with many foreign mutual funds setting up funds in India and also the industry has witnessed several mergers and acquisitions. At the end of March 2008, there were 1144 mutual funds with total assets of Rs. 6,00,000 crore; the UTI with Rs. 48,983 crore of asset under management was way ahead of other mutual funds in the public sector, while the Reliance Mutual Fund with an asset under management of Rs. 90,938 crore is leading the list.[20]

The growth of the Indian mutual fund industry in terms of number of mutual fund schemes and the number of asset management companies during 1998-99 to 2007-08 is provided in Table – 3.5.

Table – 3.5 Number of Asset Management Companies and Mutual Fund Schemes in India during 1998-99 to 2007-08

(Rupees in Crore)

Year	*No. of Asset Management Companies*	*No. of Mutual Fund Schemes*
1996-97	30	192
1997-98	31	235
1998-99	32	271
1999-2000	32	335
2000-01	35	376
2001-02	35	448
2002-03	33	498
2003-04	31	544
2004-05	29	641
2005-06	29	830
2006-07	30	1043
2007-08	33	1144

Source: Accessed at www.amfi.com

Household Sector's Mutual Fund Investments

This section analyses the investments made by the household sector in the Indian mutual fund industry, classified under investment in the UTI and in the mutual funds other than the UTI. Table – 3.6 presents the growth of these two components of the industry in terms of net resource mobilised through the household sector during 1993-94 to 2006-07.

A cursory glance at the table clearly indicates that the net resource mobilised from the household sector by the UTI fluctuated heavily as it declined from Rs. 4705 crore in 1993-94 to Rs. 262 crore in 1995-96, before increasing to Rs. 8242 crore in 1999-2000. But in the very next year, it became negative to Rs. 2301 crore implying the fact that total redemption exceeded total investment. This negative trend continued till 2003-04, the worst years of the UTI. This trend was reversed in 2004-05 as the net resource mobilised became

Table – 3.6 Resource Mobilisation by Mutual Funds from Household Sector between 1993-94 to 2006-07

(Rupees in Crore)

Year	*UTI*		*MF otherthan UTI*		*Total*	
	Amount	*Annual Growth Rate %*	*Amount*	*Annual Growth Rate %*	*Amount*	*Annual Growth Rate %*
1993-94	4705	——	1272	——	5977	——
1994-95	3908	-16.94	1647	29.48	5555	-7.06
1995-96	262	-93.30	344	-79.11	606	-89.09
1996-97	3776	1341.22	531	54.36	4307	610.73
1997-98	595	-84.24	1881	254.24	2476	-42.51
1998-99	1887	217.14	2108	12.07	3995	61.35
1999-2000	8242	336.78	7983	278.70	16225	306.13
2000-01	-2301	-127.92	3196	-59.96	895	-94.48
2001-02	-5359	-132.90	5079	58.92	-280	-131.28
2002-03	-1193	-377.74	4293	-15.48	3100	-1207.14
2003-04	-5105	-327.91	4519	5.26	-586	-118.90
2004-05	728	701.25	1550	-65.70	2278	-488.74
2005-06	3967	444.92	21139	1263.81	25106	1002.11
2006-07	1735	-56.26	36700	73.61	38435	53.09
Mean	**1132**	**140.31**	**6589**	**141.25**	**7720**	**11.22**
SD	**3787**	**4.04**	**10152**	**3.55**	**11300**	**5.18**

Source: National Income Accounts, Central Statistical Organisation, New Delhi, Various Years.

positive with Rs. 728 crore which further increased to Rs. 3967 crore in 2005-06 before declining to Rs. 1735 crore in 2006-07. This fluctuating trend of UTI's resource mobilisation is clearly captured by the annual growth rate which began with a negative rate of 16.94 per cent in 1994-95 followed by a huge 93.30 per cent fall in 1995-96, though in the next year, the growth rate touched 1341.22 per cent. This sort of positive and negative trends is the prominent feature of the net resource mobilisation by the UTI. Thus, the mean score of net resource mobilised stands at Rs. 1132 crore.

In the case of the mutual funds other than UTI too, the net resource mobilised fluctuated but importantly it never became negative during the period 1993-94 to 2006-07. It increased moderately from Rs. 1272 crore in 1993-94 to Rs. 1647 crore in 1994-95 before declining to Rs. 531 crore in 1996-97. It again went up to Rs. 1881 crore in 1997-98 and then to Rs. 7983 crore in 1999-2000. Though it touched Rs. 1550 crore in 2004-05, in the next two subsequent years it mobilised Rs. 21139 crore and Rs. 36700 crore. Thus, the mean score of the net resource mobilised by the mutual funds other than the UTI stands at Rs. 6589 crore. Thus, its annual growth rate shows only moderate fluctuations.

The net resource mobilised by the mutual fund industry as a whole through the household sector decreased slightly from Rs. 5977 crore in 1993-94 to Rs. 5555 crore in 1994-95 and further to Rs. 606 crore in 1995-96. From 1996-97 to 2000-01, the industry showed a positive trend in resource mobilisation, though in 2001-02, total redemption exceeded total investment resulting in negative mobilisation to the extent of Rs. 280 crore. This was absolutely prompted by the down fall of the UTI and the scale of fall (Rs. 5359 crore) is such that it out-weighed the positive mobilisation made by the mutual funds other than UTI to the extent of Rs. 5079 crore. But, the opposite occurred in 2002-03 when the negative mobilisation of the UTI (Rs. 1193 crore) was out-weighed by the positive mobilisation (Rs. 4293 crore) of the other mutual funds, resulting in the positive mobilisation by the overall industry to the level of Rs. 3100 crore. In 2003-04, the industry's mobilisation again turned negative by Rs. 586 crore, but only to become positive in the next three years, that is since 2004-05. Hence, resource mobilisation of the industry also portrays considerable swings in both directions. The growth trends of the Indian mutual fund industry are graphically presented in Chart – 3.5.

Chart – 3.5 Resource Mobilisation by Mutual Funds from Household Sector between 1993-94 to 2006-07

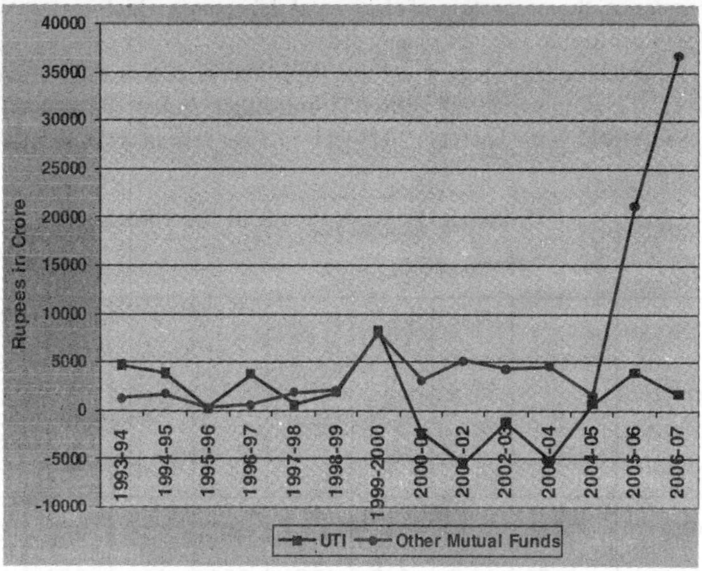

Source: Based on Table – 3.6.

The degree and nature of correlation of UTI and other mutual funds with total investment is presented in Table – 3.7. It shows a very weak (0.14) correlation between the UTI and the total investment, while the correlation between other mutual funds and total investment in considerably strong (0.94). However, there is again a weak correlation between the UTI and other mutual funds which indicates that these two components are not significantly correlated, though the relationship is positive.

Table – 3.7 Correlation of UTI and Other Mutual Funds with Total Investment

Components	*Total Investment*	*UTI*	*MF other than UTI*
Total Investment	1.00		
UTI	0.14	1.00	
MF other than UTI	0.94	0.13	1.00

Source: Computed from Table – 3.6.

It is also equally important to analyse the trends in relative shares of each component of financial savings to understand the proportionate dominance of one on the other. The relative growth trends of the components of FS are presented in Table – 3.8.

It portrays a clear trend implying the fact the Indian household sector is now moving towards more risk-oriented products, though very cautiously. For instance, the proportion of shares and debentures which was at a high of 15.59 per cent in 1993-94 plummeted to a low of 1.27 per cent in 2003-04, but rebounded equally sharply and stood at 10.68 per cent in 2006-07. Along with it, the proportions of both UTI and other mutual funds too have changed, reaching the lowest in 2003-04 (-1.63 per cent for UTI and 1.44 per cent for

Table – 3.8 Household Sector's Financial Asset Performance

(in percentage)

Year	*Net Deposits*	*Shares & Debentures*	*LIC Funds*	*Provident & Pension Funds*	*UTI*	*MF other than UTI*	*Investment In Govt. Security*	*Investment in Small Savings*
1993-94	34.67	15.59	9.71	19.34	4.97	1.34	0.48	6.81
1994-95	34.97	14.40	9.12	17.74	3.24	1.36	0.07	10.85
1995-96	32.64	8.65	12.86	21.25	0.25	0.33	0.42	8.70
1996-97	42.18	7.37	11.04	21.53	2.68	0.38	0.49	7.87
1997-98	39.87	3.36	12.35	21.48	0.40	1.25	1.86	12.89
1998-99	34.79	3.85	11.73	24.08	0.98	1.10	0.70	13.95
1999-2000	25.04	11.88	13.40	26.10	3.99	3.86	1.06	12.97
2000-01	33.63	4.11	15.18	22.26	-1.07	1.48	1.95	16.18
2001-02	28.70	1.81	18.63	18.84	-2.17	2.05	6.80	14.18
2002-03	29.00	2.34	16.33	18.96	-0.47	1.70	3.20	18.95
2003-04	24.80	1.27	15.89	16.45	-1.63	1.44	9.09	18.80
2004-05	13.46	2.78	20.87	17.67	0.23	0.49	6.70	26.74
2005-06	23.90	8.00	20.05	14.88	0.94	5.02	3.42	17.29
2006-07	30.61	10.68	22.23	14.02	0.37	7.84	0.35	8.02

Note: Share in terms of financial savings.

Source: National Income Accounts, Central Statistical Organisation, New Delhi, Various Years.

other mutual funds) and turning the corners similarly. But, in between UTI and other mutual funds, there is a vast difference, as the latter's share has gone up to 7.84 per cent in 2006-07, while that of the former has not gone beyond 1 per cent. This vouches for the fact of investors' increased risk taking ability, of late. Among others, except the proportion of Life Insurance Corporation funds, those of all other financial instruments have declined, particularly in a long term perspective. This points to a possibility of close correlation among the products which needs further analysis.

Growth Trends in the Indian Mutual Fund Industry

The growth of mutual fund industry depends not only on the liberalisation of the financial sector and privatisation of the industry, but more on the performance of the stock market. The number of new funds launched, total sales volume of the funds etc., change more or less with the

Table – 3.9 Growth Trends of Mutual Funds during the years, 1998-99 to 2006-07*

Year	*Schemes Launched*	*New Scheme Sales*	*Existing Scheme Sales*	*Total Sales*	*Total Redemption*	*Total Net Investment*	*Asset Under Management*
	Rupees in Crore						
1998-99	36	5736	14262	19998	21221	-1223	68472
1999-2000	64	8395	53146	61541	41196	20345	113005
2000-01	41	3392	90183	93575	83829	9746	93101
2001-02	72	2271	138533	140804	127435	13369	100594
2002-03	50	3768	275492	279260	268982	10278	87190
2003-04	46	8549	583223	591772	542860	48912	134279
2004-05	97	25811	814904	840715	837508	3207	149189
2005-06	189	70583	1027566	1098149	1045370	52779	230632
2006-07	213	140298	1798294	1938592	1844512	94080	356835
Mean	**112**	**29867**	**532845**	**562712**	**534768**	**27944**	**148144**
SD	**122**	**46785**	**596333**	**640510**	**613913**	**31238**	**91609**

Note: *Figures relate to calendar year.

Source: Monthly Review of the Indian Economy, Centre for Monitoring Indian Economy, Mumbai, Various Issues.

changes in the stock market. The number of investors in the Indian mutual fund industry increased from 2.79 crore in January 31, 2007 to 4.37 crore in March 31, 2008.[21] The changing scenario of the mutual fund industry since 1998-99 is analysed with the data provided in Table – 3.9. Chart – 3.6 provides the graphical view of total sales and total redemption of the mutual fund industry.

The table shows that the number of schemes launched fluctuated on a year-to-year basis, ranging from the lowest of 36 in 1998-99 to the highest of 413 in 2006-07. The sales volume of the new schemes also fluctuated, though not in the same manner. In 1998-99, when only 36 schemes were launched, it amassed Rs.5,736 crore, whereas double the number of the schemes in 2001-02, had accounted only for Rs.2,271 crore and 46 new schemes in 2003-04 were able to gather Rs.8,549 crore. When compared with the changes in the investments made in shares and debentures (Table –3.6), its comparison with new schemes' sales volume is marginally higher than the correlation between shares and debentures and the number of new schemes launched. This again brings out the fact that the Indian investors are more cautious in investing as they are not enamoured just by the number of schemes launched rather than by the performance of the stock market. The industry was flooded with 413 new schemes during 2006-07, when the stock market also peaked. The new schemes' sales volume hit a high of Rs.1,40,298 crore. This presents a rosy picture on the growth of the MF industry in India.

Apart from sales of the new schemes, the industry also attracts huge amount of investment from the sales of existing schemes. There is a consistent rise in the existing schemes' sales volume from Rs.14,262 crore in 1998-99 to Rs.17,98,294 crore in 2006-07. Thus, total sales consisting of the sales volume of new and existing schemes moved up from Rs.19,998 crore in 1998-99 to Rs.19,38,592 crore in 2006-07. The industry, as in the case of the stock market also involves redemption every year to a substantial scale. Total redemption was Rs.21,221 crore (which outweighed the total sales) in 1998-99, which increased to Rs.18,44,512 crore in 2006-07. Total net investment fluctuated from a negative volume of Rs.1,223 crore in 1998-99 to Rs.94,080 crore in 2006-07. The year-wise asset under management of the total mutual fund industry also gone up from Rs.68,472 crore in 1998-99 to Rs.3,57,691 crore in 2006-07.

The table also provides the mean and standard deviation details for all the variables. The mean score of the number of schemes launched was 112 which fetched a mean sales volume of Rs.29,867 crore, while the mean score of sales volume from the existing schemes stood at Rs.5,32,845 crore. The mean score of redemption was however less than the mean score of total

Chart – 3.6 Total Sales and Redemption of Mutual Fund Industry during 1998-99 to 2006-07

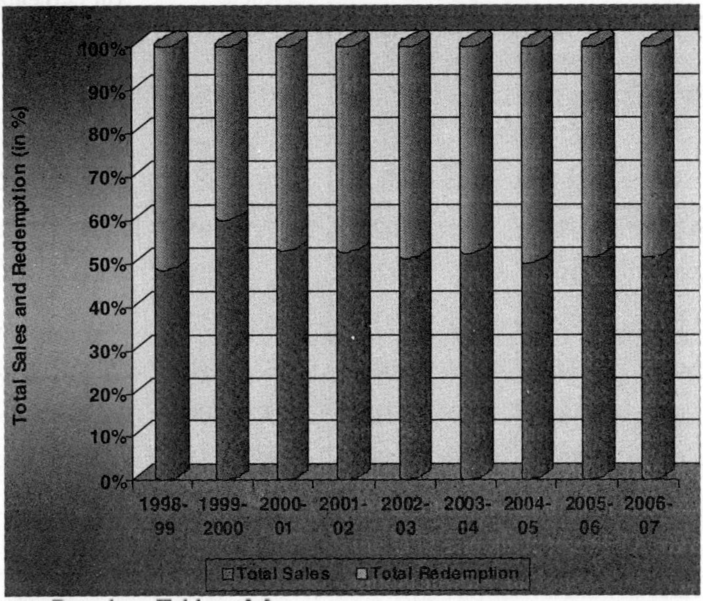

Source: Based on Table – 3.9.

sales volume, leaving a positive figure for the mean net sales volume at Rs.27,911 crore, which indicates a sizeable growth of the industry. However, there is huge amount of variation as well in all the variables, as indicated by the standard deviation. The rate of deviation is higher in the sales volume of new schemes compared to that of other variables.

To understand the growth trends of the variables, the annual growth rates are presented in Table – 3.10.

The table shows that there have been wide differences in the annual growth rates of all the variables over the period. The growth rate of the number of new schemes launched has varied from -35.9 per cent in 2000-01 to 118.5 per cent in 2006-07 and that of the new schemes' sales volume too oscillated from a low of -59.6 per cent in 2000-01 to the high of 201.9 per cent in 2004-05. In the case of the existing schemes' sales volume, though the growth rate has not gone negative, still it swung from 272.6 per cent in 1999- 2000 to 26.1 per cent in 2005-06. Similar kind of variations can also be found in other variables. In many years, the growth rate of total net investment has been negative, though total sales volume remained positive, which indicates the dominance of the growth rate of total redemption. Data indicate that asset under management has grown tremendously particularly

Table – 3.10 Growth Trends of Mutual Funds during the years 1999-2000 to 2006-07

(in percentage)

Year	*Schemes Launched*	*New Scheme Sales*	*Existing Scheme Sales*	*Total Sales*	*Total Net Investment*	*Total Redemption*	*Asset Under Management*
1999-2000*	77.8	46.4	272.6	207.7	94.1	-1763.5	65.0
2000-01	-35.9	-59.6	69.7	52.1	103.5	-52.1	-17.6
2001-02	75.6	-33.0	53.6	50.5	52.0	37.2	8.0
2002-03	-30.6	65.9	98.9	98.3	111.1	-23.1	-13.3
2003-04	-8.0	126.9	111.7	111.9	101.8	375.9	54.0
2004-05	110.9	201.9	39.7	42.1	54.3	-93.4	11.1
2005-06	94.8	173.5	26.1	30.6	24.8	1545.7	54.6
2006-07	118.5	98.8	75.0	76.5	76.4	78.3	54.7

Note: * Based on the data pertaining to the year 1998-99.

Source: Calculated from Table – 3.9.

in the last four years. However, the extent of fluctuation in the annual growth rates of the variables in the mutual fund industry signifies the risk involved in this industry.

Growth Trends in Asset under Management of asset Management Companies

The financial sector liberalisation that was unleashed since 1991 in India has increased competition in the mutual fund industry by leaps and bounds. It has not only resulted in many new entrants, but also in acquisitions and mergers of many existing funds. Thus, on March 31, 2008 there were 33 asset management companies in India including the latest entrant Mirae Asset. In this section, the growth of asset under management of these asset management companies (excluding Mirae Asset) is analysed.

Table – 3.11 Fund-wise Growth in Asset Under Management

(in Rupees Crore)

Sl. No.	*Fund's Name*	*Oct-2003*	*March 2004*	*March 2005*	*March 2006*	*March 2007*	*March 2008*
	Public Sector Funds						
1	BOB	242	454	145	191	111	72
2	Canara Robeco	790	550	1562	2079	2152	2885
3	LIC	3153	4133	2888	5227	10819	14056
4	SBI	3322	5208	6595	13186	18984	29179
5	UTI	17045	20617	20740	29519	37613	48983
Group Total		**24552**	**30962**	**31930**	**50202**	**69679**	**95175**
	Private Sector Funds						
6	ABN AMRO	NA	NA	922	2769	4910	6400
7	AIG Global	NA	NA	NA	NA	NA	3131
8	Benchmark	24	71	487	982	4250	3320
9	Birla Sun Life	8015	8390	10373	14791	22014	35906
10	DBS Chola	720	1042	1024	2007	2499	2372
11	Deutsche	1478	1656	1670	2394	6110	12912
12	DSP M L	1477	3139	5502	10795	12849	16675
13	Escorts	117	161	130	164	106	143
14	Fidelity	NA	NA	NA	3663	5692	8359
15	Franklin Temp.	13833	15133	15354	17827	22364	26842
16	HDFC	13752	14985	15010	21550	31959	44773
17	HSBC	2856	4528	6247	9220	12782	14888
18	ICICI Prudential	14123	13755	15201	23502	43750	54322
19	ING	1021	1551	1191	1961	3958	8608
20	JM Financial	3851	3141	4061	2596	3522	12945
21	JPMorgan	NA	NA	NA	NA	NA	2171
22	Kotak Mahindra	4189	5253	6404	9232	10929	18071
23	Lotus India	NA	NA	NA	NA	1424	7925
24	Morgan Stanley	1166	1361	1544	2892	2822	3205
25	PRINCIPAL	2584	3633	5462	6489	10862	13207
26	Quantum	NA	NA	NA	11	50	64
27	Reliance	6714	7241	9543	24670	47665	90938
28	Sahara	233	348	239	282	179	179
29	Stan. Chart.	8107	7152	6776	9412	13968	12733
30	Sundaram BNP	18	2018	1856	3273	7730	12564
31	Tata	2872	4014	6784	9717	14492	19679
32	Taurus	129	130	158	232	272	320
Group Total		**87279**	**98702**	**115938**	**180431**	**287158**	**432652**
GRAND TOTAL		**114335**	**134279**	**149189**	**230632**	**356835**	**528936**

Note: Figures for the month-end as specified; For 2003, data are available only from October onwards. Includes all those funds which existed as on March 31, 2008, except Mirae Asset as it entered only in 2008; NA – Not Available.

Source: Accessed at www.amfi.com

Table – 3.11 presents the growth of asset management companies in terms of asset under management, from October 2003 to March 2008, the period for which the asset under management data are available for all the asset management companies. Among the public sector asset management companies, Bank of Baroda has eroded in terms of its asset under management, which has declined from Rs. 242 crore in October 2003 to Rs.72 crore in March 2008. However, during the same period the asset under management of Life Insurance Corporation of India and State Bank of India has gone up quite remarkably. The asset under management of UTI too has grown but the rate of increase has left much to be desired. Thus, the total asset under management of the public sector funds has nearly quadrupled from Rs.24,552 crore to Rs.95,175 crore.

Among the private asset management companies too, not all the funds have witnessed growth uniformly. For instance, ABN AMRO which entered in 2005, has amassed asset worth of Rs.6,400 crore, while the asset of Escorts has struck between Rs.117 crore and Rs.143 crore during October 2003 and March 2008. This kind of sluggish growth can be seen in the case of Quantum and Taurus as well. But, there are market toppers who have blown up the growth chart like Reliance, whose asset under management has galloped from Rs.6,714 crore in October 2003 to Rs.90,938 crore in March 2008. Similarly, the asset under management of Sundaram BNP Paribas has gone up from Rs.18 crore to Rs.12,564 crore and that of Tata from Rs.2,872 crore to Rs.19679 crore. The total asset under management of the private sector has thus grown by around five times from Rs. 87,279 crore to Rs.4,32,652 crore.

Table – 3.12 shows the annual growth rates of the funds during the last five years. The overall growth rates of both the public and private sectors show huge variations, particularly in the case of the latter. But, during the last four years, the private asset management companies have not only showed more stable growth, but also outperformed the public sector asset management companies on a year-to-year basis. Moreover, since March 2006, the public sector asset management companies are growing at a declining rate. The overall growth rate of the mutual fund industry indicates that the industry has been growing at nearly 50 per cent per annum during 2005-06 to 2007-08, which is quite remarkable. However, there have also been negative growths in both the sectors, particularly during 2006-07 and 2007-08, though in general these two are very strong growth years for the industry. At the individual fund level, the cases of State Bank of India, Birla Sun Life, Deutsche, ING, Reliance and Sundaram BNP Paribas can be cited for their spectacular growth performance.

Table – 3.12 Annual Growth Rates of Asset Under Management of Mutual Funds

(in percentage)

Sl. No.	Fund's Name	March 2004*	March 2005	March 2006	March 2007	March 2008
Public Sector Funds						
1	BOB	87.49	-68.09	31.75	-42.02	-34.58
2	Canara Robeco	-30.38	183.81	33.12	3.50	34.09
3	LIC	31.07	-30.13	81.02	106.98	29.92
4	SBI	56.80	26.64	99.92	43.97	53.70
5	UTI	20.96	0.59	42.33	27.42	30.23
All	**Average**	**33.19**	**22.56**	**57.63**	**27.97**	**22.67**
Private Sector Funds						
6	ABN AMRO	NA	NA	200.36	77.31	30.35
7	Benchmark	198.08	588.64	101.78	332.61	-21.88
8	Birla Sun Life	4.67	23.65	42.59	48.83	63.11
9	DBS Chola	44.64	-1.69	95.94	24.47	-5.07
10	Deutsche	12.01	0.82	43.42	155.20	111.31
11	DSP M L	112.54	75.27	96.21	19.02	29.78
12	Escorts	37.73	-19.08	25.73	-35.32	35.22
13	Fidelity	NA	NA	NA	55.39	46.85
14	Franklin Temp.	9.40	1.46	16.11	25.45	20.03
15	HDFC	8.97	0.16	43.57	48.30	40.09
16	HSBC	58.56	37.96	47.59	38.61	16.48
17	ICICI Prudential	-2.60	10.51	54.61	86.15	24.17
18	ING	51.86	-23.21	64.61	101.85	117.51
19	JM Financial	-18.42	29.28	-36.07	35.66	267.52
20	Kotak Mahindra	25.39	21.92	44.14	18.39	65.35
21	Lotus India	NA	NA	NA	NA	456.50
22	Morgan Stanley	16.71	13.48	87.27	-2.43	13.58
23	PRINCIPAL	40.58	50.32	18.82	67.38	21.59
24	Quantum	NA	NA	NA	344.56	26.98
25	Reliance	7.84	31.79	158.52	93.21	90.78
26	Sahara	49.15	-31.29	17.84	-36.42	-0.17
27	Stan. Chart.	-11.79	-5.25	38.90	48.41	-8.84
28	Sundaram BNP	11296.10	-8.03	76.32	136.17	62.54
29	Tata	39.74	69.01	43.23	49.15	35.79
30	Taurus	1.09	20.86	47.34	16.99	17.82
All Average		**570.58**	**42.22**	**60.40**	**72.87**	**62.30**
Overall Average		**17.44**	**11.10**	**54.59**	**54.72**	**48.23**

Note: *March 2004 growth rates were based on October 2003 figures. AIG Global and JP Morgan are not included, as they have figures only from 2008.

Source: Computed from Table – 3.11.

Changes in the annual growth rates of the asset management companies have also led to changes in their relative market share over the years. Table – 3.13 provides the data on the asset management companies year-wise market shares. In the public sector, the market shares of all the funds except that of State Bank of India have come down; this is quite dramatic in the case of UTI. Thus, the overall market share of the public sector funds has dropped from 21.48 per cent in October in 2003 to 18 per cent in March 2008. Correspondingly, the market share of the private sector asset management companies put together has increased from 78.52 per cent to 82 per cent during the same period. The UTI, which once dominated the industry as monopoly, now commands around one-tenth of the total market, while ICICI Prudential and Reliance boast of more than 10 per cent share each. But, the level of competition has reduced the share of many private funds, notably that of Franklin Templeton (from 12.10 per cent in October 2003 to 5.07 per cent in March 2008), HDFC (from 12.03 per cent to 8.46 per cent and ICICI Prudential (12.35 per cent to 10.27 per cent). The share of State Bank of India has gone up from 2.91 per cent to 5.52 per cent and that of Reliance from 5.87 per cent to 17.19 per cent, which is the market leader as on March 31, 2008.

Table – 3.13 Year-wise Market Share of Asset Management Companies

(in percentage)

Sl. No.	Fund's Name	Oct-2003	March 2004	March 2005	March 2006	March 2007	March 2008
Public Sector Funds							
1	BOB	0.21	0.34	0.10	0.08	0.03	0.01
2	Canara Robeco	0.69	0.41	1.05	0.90	0.60	0.55
3	LIC	2.76	3.08	1.94	2.27	3.03	2.66
4	SBI	2.91	3.88	4.42	5.72	5.32	5.52
5	UTI	14.91	15.35	13.90	12.80	10.54	9.26
Group Total		**21.48**	**23.60**	**21.41**	**21.77**	**19.52**	**18.00**

	Private Sector Funds						
6	ABN AMRO	NA	NA	0.62	1.20	1.38	1.21
7	AIG Global	NA	NA	NA	NA	NA	0.59
8	Benchmark	0.02	0.05	0.33	0.43	1.19	0.63
9	Birla Sun Life	7.01	6.25	6.95	6.41	6.17	6.79
10	DBS Chola	0.63	0.78	0.69	0.87	0.70	0.45
11	Deutsche	1.29	1.23	1.12	1.04	1.71	2.44
12	DSP M L	1.29	2.34	3.69	4.68	3.60	3.15
13	Escorts	0.10	0.12	0.09	0.07	0.03	0.03
14	Fidelity	NA	NA	NA	1.59	1.60	1.58
15	Franklin Temp.	12.10	11.27	10.29	7.73	6.27	5.07
16	HDFC	12.03	11.16	10.06	9.34	8.96	8.46
17	HSBC	2.50	3.37	4.19	4.00	3.58	2.81
18	ICICI Prudential	12.35	10.24	10.19	10.19	12.26	10.27
19	ING	0.89	1.16	0.80	0.85	1.11	1.63
20	JM Financial	3.37	2.34	2.72	1.13	0.99	2.45
21	JPMorgan	NA	NA	NA	NA	NA	0.41
22	Kotak Mahindra	3.66	3.91	4.29	4.00	3.06	3.42
23	Lotus India	NA	NA	NA	NA	0.40	1.50
24	Morgan Stanley	1.02	1.01	1.04	1.25	0.79	0.61
25	PRINCIPAL	2.26	2.71	3.66	2.81	3.04	2.50
26	Quantum	NA	NA	NA	0.00	0.01	0.01
27	Reliance	5.87	5.39	6.40	10.70	13.36	17.19
28	Sahara	0.20	0.26	0.16	0.12	0.05	0.03
29	Stan. Chart.	7.09	5.33	4.54	4.08	3.91	2.41
30	Sundaram BNP	0.02	1.50	1.24	1.42	2.17	2.38
31	Tata	2.51	2.99	4.55	4.21	4.06	3.72
32	Taurus	0.11	0.10	0.11	0.10	0.08	0.06
Group Total		**78.52**	**76.40**	**78.59**	**78.23**	**80.48**	**82.00**
GRAND TOTAL		**100**	**100**	**100**	**100**	**100**	**100**

Source: Computed from Table – 3.11.

Regulation of Mutual Fund Industry in India [22]

Initially, there was no uniform regulation of the mutual fund industry in India. The UTI was regulated by a special Act of Parliament while funds promoted by public sector banks were subject to RBI Guidelines of July 1989. The SEBI was formed in 1988 and was given the statutory power in 1992 and it became a capital market regulator only in 1993. One of its responsibilities was to regulate the mutual fund industry and it came up with comprehensive regulations for the industry in 1993.

SEBI (Mutual Fund) Regulations, 1993

For the first time in the history of the Indian mutual fund industry mutual funds were begun to be governed by a uniform set of regulations which required them to be formed as trusts and managed by a separate asset management company and supervised by a board of trustees or trustee company. SEBI (Mutual Fund) regulations 1993 provided for arms length relationship between the various constituents of the mutual fund and thus brought about a structural change which would ensure qualitative improvement in the functioning of the mutual funds. The regulations laid down certain eligibility criteria for the sponsors of mutual funds and required that the asset management companies had a minimum net worth of Rs.6 crore of which the sponsors must contribute at least 40 per cent. The SEBI (Mutual Fund) Regulations also provided for an approval of the offer documents of schemes by SEBI. The regulations prescribed the minimum amount to be raised by each scheme. A closed ended scheme of a mutual fund must raise a minimum of Rs.20 crore and open ended scheme of Rs.50 crore. The entire subscription amount must be refunded within six weeks of the closure of the scheme in case the amount collected by the scheme fell short of the prescribed amount. There would also be certain investment restrictions for asset management companies. The advertisement code prescribed norms for fair and truthful disclosure by mutual funds in advertisements and publicity materials. The Regulations were intended to ensure that the mutual funds grow on healthy lines and investors' interests are protected.

Revisions to SEBI Regulations, 1996

The SEBI (Mutual Funds) Regulations, 1993 were revised on the basis of the recommendations of the Mutual Funds 2000 Report prepared by SEBI.[23] The revision had been carried out with the objective of improving investor protection, facilitating competition, imparting a greater degree of flexibility and promoting innovation. The existing asset management companies were required to increase their net worth from Rs.5 crore to Rs.10 crore within 1 year from the date of notification of the regulations. The asset management companies can also have cross trusteeship and cross directorship, provided, there is no conflict of interest. They were also allowed to do other fund based businesses such as providing investment management services to offshore funds, other mutual funds, venture capital funds and insurance companies. The revised regulations for mutual funds, however, retained the present fee structure of the asset management companies of 1.25 per cent of weekly average NAV upto Rs.100 crore, and 1 per cent of NAV for net assets in excess of Rs.100 crore.

Further, the consent of investors had to be obtained for bringing about any change in the "fundamental attributes" of a scheme on the basis of which the unit holders had made initial investments. The revised regulations also provided for portfolio disclosure, standardisation of accounting policies, valuation norms for NAV and pricing. The payment of early bird incentive for various schemes had been allowed provided they are viewed as interest payments for early investment with full disclosures.

The various mutual fund schemes would be allowed to mention an indicative return for schemes for fixed income securities. This would be subject to a variety of disclosures, including:

(i) That the returns be based on the current yields of instruments which may change from time to time, depending upon the interest rates prevailing in the market, RBI policy and other relevant factors.

(ii) In case a portfolio of securities is disclosed, it should also be mentioned that such a portfolio is a purely an illustrative example, and the scheme does not assure that it would maintain this portfolio.

(iii) The returns mentioned are only indicative and not assured. The actual returns will be based on the actual NAV which may go up or down depending on the market conditions.

In all 31 mutual funds (excluding the Unit Trust of India) were registered with SEBI as of December 1996, under the SEBI (Mutual Funds) Regulations, 1993. Of these, 10 belonged to the public sector and 21 were in the private sector. 16 private sector mutual funds and 1 public sector mutual fund had foreign participation in their asset management companies.

The different entities such as the Mutual Fund, the asset management company and the Custodian operate as per the provisions of the SEBI Mutual Fund Regulation 1996 and the rules and guidelines issued by SEBI. Each of these entities has independent Boards of Directors and separate auditors. SEBI keeps a close watch on the mutual funds through periodical reports and every three months, each mutual fund submits to SEBI a report conforming compliance with regulatory provisions and mutual funds are required to record their investment decisions. Any deficiency or non-compliance is dealt with suitably by SEBI.

Every year, each mutual fund is inspected by SEBI and such inspection is both a detailed scrutiny of operations and a rectification exercise. Thus, the mutual funds are strictly supervised and regulated entities and the regulatory provisions match with international standards. The Association of Mutual Funds in India (AMFI) is also engaged in upgrading professional standards and in promoting best industry practices in diverse areas such as valuation, disclosure, transparency, etc.

Association of Mutual Funds in India (AMFI)

With the increase in mutual fund players in India, a need for mutual fund association in India was generated to function as a non-profit organisation. The AMFI was incorporated on 22nd August, 1995.

The AMFI is an apex body of all asset management companies which has been registered with SEBI. Till date all the asset management companies that have launched mutual fund schemes are its members. It functions under the supervision and guidelines of its Board of Directors. The AMFI has brought the Indian mutual fund Industry to a professional and healthy market with ethical lines maintaining and enhancing standards. It follows the principle of both protecting and promoting the interests of mutual funds as well as their unit holders.

The AMFI Code of Ethics

One of the objects of the AMFI is to promote the investors' interest by defining and maintaining high ethical and professional standards in the mutual fund industry. The AMFI Code of Ethics, (ACE) sets out the standards of good practices to be followed by the asset management companies in their operations and in their dealings with investors, intermediaries and the public. SEBI (Mutual Funds) Regulation 1996 requires all asset management companies and Trustees to abide by the Code of conduct as specified in the Fifth Schedule of the Regulation. The AMFI Code has been drawn up to supplement that schedule, to encourage standards higher than those prescribed by the Regulator for the benefit of investors in the industry. The following are the salient features of the Code of Ethics set by the AMFI.

Integrity

Members and their key personnel, in the conduct of their business shall observe high standards of integrity and fairness in all dealings with investors, issuers, market intermediaries, other members and regulatory and other government authorities. Mutual fund schemes shall be organized, operated, managed and their portfolios of securities selected, in the interest of all classes of unit holders and not in the interest of:

- sponsors;
- directors of Members;
- members of Board of Trustees or directors of the Trustee company;
- brokers and other market intermediaries;
- associates of the Members; and
- a special class selected from out of unit holders.

Due Diligence

Members in the conduct of their asset management business shall at all times:

- render high standards of service;
- exercise due diligence; and
- exercise independent professional judgment.

Members shall have and employ effectively adequate resourccs and procedures which are needed for the conduct of asset management activities.

Disclosures

Members shall ensure timely dissemination to all unit holders of adequate, accurate, and explicit information presented in a simple language about the investment objectives, investment policies, financial position and general affairs of the scheme. Members shall disclose to unit holders investment pattern, portfolio details, ratios of expenses to net assets and total income and portfolio turnover wherever applicable in respect of schemes on annual basis.

Members shall in respect of transactions of purchase and sale of securities entered into with any of their associates or any significant unit holder:

- submit to the Board of Trustees details of such transactions, justifying its fairness to the scheme; and
- disclose to the unit holders details of the transaction in brief through annual and half yearly reports.

All transactions of purchase and sale of securities by key personnel who are directly involved in investment operations shall be disclosed to the compliance officer of the member at least on half yearly basis and subsequently reported to the Board of Trustees if found having conflict of interest with the transactions of the fund.

Professional Selling Practices

Members shall not use any unethical means to sell, market or induce any investor to buy their products and schemes. Members shall not make any exaggerated statement regarding performance of any product or scheme.

Members shall endeavour to ensure that at all times –

* investors are provided with true and adequate information without any misleading or exaggerated claims to investors about their capability to render certain services or their achievements in regard to services rendered to other clients;
* investors are made aware of attendant risks in members' schemes before any investment decision is made by the investors;
* copies of prospectus, memoranda and related literature is made available to investors on request;
* adequate steps are taken for fair allotment of mutual fund units and refund of application money without delay and within the prescribed time limit; and,
* complaints from investors are fairly and expeditiously dealt with. Members in all their communications to investors and selling agents shall:
* not present a mutual fund scheme as if it were a new share issue;
* not create unrealistic expectations;
* not guarantee returns except as stated in the Offer Document of the scheme approved by SEBI, and in such case, the Members shall ensure that adequate resources will be made available and maintained to meet the guaranteed returns;
* convey in clear terms the market risk and the investment risks of any scheme being offered by the Members;
* not induce investors by offering benefits which are extraneous to the scheme; and
* not misrepresent either by stating information in a manner calculated to mislead or by omitting to state information which is material to making an informed investment decision.

Investment Practices

Members shall manage all the schemes in accordance with the fundamental investment objectives and investment policies stated in the offer documents and take investment decisions solely in the interest of the unit holders. Members shall not knowingly buy or sell securities for any of their schemes from or to:

- any director, officer, or employee of the member; and
- any trustee or any director, officer, or employee of the Trustee Company.

Operations

Members shall avoid conflicts of interest in managing the affairs of the schemes and shall keep the interest of all unit holders paramount in all matters relating to the scheme.

Members or any of their directors, officers or employees shall not indulge in front running (buying or selling of any securities ahead of transaction of the fund, with access to information regarding the transaction which is not public and which is material to making an investment decision, so as to derive unfair advantage). Members or any of their directors, officers or employees shall not indulge in self dealing (using their position to engage in transactions with the fund by which they benefit unfairly at the expense of the fund and the unit holders).

Members shall not engage in any act, practice or course of business in connection with the purchase or sale, directly or indirectly, of any security held or to be acquired by any scheme managed by the Members, and in purchase, sale and redemption of units of schemes managed by the Members, which is fraudulent, deceptive or manipulative.

Members shall not, in respect of any securities, be party to –

- creating a false market;
- price rigging or manipulation; and
- passing of price sensitive information to brokers, Members of stock exchanges and other players in the capital markets or take action which is unethical or unfair to investors.

Employees, officers and directors of the Members shall not work as agents / brokers for selling of the schemes of the Members, except in their capacity as employees of the Member or the Trustee Company. Members shall not make any change in the fundamental attributes of a scheme, without the prior approval of unit holders except when such change is consequent on changes in the regulations. Members shall avoid excessive concentration of business with any broking firm, and excessive holding of units in a scheme by few persons or entities.

Reporting Practices

Members shall follow comparable and standardized valuation policies in accordance with the SEBI Mutual Fund Regulations. Members shall follow uniform performance reporting on the basis of total return. Members shall ensure scheme-wise segregation of cash and securities accounts.

Unfair Competition

Members shall not make any statement or become privy to any act, practice or competition, which is likely to be harmful to the interests of other Members or is likely to place other members in a disadvantageous position in relation to a market player or investors, while competing for investible funds.

Observance of Statutes, Rules and Regulations

Members shall abide by the letter and spirit of the provisions of the Statutes, Rules and Regulations which may be applicable and relevant to the activities carried on by the Members.

Enforcement

Members shall:

- widely disseminate the AMFI Code to all persons and entities covered by it;
- make observance of the Code a condition of employment;
- make violation of the provisions of the code, a ground for revocation of contractual arrangement without redress and a cause for disciplinary action;
- require that each officer and employee of the Member sign a statement that he / she has received and read a copy of the Code;
- establish internal controls and compliance mechanisms, including assigning supervisory responsibility;
- designate one person with primary responsibility for exercising compliance with power to fully investigate all possible violations and report to competent authority;

- file regular reports to the Trustees on a half yearly and annual basis regarding observance of the Code and special reports as circumstances require;
- maintain records of all activities and transactions for at least three years, which records shall be subject to review by the Trustees; and
- dedicate adequate resources to carry out the provisions of the Code.

Amendment to Mutual Funds Regulations, 2006

The SEBI has amended its regulations to allow mutual funds to invest in both gold and gold related instruments. According to the amended regulations called Securities and Exchange Board of India (Mutual Funds) (Amendment) Regulations, 2006, a Gold Exchange Traded Fund (GETF), which means a mutual fund scheme that invests primarily in gold and gold related instruments, shall be allowed subject to certain investment restrictions.

Initial issue expenses in respect of any GETF scheme shall not exceed six per cent of the funds raised under that scheme. The funds of such schemes shall be invested only in gold or gold-related instruments in line with its investment objective except to such extent that is necessary to meet the liquidity requirements for honouring repurchases or redemption as disclosed in the offer document, it added. In case of delay in deploying funds, mutual funds may invest such funds in short term deposits of scheduled commercial banks.

Conclusion

The mutual fund industry in India which was created with the establishment of the UTI in 1963 has gone through many phases, right from a state of monopoly to that of being controlled by market forces. Many new asset management companies have entered in the process and some existing ones have been acquired or got merged with others. This industry, through its unique aspect of less risk (compared to stock market) and better returns (vis-à-vis the traditional financial products) has come as a boon to the middle class and has attracted huge amount of investment. However, analysis shows that the Indian investors' preference for physical assets still outweighs, albeit negligibly, the financial products. At the same time, among the financial products, attraction towards shares and debentures and mutual funds is on the rise, notably in the last three years.

The asset under management has increased manifold in many asset management companies, while in some others, the quantum of assets has declined and this has occurred in both public and private sectors. There have been huge fluctuations in the growth rates and also the market shares of many asset management companies. This indicates a dynamic scenario unfolding in the Indian mutual fund industry. This warrants an in-depth study about the performance of the asset management companies in both the public and private sectors, which is undertaken in the forthcoming chapters.

References

1. Neal, L., (1990), "The Rise of Financial Capitalism: International Capital Markets in the Age of Reason", Cambridge: Cambridge University Press, pp. 56-59.
2. Ibid., pp. 62-64.
3. In a tontine, a borrower promises to pay to a group of individuals an annuity which will be divided among the surviving members. As members die, the payout to the survivors increases.
4. Riley, J., (1980), "International Government Finance and the Amsterdam Capital Market 1740–1815", Cambridge: Cambridge University Press, pp. 85-89.
5. Kuchhal S.K., (1990), "Corporation Finance: Principles and Problems", (Chaitanya Publishing House, Allahabad, pp. 358-371.
6. Rouwenhorst, K. Geert, (2004), "The Origins of Mutual Funds", Yale International Centre for Finance Working Paper No. 04-48, December. Accessed at www.ssrn.com
7. Khan M.Y., (1980), Indian Financial Sytem, Vikas Publishing House, New Delhi, pp. 63-89.
8. Mutual Fund Fact Book, (1995), Investment Company Institute, Washington, pp. 22-23.
9. Khorana, Ajay, Henri Servaes, B.C., Peter Tufanod, E, (2005), "Explaining the size of the mutual fund industry around the world", Journal of Financial Economics, October, pp. 145-185.
10 Indian Central Banking Enquiry Committee, (1931), Minority Report, p. 325.
11. Kuchhal S.K., op.cit., p.367.
12. Hanifa K.M., (1960), Investment Trusts, RBI Bulletin, October, pp.1445-1468.
13. Annual Report of UTI, various years.
14. Information accessed at www.amfi.com
15. The Hindu, July 3, 2002, p.18.
16. Economic Survey 1993-94, Ministry of Finance, Govt. of India, New Delhi, p.53.

17. Economic Survey 1996-97, Ministry of Finance, Govt. of India, New Delhi, p.66.
18. Accessed at www.icmrindia.org
19. Economic Survey 2003-04, accessed at http://www.finmin.nic.in/reports/index.html
20. Information accessed at www.amfi.com
21. Financial Express, May 5, 2008.
22. This section is based on the SEBI Mutual Fund Regulation Act, 1996, accessed at www.mutualfundsinindia.com
23. Economic Survey 1996-97, op. cit., p.67.

4

RETURNS AND RISK OF THE SAMPLE SCHEMES

Introduction

Generally, the main objective of investing in any portfolio is to earn some income. Investment in mutual funds enables the investor to earn more than the conventional products like provident fund, post office and bank deposits, etc., while at the same time not exposing to the kind of risk as seen in the stock market. It should also be noted that the degree of risk involved in mutual fund is higher than that of the conventional products. Thus, return and risk are the two most important aspects of mutual fund investment. In this chapter, these two aspects are analysed for the sample mutual fund schemes.

Household Sector's Savings in India

This section analyses the growth of the household sector savings in India since 1993-94, which begins with an analysis about the savings and investment patterns of the household sector in India.

Savings and investment preferences of the investors have undergone remarkable changes especially during the liberalised era in India. The arrival of multinational companies, privatisation of the industrial and service sectors have all opened up the floodgates for new competitive spirit in the country. This has resulted in a quantum jump in the salary levels and thus a paradigm shift has taken place in the savings and investment preferences. The trends in Gross Domestic Savings (GDS), household sector savings (HSS), savings in physical assets (PS) and financial savings (FS) are discussed with the help of the data presented in Table – 4.1.

Table – 4.1 Trends in Household Sector Savings

(in Rupees Crore)

Year	GDS	HSS		PS		FS	
		Amount	As% of GDS	Amount	As% of HSS	Amount	As% of HSS
1993-94	193621	158310	81.76	63572	40.16	94738	59.84
1994-95	251463	199358	79.28	78625	39.44	120733	60.56
1995-96	298195	215588	72.30	110422	51.22	105166	48.78
1996-97	316923	232914	73.49	91786	39.41	141128	60.59
1997-98	358250	271383	75.75	121185	44.65	150198	55.35
1998-99	386732	336469	87.00	143958	42.78	192511	57.22
1999-2000	484256	412516	85.19	205914	49.92	206602	50.08
2000-01	499033	454853	91.15	239634	52.68	215219	47.32
2001-02	534885	504165	94.26	256689	50.91	247476	49.09
2002-03	647970	569134	87.83	315879	55.50	253255	44.50
2003-04	821026	670776	81.70	357516	53.30	313260	46.70
2004-05	1000424	725110	72.48	406846	56.11	318264	43.89
2005-06	1227348	866756	70.62	445915	51.45	420841	48.55
2006-07	1441423	985822	68.39	517837	52.53	467985	47.47
Mean	**604396**	**471654**	**80.09**	**239698**	**48.58**	**231955**	**51.42**
SD	**382539**	**261942**	**8.18**	**148765**	**6.01**	**114632**	**6.01**

Note: SD – Standard Deviation. HSS – Household Sector Savings; PS – Physical Savings; FS – Financial Savings.

Source: National Income Accounts, Central Statistical Organisation, New Delhi, Various Years.

The GDS has increased from Rs.1,93,621 crore in 1993-94 to Rs. 4,84,256 crore in 1999-2000 and further to Rs. 14,41,423 crore in 2006-07. The household sector savings, which is a component of GDS has also increased correspondingly over the years. It has consistently increased from Rs. 1,58,310 crore in 1993-94 to Rs. 4,12,516 crore in 1999-2000 and again to Rs. 9,85,822 crore in 2006-07. But the relative share of HSS in GDS has not been consistent. To begin with, it declined from 81.76 per cent in 1993-94 to 72.30 in 1995-96. It increased thereafter and touched the highest level of 94.26 per cent in 2001-02. The relative share of HSS, since then climbed down and stood at 68.39 per cent in 2006-07.

The savings of the household sector consists of savings made in physical assets and financial assets. In a feudal set up, it is natural that people tend to prefer PS over FS to a greater extent, mainly due to lack of awareness, lack of risk-taking ability and the underdevelopment of the financial market. With the development of the economy, increased monetisation and the arrival of market forces, financial market and its related products develop, which tremendously increase the portfolio of choices to the investors. Table – 4.1 also shows the trend in FS and its relative share in HSS. In absolute terms, FS went up from Rs.94,783 crore in 1993-94 to Rs.2,06,602 crore in 1999-2000 and further to Rs.4,67,985 crore in 2006-07. This consistent rise, however has not replicated in its relative share in HSS. It accounted for 60.56 per cent in 1994-95, but nosedived to 48.78 per cent in the subsequent year (declined even in absolute terms), but again got restored to that level in the next year, 1996-97. In the remaining years too, the share of FS has undergone huge fluctuations. In 2004-05, it has touched the lowest level of 43.89 per cent and clocked 47.47 per cent in 2006-07. Meanwhile, savings in physical assets increased from Rs.63,572 crore in 1993-94 to Rs.1,10,422 crore in 1995-96, in which years its share in HSS crossed the 50 per cent mark. Though people's preferences for PS declined to Rs.91,786 crore in the next year, it did not last long. Since 1997-98 onwards, there is a continuous and consistent rise in PS from Rs.1,21,185 crore in that year to a whopping Rs.5,17,837 crore in 2006-07.

The table also provides the mean and standard deviation of all the variables. The mean score of HSS was Rs. 4,71,654 crore, that of PS was Rs. 2,39,698 crore and FS was Rs. 2,31,955 crore. However, the mean share of FS (51.42) is marginally higher than that of PS (48.58), mainly due to the higher share of the former compared to that of the latter during the 1990s.

The trends in HSS, PS and FS are graphically presented in Chart – 4.1. It depicts that HSS as a proportion of GDS, with lot fluctuations in its growth rate peaked in 2001-02, and started to decline rather swiftly, though its rate of decline somewhat moderated since 2004-05. The trend in PS indicates that it was lying low till 1999-2000, in which year it was on par with the FS and gone past the latter since then. This suggests that even after liberalisation of the financial sector in India, and the resultant arrival of plethora of portfolios, the dominance of physical sector products which includes gold, land and others still dominates the HSS. The trend of the FS is the mirror image of the PS, as the former is only the reciprocal of the latter.

Chart – 4.1 Trends in Household Sector Savings in India

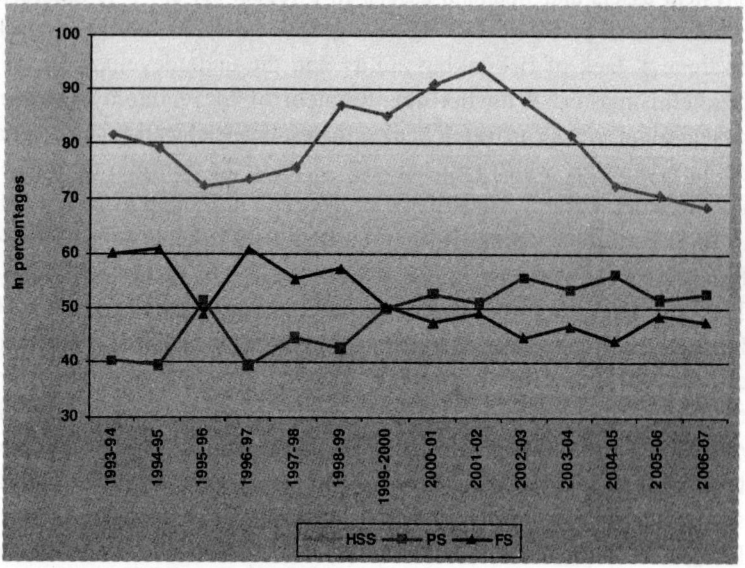

Note: HSS in terms of GDS; PS and FS are in terms of HSS.
Source: Based on Table – 4.1.

Returns from Sample Schemes

Investment in mutual funds by the investors is made with the expectation of earning more by exploiting the expertise of the fund manager. This helps in evaluating the performance of the fund manager or the AMC's in the backdrop of the fund's objectives. The notion behind this evaluation is to compare the returns obtained by the mutual fund scheme with the returns that would have been obtained by the investor had one or more alternative portfolios been chosen for investment. Such portfolios chosen for comparison are often referred to as 'benchmark portfolios'. Stock market index can be considered as one such benchmark.

To measure the returns, month-end NAVs of the selected sample schemes as announced by the asset management companies have been used. Though NAVs are available on daily basis, it has been proved that monthly NAVs make for more normal distribution.[1] Evaluation can also be made on the basis of market prices. But, in the Indian context, the scrips of the mutual funds are very thinly traded and the secondary market for mutual fund units is rather weak. Hence, NAVs are considered as appropriate.

For each mutual fund scheme in the sample, the returns have been calculated taking month-end NAVs since April 2003 to March 2008. The NAVs are adjusted for dividends, by assuming that they are reinvested at the ex-dividend NAV. The returns are computed as:

$$R_{pt} = \ln (NAV_t / NAV_{t-1})$$

where, R_{pt} is the return of the scheme 'p' based on NAV in period 't', where 't' is the given month-end and 'ln' is the natural logarithm to the base 'e'. The average return of the scheme is computed as follows:

$$AR_p = \sum_{t=1}^{n} R_{pt} / n$$

where AR_p is the average return of the scheme and 'n' is the total number of observations.[2] The average returns of the selected sample schemes in the study period (April 2003 to March 2008) are presented in Appendix A-2 and they are classified and tabulated in Table – 4.2.

Table – 4.2 Sector-wise and Category-wise Average Returns of the Sample Schemes, April 2003 to March 2008

Sector	Category	AVERAGE RETURNS (in percentage)							Total
		Below 0	0.01-1.0	1.01-2.0	2.01-3.0	3.01-5.0	5.01-8.0	More than 8.0	
Private	Income	Nil	9	6	7	7	Nil	Nil	29
	Balance	Nil	Nil	2	2	4	5	7	20
	Growth	2	4	8	1	3	7	3	28
	ELSS	1	Nil	7	1	1	2	1	13
	All	**3**	**13**	**23**	**11**	**15**	**14**	**11**	**90**
Public	Income	Nil	5	4	Nil	3	2	Nil	14
	Balance	2	2	2	2	Nil	Nil	Nil	8
	Growth	2	2	3	3	2	Nil	Nil	12
	ELSS	2	Nil	3	1	Nil	Nil	Nil	6
	All	**6**	**9**	**12**	**6**	**5**	**2**	**Nil**	**40**
Total	Nil	**14**	**10**	**7**	**10**	**2**	Nil	**43**	
	Balance	**2**	**2**	**4**	**4**	**4**	**5**	**7**	**28**
	Growth	**4**	**6**	**11**	**4**	**5**	**7**	**3**	**40**
	ELSS	**3**	Nil	**10**	**2**	**1**	**2**	**1**	**19**
	All	**9**	**22**	**35**	**17**	**20**	**16**	**11**	**130**

Source: Computed from Appendix A-2.

The AR_p of the sample schemes indicates that, out of the 43 income schemes, 31 schemes (72.1 per cent) generate 3 per cent return or less and the remaining 12 schemes (27.9 per cent) yield 3 per cent or more as average return. This clearly indicates that the level of average return of the income schemes is rather restricted, basically due to its objective. In the case of balanced and growth schemes, however, the monthly average returns are more widespread. Out of the 28 balanced schemes, 2 schemes yield negative returns, 10 schemes (35.7 per cent) provide positive returns less than 3 per cent. Rest of the 16 schemes (57.1 per cent) produce more than 3 per cent return per month, which also includes 7 schemes (25 per cent) that generate more than 8 per cent return. This suggests that balanced schemes which depend also on the equity market to a considerable extent are able to generate a return which is markedly higher than that of the income schemes.

In the case of 40 growth schemes, 4 schemes (10 per cent) yield negative returns, while there are 21 schemes (52.5 per cent) in the range of 0.01-3.0 per cent return class and 15 schemes (37.5 per cent) yield more than 3 per cent per month. This includes 10 schemes (25 per cent) with 5 per cent or more return. Thus, the number of growth schemes in the higher return classes is more as in the case of balanced schemes. This underscores the fact that the growth scheme which is totally oriented towards the equity market yields higher returns.

In the case of 19 ELS schemes, 3 schemes (15.8 per cent) yield negative return and there are as many as 12 schemes (63.2 per cent) with an average monthly return of 3 per cent or less, while 4 schemes (21 per cent) are in the higher return classes of 3 per cent or more. Hence, the returns on the ELS schemes are quite widespread, though majority of the schemes yield less returns, during the study period.

Sector-wise, out of the 29 income schemes in the private sector, though none of them yield negative return, 22 schemes (75.9 per cent) generate return only up to 3 per cent per month. However, there are 7 schemes (24.1 per cent) each in the 3.01 – 5.0 per cent return class. In the case of 20 balanced schemes, only 4 schemes (20 per cent) yield up to 3 per cent return, while the remaining 16 schemes (80 per cent) generate more than that, which also consists of 7 schemes (35 per cent) with more than 8 per cent return.

As far as the 28 growth schemes are concerned, there are 2 schemes (7.1 per cent) in the negative return class, while 13 schemes (46.4 per cent) generate a return of 3 per cent or less and an equal number of schemes yield more than 3 per cent, which also include 10 schemes (35.7 per cent) with more than 5 per cent return. The returns of the ELS schemes in this sector suggests that a majority of them, 7 schemes (53.8 per cent) account for only

1.01 – 2.0 per cent return per month, while the returns of the remaining schemes are distributed in all other return classes, except that of 0.01 – 1.0 per cent.

The returns of the public sector schemes generally indicate that the returns are quite narrowly distributed. Among the 14 income schemes, 9 schemes (64.3 per cent) generate a monthly return of up to 2 per cent, though there is no negative yield. The remaining 5 schemes (35.7 per cent) produce more than 3 per cent return. The return of 8 balanced schemes ranges only up to 3 per cent with negative returns from 2 schemes. Similarly, in the case of 12 growth schemes, the higher return is 3.01 – 5.0 per cent in which there are 2 schemes, and there is equal number of schemes in the negative return class and also in the 0.01 – 1.0 return class. There are 6 schemes in the ELSS category, of which 2 schemes yield negative return, 3 schemes generate only 1.01 – 2.0 per cent monthly return.

This comparative analysis of the schemes' returns in the two sectors exposes the fact that the returns of the private sector schemes are much more spread out than the returns of public sector schemes. Moreover, in the case of the latter, not many of the schemes yield more than 5 per cent return, while in the case of the former, considerable number of schemes produce not only more than 5 per cent, but also more than 8 per cent as average return. This occurs across all categories.

Risk Associated with Sample Schemes

Performance of the mutual fund schemes cannot be evaluated in the isolation of return. The comparatively higher returns which are associated with mutual funds are blended with substantial degree of risk, which is the hallmark of stock market. Risk, with regard to investment, can be defined as the degree of probability of variations in the expected returns of the portfolios. This is considered as the basis of measuring or quantifying risk. Studies have mentioned that variability of returns measured in terms of standard deviation is the widely used measure of risk. Standard deviation is a statistical measure of dispersion of returns around average return. Smaller the deviation smaller will be the spread of distribution and hence, lower will be the degree of risk. In this study, standard deviation (total risk) of the scheme's return is calculated for the entire sample of schemes, which are presented in Appendix A-2. The total risk or standard deviation of returns is measured as:

$$\sigma_p = 1/n\left(\sum_{t=1}^{n}\{R_{pt} - AR_p\}^2\right)^{1/2}$$

where σ_p is the standard deviation of the sample scheme which indicates the scheme's total risk, R_{pt} is the return over a period of time and AR_p is the average return of the portfolio 'p'. The calculated risk is classified into different classes and shown in Table – 4.3.

Table – 4.3 Sector-wise and Category-wise Total Risk of the Sample Schemes, April 2003 to March 2008

Sector	Category	TOTAL RISK (in percentage)						
		Below 2.0	2.01-3.0	3.01-4.0	4.01-6.0	6.01-8.0	More than 8.0	Total
Private	Income	12	8	8	1	Nil	Nil	29
	Balance	Nil	5	9	4	2	Nil	20
	Growth	Nil	3	12	8	4	1	28
	ELSS	Nil	3	2	6	1	1	13
	All	**12**	**19**	**31**	**19**	**7**	**2**	**90**
Public	Income	2	2	8	2	Nil	Nil	14
	Balance	2	3	3	Nil	Nil	Nil	8
	Growth	Nil	1	Nil	Nil	7	4	12
	ELSS	Nil	Nil	4	2	Nil	Nil	6
	All	**4**	**6**	**15**	**4**	**7**	**4**	**40**
Total	**Income**	**14**	**10**	**16**	**3**	**Nil**	**Nil**	**43**
	Balance	**2**	**8**	**12**	**4**	**2**	**Nil**	**28**
	Growth	**Nil**	**4**	**12**	**8**	**11**	**5**	**40**
	ELSS	**Nil**	**3**	**6**	**8**	**1**	**1**	**19**
	All	**16**	**25**	**46**	**23**	**14**	**6**	**130**

Source: Computed from Appendix A-2.

The table indicates that out of the 43 income schemes, the total risk as measured by standard deviation of as many as 40 schemes (93 per cent) is 4 per cent or less. In this, 14 schemes (32.6 per cent) have a very low risk of 2 per cent. Thus, only 3 schemes (7 per cent) have a marginally higher risk level of 4.01 – 6.0 per cent. This is quite understandable given the fact that income schemes rely absolutely on secured portfolios like government securities and thus boast of lower risk level. In the case of 28 balanced schemes, 22 schemes (78.6 per cent) have a risk of 4 per cent or less. The remaining 6 schemes (21.4 per cent) bear a risk level of more than 4 per cent.

Hence, compared to the income schemes, the degree of risk of the balanced schemes is higher, as they are exposed to the stock market.

The growth schemes, which are totally tied to the stock market, theoretically and also practically, are much riskier than other schemes. The table shows that out of the 40 schemes, only 16 schemes (40 per cent) have a risk level of 4 per cent or less, of which none fall in the lowest risk class of below 2 per cent. Of the other 24 schemes, 16 schemes (40 per cent) exhibit a risk level of 6 per cent or more and 8 more schemes are in the 4.01 - 6.0 per cent risk class. In the case of ELS schemes also, the degree of risk is more or less similar to that of growth schemes, particularly in the lower risk classes. In the higher risk classes like 6.01 – 8.0 per cent and more than 8 per cent, however, there is only one scheme each.

Sector-wise, out of the 29 income schemes in the private sector, all but one scheme falls in the lower risk classes of 4 per cent or less. In the case of 14 income schemes in the public sector, 12 schemes (85.7 per cent) fall in the 4 per cent or less risk class, while 2 schemes are in the 4.01 - 6.0 per cent class.

There are 20 balanced schemes in the private sector, of which no scheme falls in the lowest risk class, while 14 schemes (70 per cent) bear a risk level of 4 per cent or less and the remaining 30 per cent schemes bear 4 per cent or more risk level, while none falls in the highest risk class. However, in the case of 8 public sector balanced schemes, all fall in the 4 per cent or lesser level of risk, with 2 schemes falling in the lowest level of risk.

The degree of risk of 28 private sector growth schemes is even greater than that of the balanced schemes, with no scheme falling in the lowest risk level. Only 15 schemes (53.6 per cent) bear the risk of less than 4 per cent. However, the remaining 13 schemes bear greater risk, as 8 schemes (28.6 per cent) are in the 4.01 – 6.0 per cent risk class, 4 schemes (14.3 per cent) in the 6.01 – 8.0 per cent class and one scheme falls in the highest risk class of more than 8 per cent. In the case of 12 public sector growth schemes, one is in the 2.01 – 3.0 per cent risk class, while 7 schemes (58.3 per cent) are in the 6.01 – 8.0 per cent level of risk and 4 schemes (33.3 per cent) bear the highest level of risk. Hence, while the risk level of the growth schemes are the highest, public sector growth schemes are much riskier than the private sector growth schemes.

In the ELSS category, there are 13 private sector schemes, of which 5 schemes (38.5 per cent) have a risk of 4 per cent or less, 6 schemes (46.2 per cent) are in the 4.01 – 6.0 per cent class and there is one scheme each in the 6.01 – 8.0 and more than 8 per cent risk classes. Thus, the risk levels of the private sector ELS schemes are mostly similar to that of the growth schemes of that sector. In the case of 6 public sector ELS schemes, 4 schemes (66.7 per cent) bear a risk level of 3.01 – 4.0 per cent and 2 schemes (33.3 per cent) have a 4.01 – 6.0 per cent risk. Hence, comparatively, the public sector ELS schemes are less risky than their counterparts in the private sector. Thus, this analysis of the sector-wise risk of the schemes suggests that in the private sector, income schemes and growth schemes are less risky, while the other two categories viz., balanced schemes and ELS schemes are less risky in the public sector.

In this section, the average returns of the sample schemes and their total risk are analysed combinedly. The overall returns and risk of the schemes are presented in Table – 4.4.

Table – 4.4 Returns and Risk of the Sample Schemes, April 2003 to March 2008

	Total Risk (in percentage)						
Average Return (in%)	*Below 2.0*	*2.01-3.0*	*3.01-4.0*	*4.01-6.0*	*6.1-8.0*	*More than 8.0*	*Total*
Below 0	1	Nil	4	Nil	3	1	**9**
0.01-1.0	8	3	5	5	Nil	1	**22**
1.01-2.0	4	8	7	6	1	2	**28**
2.01-3.0	1	3	6	4	2	1	**17**
3.01-5.0	2	5	8	3	2	Nil	**20**
5.01-8.0	Nil	3	7	3	3	Nil	**16**
More than 8.0	Nil	3	9	2	3	1	**18**
Total	**16**	**25**	**46**	**23**	**14**	**6**	**130**

Source: Computed from Appendix A-2.

The table indicates that out of the 130 sample schemes, 16 schemes (12.3 per cent) bear the lowest risk of below 2 per cent. Out of these 16 schemes, the average monthly return of 13 schemes is less than 2 per cent, while none generates more than 5 per cent return. In the next risk class of 2.01 – 3.0 per cent, there are 25 schemes, of which 11 yield up to 2 per cent return, 8 schemes produce a return in the range of 2.01 – 5.0 per cent and the remaining 6 schemes earn more than 5 per cent return per month. Bulk of the sample schemes (46 out of 130, 35.4 per cent) fall in the risk range of 3.01 – 4.0 per cent. The 46 schemes are distributed in all the return classes, though 24 schemes provide more than 3 per cent return per month. In the risk class of 4.01 – 6.0, there are 23 schemes (17.7 per cent), of which 15 schemes earn less than 3 per cent return.

Theoretically, as the level of risk goes up, the level of return is also expected to go up, since fund managers in the pursuit of earning more, will take more risk. But, during the study period, among the sample schemes, this hypothesis has not been proved nor disproved. In the successive risk classes, the proportion of schemes earning higher returns does not go up. For instance, in the risk class of 6.01 – 8.0 per cent, out of the 14 schemes, 6 schemes earn only up to 3 per cent, while in the highest risk class of more than 8 per cent, of the 6 schemes, 5 schemes generate a return of only 3 per cent or less. Thus, this suggests a mixed trend between return and risk of the sample schemes and there is no clear evidence to believe that higher return is associated with higher risk or *vice versa.* This would have happened as the fund managers compete for better returns, increase the risk quotient, though they fail in attaining the former. The return and risk of the sample schemes is analysed sector-wise with the help of Table – 4.5.

Table – 4.5 Sector Returns and Risk of the Sample Schemes, April 2003 to March 2008

Sector	*Average Return (in %)*	*TOTAL RISK (in percentage)*						Total
		Below 2.0	*2.01-3.0*	*3.01-4.0*	*4.01-6.0*	*6.01-8.0*	*More than 8.0*	
Private	Below 0	Nil	Nil	1	Nil	1	1	3
	0.01-1.0	6	1	2	4	Nil	Nil	13
	1.01-2.0	4	6	2	4	Nil	Nil	16
	2.01-3.0	1	3	4	3	Nil	Nil	11
	3.01-5.0	1	4	7	3	Nil	Nil	15
	5.01-8.0	Nil	2	6	3	3	Nil	14
	More than 8.0	Nil	3	9	2	3	1	18
	Total	**12**	**19**	**31**	**19**	**7**	**2**	**90**
Public	Below 0	1	Nil	3	Nil	2	Nil	6
	0.01-1.0	2	2	3	1	Nil	1	9
	1.01-2.0	Nil	2	5	2	1	2	12
	2.01-3.0	Nil	Nil	2	1	2	1	6
	3.01-5.0	1	1	1	Nil	2	Nil	5
	5.01-8.0	Nil	1	1	Nil	Nil	Nil	2
	More than 8.0	Nil	Nil	Nil	Nil	Nil	Nil	Nil
	Total	**4**	**6**	**15**	**4**	**7**	**4**	**40**

Source: Computed from Appendix A-2.

The table shows that in the private sector, out of the 90 schemes, 62 schemes (68.9 per cent) bear a lower risk level of 4 per cent or less, of which just under 50 per cent (30 schemes) yield up to 3 per cent or less. In the higher risk classes such as 4.01 – 6.0, 6.01 – 8.0 and more than 8 per cent, there are 28 schemes (31.1 per cent), in which 15 schemes (53.6 per cent) earn more than 3 per cent per month. Thus, in the private sector, in the lower risk ranges, 50 of the schemes earn less than 3 per cent and the other half earn more than that, while in the higher risk classes, 53.6 per cent schemes generate more than 3 per cent return.

In the public sector, out of the 40 schemes, 25 schemes (62.5 per cent) fall in the risk range of 4 per cent or less, of which 20 schemes produce less than 3 per cent return per month. And, of the remaining 15 schemes, only 2 schemes yield more than 3 per cent return. This indicates that the private sector schemes perform better, though only marginally, compared to the public sector schemes. The average return of the later schemes is less even in the higher risk classes, while in the case of private sector schemes, a greater proportion of schemes earn higher in the higher risk ranges.

Return and Risk of Benchmark Indices

The return and risk of the mutual fund schemes, especially those of balanced and growth schemes depend to a great deal on the performance of the stock market. Hence, to explore the performance of the sample schemes further, it is pertinent to compare the return and risk of the sample schemes with that of the stock market, which is taken as the benchmark. Here, the Sensitivity Index (Sensex) of the Bombay Stock Exchange and Nifty of the National Stock Exchange are taken as the benchmark indices. Though both these indices provide the market prices of more or less the same stocks, trading volume and the stock prices differ between these two indices. Hence, in this analysis, these two indices are used as benchmark indices. Monthly index data for both Sensex and Nifty that are provided by BSE and NSE were used here to compute their average return and total risk. The average return of the indices is computed as:

$$R_{mt} = \ln (I_t \;/\; I_{t-1})$$

where, R_{mt} is the return of the benchmark index in period 't', where 't' is the given month-end, I_t is the value of the index at time period 't' and 'ln' is the natural logarithm to the base 'e'.

The average return of the scheme is computed as follows:

$$AR_m = \sum_{t=1}^{n} R_{mt} / n$$

where AR_m is the average return of the index and 'n' is the total number of observations. Similarly, the total risk (standard deviation) of the market return is also computed:

$$\sigma_m = 1/n\left(\sum_{t=1}^{n}\{R_{mt} - AR_m\}^2\right)^{1/2}$$

where σ_m is the standard deviation of the index which indicates the market's total risk, R_{mt} is the return over a period of time.[3] The calculated average return and total risk of both the indices are presented in Appendix A-3 along with the average return and total risk of the sample schemes. In order to understand the relative performance of the sample schemes, the average returns and the total risk of the sample schemes and that of the market index (AR_p and AR_m and σ_p and σ_m) are compared under the following four groups:

ONE: $AR_p > AR_m$; $\sigma_p < \sigma_m$

The schemes which come under this group will be the best performing ones as their returns outperform the market, while they are less risky than the market.

TWO: $AR_p < AR_m$; $\sigma_p < \sigma_m$

This group exhibits lower return of the schemes along with lower risk compared to the market index and thus comes second.

THREE: $AR_p > AR_m$; $\sigma_p > \sigma_m$

In this group, not only the schemes' returns are higher than the market, but also their risk. Thus, though investors can earn more under this group, the greater risk quotient will make the investors wary.

FOUR: $AR_p < AR_m$; $\sigma_p > \sigma_m$

Group four is the worst case where the sample schemes' returns are less compared to the market, while their risk is higher. The groups of all the sample schemes are presented in Appendix A-3. The sector-wise and category-wise classification of the groups of the sample schemes is given in Table – 4.6.

Out of the 130 sample schemes, only 15 schemes (11.5 per cent) come under the first group of best performing schemes which not only outperform the market return-wise, but do so with less risk. Of these 15 schemes, none come from the income schemes, since these schemes are not expected to beat the market return, though risk-wise they are better. There are 8 balanced schemes, 2 growth schemes and 5 ELS schemes. This indicates that the balanced schemes are the best in offering higher returns at lower risk, which is followed by the ELS schemes.

Table – 4.6 Sector-wise and Category-wise Return and Risk of Sample Schemes Under Different Groups, April 2003 to March 2008

Sector	*Category*	*GROUPS*				*Total*
		One	*Two*	*Three*	*Four*	
Private	Income	Nil	28	Nil	1	29
	Balance	7	2	11	Nil	20
	Growth	2	1	18	7	28
	ELSS	3	4	6	Nil	13
	All	**12**	**35**	**35**	**8**	**90**
Public	Income	Nil	11	Nil	3	14
	Balance	1	4	2	1	8
	Growth	Nil	1	8	3	12
	ELSS	2	2	2	Nil	6
	All	**3**	**18**	**12**	**7**	**40**
Total	**Income**	**Nil**	**39**	**Nil**	**4**	**43**
	Balance	**8**	**6**	**13**	**1**	**28**
	Growth	**2**	**2**	**26**	**10**	**40**
	ELSS	**5**	**6**	**8**	**Nil**	**19**
	All	**15**	**53**	**47**	**15**	**130**

Source: Computed from Appendix A-3.

In the second group that includes schemes which provide lower return with lower risk, there are 53 schemes. This consists of 39 income schemes (73.6 per cent), which is quite expected as these schemes depend on portfolios like government securities which involves zero-risk almost. There are also 6 schemes each from the balanced and ELSS categories and 2 schemes from the growth category.

Group three involves not only higher return but also higher risk than the market, in which there are 47 schemes totally. This includes 26 growth schemes (55.3 per cent), 13 balanced schemes (27.7 per cent), 8 schemes (17 per cent) from the ELSS category and none from the income category. This suggests that growth schemes not only extend higher returns, but also involve greater risk.

Some schemes not only yield lower return, but also come with higher risk, which forms the fourth group. There are 15 schemes in this group which incorporates 10 growth schemes, 4 income schemes and also one balanced scheme. Fund managers in the quest of out-competing their rivals, expose their investors to greater risk, though could not earn better than the market. It is also significant to note that there are 4 schemes from the income category in this scenario. This might have occurred due to the preference of the portfolios which contain marginally greater risk potential.

Sector-wise, out of the 90 schemes in the private sector, 12 schemes (13.3 per cent) fall in the first group, 35 schemes (38.9 per cent) each in the second and third groups and 8 schemes (8.9 per cent) in the worst situation of group four. The first group is again dominated by the balanced schemes (7 out of 12 schemes), which also consists of 2 growth schemes and 3 ELS schemes, as there is no income scheme. In the second group, there are 35 schemes (38.9 per cent), out of which income schemes alone account for 28, while balanced, growth and ELSS categories account for 2, 1 and 4 schemes respectively. In the private sector, there are another 35 schemes in the third group. This contains 18 growth schemes, 11 balanced schemes and 6 ELS schemes. The fourth group of lower returns and greater risk has 8 schemes (8.9 per cent) and expectedly there are 7 growth schemes and 1 income scheme. Thus, in the private sector, most of the schemes fall in the second and third groups. The second group is dominated by the income schemes, while in the third and fourth, there are more growth schemes. This unfailingly underlines the risky nature of the growth schemes.

In the public sector, out of the 40 schemes, only 3 schemes (7.5 per cent) come under the first group, which comprises of 1 balanced scheme and 2 ELS schemes. Thus, no growth scheme from the public sector could beat the market in terms of return and risk simultaneously. In the second group, there are 18 schemes (45 per cent) that underperform the market return-wise, though better risk-wise. These 18 schemes include 11 income schemes, 4 balanced, 1 growth and 2 ELS schemes. Hence, as in the case of private sector, here too, only income schemes dominate the second group. There are 12 schemes (30 per cent) in the third group of greater risk group which is flooded with the growth schemes (8 out of 12) and 2 schemes each from balanced and ELSS categories also fall in this group. The fourth group that involves lower return with greater risk incorporates 7 schemes (17.5 per cent), of which there are 3 schemes each from the income and growth category along with 1 balanced scheme.

The overall picture shows that there are more private sector schemes in the first group which possesses greater proportion of balanced schemes. The second group has more schemes than the third, which is markedly influenced by the income schemes. In both private sector and public sector, most of the growth schemes come under the umbrella of third and fourth groups. This shows the risky nature of the growth schemes.

Components of Risk and Return

The risk associated with the volatility in the returns of the mutual fund schemes is measured in terms of standard deviation (σ) of the scheme which is called as the total risk. This total risk comprises of two types or emanates from two sources, viz., the market itself and from the concerned portfolio. Moreover, when earlier researchers wanted to study the performance of the mutual fund schemes, they devised, what is known as risk adjusted return. The different components of return are:

- Risk-free return: R_f – which is the return that the investors would have earned, had they invested in portfolios such as government securities, savings certificates, etc., which involve zero risk and is represented by the 91-day Treasury Bill rate, in this study.
- Market return: R_m – which is the return provided by the market, measured from the market index.
- Risk premium: $(R_p - R_f)$ – which is the return earned over and above the risk-free rate of return.
- Systematic risk: (beta – β), is the risk associated with the return of the scheme, that is due to the variability in the market return. Thus, irrespective of what the fund managers attempt, this part of the risk cannot be wished away by them, as it is external to them.
- Unique risk: This is the risk, which is also termed as the unsystematic risk that can be reduced or even be eliminated totally by the fund managers through diversification of the investment portfolio. This is measured by R^2, which is derived from the estimation of the market version of the CAPM.

Systematic Risk

Systematic risk of the portfolio is explained as that part of the total variability, which is linked with the variability of the overall stock market. This shows the way in which the scheme's return varies systematically with the variation in the market return. It indicates the relationship between portfolio return and market return. The fund managers cannot be expected to control those forces which are external to their companies, which impact the securities in the stock market. These external forces are the sources of systematic risk. In the words of Fisher and Jordan, (1995)[4] systematic risk refers to that portion of total variability in return which is caused by the factors affecting the prices of all securities in the market as a whole. This impact of volatility in market return on the return of the scheme can be statistically measured by modelling for the latter. This is done by applying the linear regression model (which is the market version of the CAPM in which the market return is taken as the explanatory variable. The model is:

$$R_{pt} = \alpha + \beta_p R_{mt} + e_{pt}$$

where α is the constant term, β is the systematic risk and 'e' is the error term. This explains the systematic component (β_p) of the total risk (σ_p) of the scheme in terms of market return (R_{mt}). Beta can either be positive or negative and the sign indicates the direction in which the portfolio's return will move for a given one unit change in the market return. Its implications are as follows:

If $\beta < 0$, then there is an inverse relationship between the scheme's return and market return.

If $\beta = 0$, then the return of the scheme is independent of the market return. That is, the variability in the market return will not affect the return of the scheme.

If $0 < \beta < 1$, then the return of the scheme is positively associated with the market return, but the former will be less volatile compared to the latter.

If $\beta = 1$, the volatility in the return of the schemes is totally equal to that of the market return and both will vary by the same margin.

If $\beta > 1$, then the return of the scheme is more volatile than the market return and thus, the former will change more than proportionately for a given change in the latter.[5]

The beta values of all the sample schemes are calculated and presented in Appendix A-4.

Beta of the Sample Schemes in Relation to Sensex

To begin with, the classified beta values (in terms of Sensex) are analysed with the help of Table – 4.7.

Out of the total of 130 sample schemes, 20 schemes (15.4 per cent) produce negative beta values underlying the fact that these schemes' returns are inversely correlated with the market return. Of the 20 schemes, 18 are income schemes and only 2 are from the ELSS category. The negative relationship of the income schemes indicates lack of any direct link between these schemes' returns and market return. This is furthermore underscored by the fact that out of the 43 income schemes, apart from the 18 which are negatively correlated, 23 schemes are positively correlated, but with a negligible beta value of 0.01 - 0.10.

Table – 4.7 Sector-wise and Category-wise Beta of the Sample Schemes in Relation to Sensex, April 2003 to March 2008

Sector	*Category*	*BETA (Sensex)*					*Total*
		Upto 0.00	*0.01-0.10*	*0.11-0.40*	*0.41-0.50*	*More than 0.50*	
Private	Income	11	16	2	Nil	Nil	29
	Balance	Nil	3	13	3	1	20
	Growth	Nil	2	7	4	15	28
	ELSS	2	Nil	1	4	6	13
	All	**13**	**21**	**23**	**11**	**22**	**90**
Public	Income	7	7	Nil	Nil	Nil	14
	Balance	Nil	Nil	6	1	1	8
	Growth	Nil	2	3	5	2	12
	ELSS	Nil	Nil	3	1	2	6
	All	**7**	**9**	**12**	**7**	**5**	**40**
Total	**Income**	**18**	**23**	**2**	**Nil**	**Nil**	**43**
	Balance	**Nil**	**3**	**19**	**4**	**2**	**28**
	Growth	**Nil**	**4**	**10**	**9**	**17**	**40**
	ELSS	**2**	**Nil**	**4**	**5**	**8**	**19**
	All	**20**	**30**	**35**	**18**	**27**	**130**

Source: Computed from Appendix A-4.

In the beta range of 0.01 - 0.10, there are 30 schemes, of which 23 are income schemes, 3 are balanced schemes and 4 schemes are from the growth category. When the beta range goes up to 0.11 - 0.40, the proportion of balanced schemes goes up to 54.3 per cent (19 out of 35 schemes). In the higher beta ranges, the proportion of balanced schemes decreases, while the proportion of growth schemes and also ELS schemes increases. For instance, in the highest beta range of more than 0.50, out of the 27 schemes, 17 schemes are from the growth category, 8 from the ELSS and 2 schemes belong to the balanced category. The exposure of the balanced schemes, ELS schemes and the growth schemes to the stock market is high in that order which directly pushes up their risk quotient. This suggests that when the schemes' dependency on the stock market increases, the degree of systematic risk too goes up. Moreover, classification of the beta values also suggests that none of them is exactly equal to zero and thus their returns are not independent of the market, though in case of income schemes the beta values are closer to zero. Similarly, the beta value of no scheme is either equal to one or greater than one and thus most of the values falls in the range of $0 < \beta < 1$. This signifies the fact that the returns of the sample schemes are volatile, but not as risky as that of the market.

Sector-wise, in the private sector, out of the 29 income schemes, 11 (37.9 per cent) fall in the negative range of upto zero and 2 schemes in the 0.11-0.40 range. Among the 20 balanced schemes, none come in the negative range, 3 schemes (15 per cent) bear a beta value between 0.01 -0.10, while as many as 13 schemes (65 per cent) fall in the 0.11 - 0.40 beta range. Three more schemes could be seen in the 0.41 - 0.50 class and one in the highest beta value of more than 0.50. In the case of 28 growth schemes in this sector, 15 schemes (53.6 per cent), are in the highest beta range, 7 schemes (25 per cent) in the middle range of 0.11 - 0.40 and 4 schemes (14.3 per cent) in the marginally higher risk range of 0.41 - 0.50. Among the 13 ELS schemes, 6 schemes (46.1 per cent) come under the highest risk class and 4 schemes (30.8 per cent) in the marginally higher class and one in the middle class.

In the case of public sector, out of the 14 income schemes, 50 per cent has a negative link, while the remaining 50 per cent has the lowest positive risk. Among the 8 balanced schemes, 6 schemes, (75 per cent) bear the middle level risk (0.11 - 0.40), and one each in the next two ranges. There are 12 growth schemes, of which only 2 schemes (16.7 per cent) fall in the highest risk class, 5 schemes (41.7 per cent) in the 0.41-0.50 risk class, and 3 schemes (25 per cent) in the middle class and there are 2 schemes even in the lowest risk class. As far as the 6 ELS schemes are concerned, only one-third bear the highest risk, 50 per cent fall in the middle class and one in the 0.41 - 0.50 risk class.

This trend indicates that the proportion of public sector schemes is higher in the lower risk classes and *vice versa*. And this has happened in almost all the categories. For instance, there are 20 schemes in the negative risk class which consists of 7 public sector schemes out of 40 (17.5 per cent) and 13 private sector schemes out of 90 (14.4 per cent). In the beta range of 0.01 - 0.10, of the 30 schemes, 9 schemes are from the public sector (22.5 per cent from that sector) and 21 from the private sector (23.3 per cent). In the 0.11 - 0.40 beta range, the 35 schemes comprise of 12 public sector schemes (30 per cent) ad 23 private sector schemes (25 per cent). But, in the highest beta range of more than 0.50, there are 27 schemes which include 5 public sector schemes (12.5 per cent) and 22 private sector schemes (24.4 per cent).

Beta of Sample Schemes in Relation to Nifty

The beta values of the sample schemes are calculated in relation to National Stock Exchange's Nifty index.

Table - 4.8 provides the beta values in terms of Nifty. Of the 130 sample schemes, 30 schemes (23.1 per cent) fall in the negative beta range which indicates a negative link between the schemes' return and market return. These 30 schemes comprise of 11 public sector schemes (27.5 per cent of that sector) and 19 private sector schemes (21.1 per cent of that sector). In the lowest positive beta value of 0.01-0.10 range, there are 62

Table – 4.8 Sector-wise and Category-wise Beta of the Sample Schemes in Relation to Nifty, April 2003 to March 2008

Sector	*Category*	*BETA (Nifty)*					*Total*
		Upto 0.00	*0.01-0.10*	*0.11-0.40*	*0.41-0.50*	*More than 0.50*	
Private	Income	13	15	1	Nil	Nil	29
	Balance	4	11	5	Nil	Nil	20
	Growth	1	11	13	1	2	28
	ELSS	1	7	2	2	1	13
	All	**19**	**44**	**21**	**3**	**3**	**90**
Public	Income	11	2	1	Nil	Nil	14
	Balance	Nil	6	2	Nil	Nil	8
	Growth	Nil	7	4	1	Nil	12
	ELSS	Nil	3	2	1	Nil	6
	All	**11**	**18**	**9**	**2**	**Nil**	**40**
Total	**Income**	**24**	**17**	**2**	**Nil**	**Nil**	**43**
	Balance	**4**	**17**	**7**	**Nil**	**Nil**	**28**
	Growth	**1**	**18**	**17**	**2**	**2**	**40**
	ELSS	**1**	**10**	**4**	**3**	**1**	**19**
	All	**30**	**62**	**30**	**5**	**3**	**130**

Source: Computed from Appendix A-4.

schemes (47.7 per cent) in which there are 18 public sector schemes (45 per cent of that sector) and 44 private sector schemes (48.9 per cent of that sector). There are 30 schemes in the 0.11 - 0.40 beta range (23.1 per cent) in which there are 9 schemes from the public sector (22.5 per cent) and 21 private sector schemes (23.3 per cent). However, in the higher beta ranges of 0.41 - 0.50 and more than 0.50, there are only a few schemes, which mostly comprises of private sector schemes. For example, in the 0.41 - 0.50 beta range, out of the 5 schemes (3.8 per cent), 2 schemes are from the public sector and 3 from the private sector, while in the more than 0.50 beta range, there are 3 schemes, all of which belong to the private sector.

Category-wise, in the negative risk class, there are 30 schemes of which 24 (80 per cent) are income schemes, 4 schemes (13.3 per cent) are from the balanced category and each one from the growth and ELSS categories also found in this class. In the lowest positive risk class, there are as many as 62 schemes, which includes 17 schemes (27.4 per cent) each from the income and balanced category, 18 (29 per cent) from the growth category and 10 schemes (16.1 per cent) from the ELSS category.

In the middle level of 0.11 - 0.40 class, out of the 30 schemes, majority of the schemes (17 schemes, 56.7 per cent) come from the growth category, 2 schemes from income, 7 schemes from the balanced and 4 from the ELSS categories could also be seen. In the higher risk classes like 0.41-0.50 and more than 0.50, there are only 5 and 3 schemes respectively.

A comparison of Table – 4.7 and 4.8 reveals a common trend in both the sectors. That is, less number of schemes falls in the higher risk classes, when beta is analysed in terms of Nifty, than when the same is done in terms of Sensex. This indicates that the sample schemes possess lesser degree of systematic risk in terms of Nifty, than under Sensex.

Market Dependency of Returns

Much of the analysis on the performance of the market fund schemes depends on the CAPM, in which the use of beta is strongly underlined. This indicates the dependency of the schemes' returns on the market. Thus, it is imperative to assess the significance of beta, which is done with the application of the market model:

$$R_{pt} = \alpha + \beta_p R_{mt} + e_{pt}$$

The calculated beta values need to be statistically significant. The summary results are given in Table – 4.9.

The number of schemes with significant beta values in terms of both the indices is presented in Table – 4.9, which shows that close to 50 per cent of the sample schemes have statistically significant betas, which implies that these beta values are statistically significant too. This underscores the dependency of the schemes or the role played by the market. Out of the 63 schemes, 43 are from the private sector (out of 90, 47.8 per cent) and 21 out of 40 from the public sector (52.5 per cent). Thus, sector-wise the proportion of schemes that have significant beta is also close to 50 per cent, though the public sector is marginally ahead of the private sector. Category-wise, only 5 income schemes have significant beta (out of 43, 11.6 per cent), 20

Table – 4.9 Number of Schemes with Significant Beta Values

Sector	*Category*	*MARKET INDEX* Sensex	Nifty	*Total*
Private	Income	3	1	4
	Balance	12	Nil	12
	Growth	18	3	21
	ELSS	10	3	13
	All	**43**	**7**	**50**
Public	Income	2	2	4
	Balance	8	1	9
	Growth	9	2	11
	ELSS	2	1	3
	All	**21**	**6**	**27**
Total	**Income**	**5**	**3**	**8**
	Balance	**20**	**1**	**21**
	Growth	**27**	**5**	**32**
	ELSS	**12**	**4**	**16**
	All	**64**	**13**	**77**

Source: Computed from Appendix A-4.

out of 28 balanced schemes (71.4 per cent), 27 out of 40 growth schemes (67.5 per cent) and 12 from 19 ELS schemes (63.2 per cent) also have significant beta values. Thus, except the income schemes, in all other categories, more than 50 per cent of the schemes depend on the market.

The table also provides the results in terms of Nifty, which is markedly different from that of Sensex. Under Nifty, only 13 out of 130 schemes (10 per cent) turn with significant beta values which comprise of 7 private sector and 6 public sector schemes. These 13 schemes include a greater proportion of ELSS and growth schemes than the balanced schemes. The number of income schemes is even higher than the balanced schemes. This analysis indicates that the schemes' dependency on the market is higher in terms of Sensex than under Nifty, which also implies the relevance of Sensex in this analysis.

Unique Risk and Diversification

Fund managers seek to cut down the risk involved in the portfolio's return, through diversification. Under efficient capital market scenario. it is held that a portfolio could be shaped in such a way that the only risk involved is the systematic risk. This can be achieved through sustained reduction in the controllable component of the risk, which can even be eliminated under extreme circumstances. Though, theoretically it sounds possible, practically it is not plausible, since fund managers are constrained by the capital market imperfections. Hence, while fund managers are unable to totally eliminate the systematic risk, they try to reduce the unsystematic (unique) risk through diversifying their investments. This implies that the degree of diversification and the degree of unique risk are inversely related.

Diversification is a process of spreading the investment in more than one security. It irons out the spikes in the values of security prices. When one more security is added to an already existing portfolio, the return on the portfolio becomes the weighted average of the returns of the securities in the portfolio. As more and more securities are added to the portfolio, dispersion among the returns of the securities gets reduced. This can be termed as the well diversified portfolio.

The extent of diversification which is used to reduce the degree of unique risk is measured by R^2 of the portfolio. In a well-diversified portfolio, the unique risk is completely eliminated and only the market part of the risk (systematic risk) is retained. In such a case, the value of R^2 will be equal to one and on the other extreme, if R^2 value is equal to zero, it implies the complete absence of diversification or zero-diversified portfolio. Hence, R^2 ranges from 0 to 1 and cannot be negative.

The R^2 is the ratio between systematic risk and total risk of the sample scheme, which is derived from the estimation of the market version of the CAPM, the linear regression model. Under the regression model, the R^2 is calculated as follows:

$$R^2 = SS_R / SS_T$$

where, SS_R is the regression sum of square and SS_T is the total sum of square. The calculated R^2 values in terms of Sensex and Nifty for all the sample schemes are presented in Appendix A-4.

R^2 Values of the Sample Schemes in Relation to Sensex

The R^2 values in terms of Sensex are provided in Table – 4.10.

The table indicates that out of the 43 income schemes totally, 31 schemes (72.1 per cent) possess a R^2 value of up to 0.02, which is the lowest, 11 schemes (25.6 per cent) have 0.02 - 0.1 range of diversification. The income schemes show least diversification, which is not surprising given the fact that these schemes have no direct link with the stock market.

Table – 4.10 Sector-wise and Category-wise R^2 Values of the Sample Schemes in Relation to Sensex, April 2003 to March 2008

Sector	Category	R^2 (Sensex)					
		Upto 0.02	*0.02-0.1*	*0.1-0.2*	*0.2-0.5*	*More than 0.5*	*Total*
Private	Income	21	7	1	Nil	Nil	29
	Balance	2	4	9	5	Nil	20
	Growth	1	2	1	16	8	28
	ELSS	Nil	1	1	9	2	13
	All	**24**	**14**	**12**	**30**	**10**	**90**
Public	Income	10	4	Nil	Nil	Nil	14
	Balance	Nil	1	4	3	Nil	8
	Growth	1	3	6	1	1	12
	ELSS	Nil	3	1	2	Nil	6
	All	**11**	**11**	**11**	**6**	**1**	**40**
Total	Income	31	11	1	Nil	Nil	43
	Balance	2	5	13	8	Nil	28
	Growth	2	5	7	17	9	40
	ELSS	Nil	4	2	11	2	19
	All	**35**	**25**	**23**	**36**	**11**	**130**

Source: Computed from Appendix A-4.

In the case of 28 balanced schemes, 2 schemes (7.1 per cent) are in the lowest R^2 range of less than 0.02, 5 schemes (17.9 per cent) in the R^2 range of 0.02 - 0.1, 13 schemes (46.4 per cent) fall in the diversification range of 0.1 - 0.2 and 8 schemes (28.6 per cent) are in the next diversification class of 0.2 - 0.5, while there is no scheme in the highest R^2 class of more than 0.5. Thus, there is considerable degree of diversification in the case of balanced schemes. Out of the 40 growth schemes, in the least diversification range of upto 0.02, there are only 2 schemes (5 per cent), in the next class of 0.02 - 0.1 there are 5 schemes (12.5 per cent), 7 schemes (17.5 per cent) fall in the 0.1 - 0.2 R^2 class, 17 schemes (42.5 per cent) come in the considerably higher diversification class of 0.2-0.5 and there are 9 schemes (22.5 per cent) in the highest diversification class of more than 0.5. This clearly underlines a greater degree of diversification that is practiced in the case of growth schemes. Similarly, in the case of ELS schemes also, the number of schemes in the lower diversification ranges is less and *vice versa*. For instance, of the 19 schemes, there is no scheme in the lowest R^2 range of less than 0.02, 4 schemes (21.1 per cent) fall in the 0.02-0.1 R^2 range, 2 schemes (10.5 per cent) come under the 0.1-0.2 R^2 class. But, in the 0.2-0.5 diversification class, there are 11 schemes (57.9 per cent) and in the highest R^2 range of more than 0.5, there are 2 schemes (10.5 per cent). This shows that the degree of diversification of the ELS schemes mostly resemble that of the growth schemes.

Sector-wise, among the 29 private sector income schemes, 21 schemes (72.4 per cent) are in the lowest R^2 range of upto 0.02, 7 schemes (24.1 per cent) fall in the 0.02-0.1 diversification class and one scheme in the 0.1 - 0.2 diversification range. Thus, there is no scheme from this category that is diversified by more than 0.2. As in the case of overall picture, here too, the degree of diversification of the income schemes is quite restricted. In the case of 20 balanced schemes, there is greater diversification, as only 2 schemes (10 per cent) and 4 schemes (20 per cent) fall in the les than 0.02 and 0.02 - 0.1 range of diversification respectively. In the 0.1 - 0.2 range of diversification, there are 9 schemes (45 per cent) and 5 schemes (25 per cent) in the 0.2 - 0.5 range of diversification. Thus, there is no scheme in the highest diversification class of more than 0.5.

Among the 28 growth schemes, there is even more diversification as only one scheme falls in the lowest class of diversification, 2 schemes (7.1 per cent) in the 0.02 - 0.1 range of diversification and again only one scheme in the 0.1 - 0.2 degree of diversification. But in the higher diversification class of 0.2 - 0.5, there are 16 schemes (57.1 per cent) and 8 schemes (28.6 per cent) fall in the more_than 0.5 range of diversification. This trend is replicated in the ELSS category as well. Of the 13 ELS schemes, there is no scheme in the lowest diversification class, while there is one scheme each in the next two classes, viz., 0.02 - 0.1 and 0.1 - 0.2. However, there are 9 schemes (69.2 per cent) in the 0.2 - 0.5 diversification class and 2 schemes (15.4 per cent) in the highest diversification class of more than 0.5.

In the public sector, of the 14 income schemes, 10 schemes (71.4 per cent) are in the less than 0.02 diversification class and 4 schemes (28.6 per cent) are in the next class of 0.02 - 0.1, while there is no scheme in the higher diversification classes. In the case of 8 balanced schemes, there is no scheme in the lowest diversification class, only one scheme in the 0.02 - 0.1 diversification class, 4 schemes (50 per cent) in the 0.1 - 0.2 class of diversification and the remaining 3 schemes (37.5 per cent) fall in the next range of 0.2 - 0.5 class. Thus, diversification of the balanced schemes in this sector does not go beyond the 0.5 level. Among the 12 growth schemes, one scheme comes in the less than 0.02 class, 3 schemes (25 per cent) fall in the 0.02 - 0.1 diversification class and 6 schemes (50 per cent) fall under the 0.1 -0.2 class of diversification. There is one scheme each in the next two classes, viz., 0.2 - 0.5 and more than 0.5. In the case of 6 ELS schemes, there is no scheme in the less than 0.02 class, whereas 3 schemes (50 per cent) are in the 0.02 - 0.1 class. Of the remaining 3 schemes, 1 scheme fall in the 0.1 - 0.2 range and the other 2 schemes fall in the 0.2 - 0.5 range of diversification. Thus, the degree of diversification of these public sector growth schemes is well spread out into all classes, though it is comparatively lower than the private sector growth schemes.

The R^2 values of ELS schemes are also typically less than that of their counterparts in the private sector, as 50 per cent of these schemes (3 out of 6 schemes) are in the 0.02 - 0.1 class, one in the 0.1 - 0.2 and 2 schemes in the 0.2 - 0.5 R^2 range. This indicates that the public sector schemes' degree of diversification is less compared to that of the private sector schemes which happen in the cases of balanced, growth and ELS schemes.

R^2 Values of the Sample Schemes in Relation to Nifty

Table – 4.11 provides the R^2 values of the sample schemes in terms of Nifty.

Table – 4.11 Sector-wise and Category-wise R^2 Values of the Sample Schemes in Relation to Nifty, April 2003 to March 2008

Sector	*Category*	*R^2 (Nifty)*					*Total*
		Upto 0.02	*0.02-0.1*	*0.1-0.2*	*0.2-0.5*	*More than 0.5*	
Private	Income	25	4	Nil	Nil	Nil	29
	Balance	17	3	Nil	Nil	Nil	20
	Growth	12	9	5	2	Nil	28
	ELSS	8	1	2	1	1	13
	All	**62**	**17**	**7**	**3**	**1**	**90**
Public	Income	12	2	Nil	Nil	Nil	14
	Balance	5	2	1	Nil	Nil	8
	Growth	10	2	Nil	Nil	Nil	12
	ELSS	3	2	Nil	1	Nil	6
	All	**30**	**8**	**1**	**1**	**Nil**	**40**
Total	**Income**	**37**	**6**	**Nil**	**Nil**	**Nil**	**43**
	Balance	**22**	**5**	**1**	**Nil**	**Nil**	**28**
	Growth	**22**	**11**	**5**	**2**	**Nil**	**40**
	ELSS	**11**	**3**	**2**	**2**	**1**	**19**
	All	**92**	**25**	**8**	**4**	**1**	**130**

Source: Computed from Appendix A-4.

Out of the 130 total sample schemes, as many as 92 schemes (70.8 per cent) fall in the lowest diversification class of less than 0.02 (whereas it is only 26.9 per cent in terms of Sensex). In this least diversification class, apart from the 37 income schemes, there is also more number of all other categories of schemes. For instance, there are also 22 balanced schemes (out of 28 in that category), another 22 growth schemes (from a total of 40 schemes) and 11 ELS schemes (from 19 schemes). Thus, in the subsequent higher R^2 ranges, except the growth schemes, the proportion of other schemes is quite less. Thus, in the 0.1-0.2 range of diversification, there are only 8 schemes out of 130, (6.2 per cent), 4 schemes (3.1 per cent) in the 0.2-0.5 diversification class and only one scheme in the highest diversification class of more than 0.5 (while there are 11 schemes in this class in terms of Sensex). This shows that the sample schemes which exhibited lower degree of systematic risk in terms of Nifty also exposes lower degree of diversification (and hence higher unique risk).

Conclusion

The analysis of return and risk of the sample schemes indicates that the public sector schemes which yield relatively less return are surprisingly much riskier than the private sector schemes. Category-wise, growth schemes are the riskiest category, while income schemes are the least risky. This implies that the schemes which are exposed to the stock market bear more risk and *vice versa*. The reason for the relatively greater underperformance of the public sector schemes *vis-à-vis* the private sector schemes can be seen from the measure of diversification. Under this measure, the private sector schemes are more diversified than the public sector schemes, while among the categories, growth schemes and ELS schemes are more diversified.

The analysis of systematic risk (beta) of the sample schemes suggests that there is common trend in both the sectors. That is, less number of schemes falls in the higher risk classes, when beta is analysed in terms of Nifty, than when the same is done in terms of Sensex. This indicates that the sample schemes possess lesser degree of systematic risk in terms of Nifty, than under Sensex. This analysis indicates that the schemes' dependency on the market is higher in terms of Sensex than under Nifty, which also implies the relevance of Sensex in this analysis. The market dependency of the sample schemes which is examined with the help of statistically significant beta values indicates that the schemes' dependency on the market is higher in terms of Sensex than under Nifty, which also implies the relevance of Sensex in this analysis.

References

1. Gali, Kanti Kumar, (1995), "Mutual Funds' Performance Appraisal ad Organizational Factors: an Analysis Based on Risk-Adjusted Returns", unpublished Ph.D. Thesis, IIM – Bangalore, p. 61.
2. Muthappan P.K. and Damodharan E., (2006), op.cit.,
3. Adhikari, Umesh and Meenal Bhosale, (1994), Risk – Return Analysis of Mutual Fund Growth Schemes", Indian Institute of Management, Working Paper, August.
4. Fisher, Donald E., and Jordan, Donald J., (1995), "Security analysis and Portfolio Management", Prentice Hall, New Delhi.
5. Govindrajan K., (2001), "Performance of Public Sector and Private Sector Mutual Funds in India, Unpublished Ph.D. Thesis, Annamalai University, Annamalai Nagar.
6. Gujarathi, Damodar N., (2003), Basic Econometrics, Mc Graw Hill, New York, p. 84.

5

PERFORMANCE EVALUATION OF THE SAMPLE SCHEMES

Introduction

Performance of the mutual funds is evaluated in terms of its net asset value through different measures viz., internal rate of return, the methods developed by Sharpe, Treynor, Jenson, Sharpe differential measure, Fama's measures, Treynor and Mazuy's market timing ability among others. These methods capture different aspects of the mutual funds like its superior returns in terms of total risk, systematic risk, stock selecting ability, impact of beta, impact of diversification, impact of selectivity and market timing ability of the fund managers. This chapter presents the performance evaluation of the sample schemes based on these methods.

Internal Rate of Return

The internal rate of return (IRR) is a simple and an important tool in the analysis of performance of investment decisions in business. In the context of investment decisions, risk is measured in terms of the expected rate of return. Thus, it is measured by discounting the cash flows with the help of time and expected return. Depending on the rate of return, accepting or rejecting of investment decisions is made. Here, the IRR for the sample schemes are analysed by taking the NAV for the period from April 2003 to March 2008.

The formula used to compute the IRR is:

$$P_0 = \frac{D_1}{(1+r)} + \frac{D_2}{(1+r)^2} + \frac{D_3}{(1+r)^3} + \ldots + \frac{D_n}{(1+r)^n} + \frac{P_n}{(1+r)^n}$$

where, P_0 is the initial investment, which is the face value of the mutual fund unit;

D_1, D_2 ... D_n represents the cash dividends received by the investor during the given period;

r is the rate of return and

P_n is the NAV at the end of the maturity period.

If no dividends are paid, IRR is calculated as:

$$P_0 = \frac{P_n}{(1 + r)^n}$$

IRR is the rate which equates the present value of the cash inflow from the holding of mutual fund units to the acquisition cost. The cash inflow includes dividends and the terminal price. These are adjusted for bonus and rights issues. It is also comparable with other alternative investment measures. The IRR is calculated by solving the equations for 'r'. The IRR has been computed for the 130 sample schemes which existed in April 2003. The returns for the schemes are computed on the assumption that the investor holds the scheme till March 2008 or up to the time of redemption of the unit. The calculated IRR of the sample schemes are presented in Appendix A-5. A snapshot of the IRR of the schemes, both sector and category-wise is presented in Table – 5.1.

Table – 5.1 IRR of the Sample Schemes

Sector	*Category*	*TOTAL RISK (in percentage)*						*Total*
		Below 0	*0.1-5.0*	*5.1-10.0*	*10.1-20.0*	*20.1-50.0*	*More than 50.0*	
Private	Income	Nil	4	15	10	Nil	Nil	29
	Balance	Nil	Nil	2	7	10	1	20
	Growth	2	1	Nil	4	12	9	28
	ELSS	1	Nil	Nil	5	5	2	13
	All	**3**	**5**	**17**	**26**	**27**	**12**	**90**
Public	Income	Nil	4	6	4	Nil	Nil	14
	Balance	2	2	3	1	Nil	Nil	8
	Growth	2	Nil	4	6	Nil	Nil	12
	ELSS	2	Nil	2	2	Nil	Nil	6
	All	**6**	**6**	**15**	**13**	**Nil**	**Nil**	**40**
Total	**Income**	**Nil**	**8**	**21**	**14**	**Nil**	**Nil**	**43**
	Balance	**2**	**2**	**5**	**8**	**10**	**1**	**28**
	Growth	**4**	**1**	**4**	**10**	**12**	**9**	**40**
	ELSS	**3**	**Nil**	**2**	**7**	**5**	**2**	**19**
	All	**9**	**11**	**32**	**39**	**27**	**12**	**130**

Source: Computed from Appendix A-5.

The IRR of the sample schemes ranges from below 0 per cent (negative) to above 50 per cent. Out of the 130 schemes, 9 schemes (6.9 per cent) gave sub-zero returns. Sector-wise, there are 3 private sector and 6 public sector schemes in this class. Category-wise, among the 9 schemes, 2 schemes belong to the balanced fund category, 4 belong to the growth fund category and 3 schemes fall in the ELSS category. Since, income fund schemes provide secured returns, none of them fall in the negative return class.

There are 11 schemes (8.5 per cent) that provide return that ranges from 0.1 per cent to 5.0 per cent of which 5 are private sector schemes and 6 are public sector schemes. Among these 11 schemes, 8 are income schemes, 2 are balanced schemes and 1 scheme comes under the growth category. Majority of the schemes' returns ranges between 5.1 - 10.0 per cent and 10.1 - 20.0 per cent. In the 5.1 - 10.0 per cent return class, there are 32 schemes (24.6 per cent) out of the 130 sample schemes. Out of these, 17 come from the private sector and the remaining 15 schemes come from the public sector funds.

In the class of 10.1 - 20.0 per cent returns, there are 39 schemes (30 per cent), in which 26 are private sector schemes and 13 are public sector schemes. Schemes' category-wise analysis shows that among the 39 schemes, 14 schemes belong to income fund category, 8 fall in the balanced category, 10 to the growth fund and 7 to the ELSS category.

In the other two return classes viz., 20.1 - 50.0 per cent and more than 50 per cent, there are only private sector schemes, as the public sector schemes, among the sample schemes could provide only up to 20 per cent return. In the class of 20.1 - 50.0 per cent returns, there are 27 schemes (20.8 per cent), in which 10 belong to the balanced fund category, 12 to the growth fund category and 5 to the ELSS category. Similarly, in the more than 50 per cent return class, there are 12 schemes (9.2 per cent) out of which one belongs to the balanced fund, 9 schemes belong to the growth fund category and 2 to the ELSS category.

The table also indicates that, of the 40 public sector sample schemes, not even one could provide more than 20 per cent return.

Schemes' category-wise analysis suggests that out of the 43 income schemes (both private and public sector), 29 schemes (67.4 per cent) provide 10 per cent or less return, while the remaining 14 schemes (32.6 per cent) are in the 10.1-20.0 per cent return class. In the case of 28 balanced schemes, the return of 9 schemes (32.1 per cent) lies below 10 per cent and the remaining 19 schemes (67.9 per cent) yield 10 per cent or more, while 11 of them generate more than 20 per cent. Thus, the returns of balanced schemes are well spread out, unlike the income schemes. This is also the case with the growth schemes. Out of the 40 schemes, as many as 31 schemes (77.5 per cent) provide more than 10 per cent return; 10 schemes could earn 10.1 - 20.0 per cent; 12 schemes earn 20.1 - 50.0 per cent and 9 schemes provide more than 50 per cent return. In the case of 19 ELS schemes, the returns of 3 schemes (15.8 per cent) are negative, 2 schemes earn 5.1 - 10.0 per cent, 7 schemes (36.8 per cent) account for 10.1 - 20.0 per cent return, 5 schemes (26.3 per cent) provide 20.1 - 50.0 per cent return and 2 schemes earn more than 50 per cent return.

The category-wise analysis of the schemes' returns indicates that the income schemes, true to their objective, yield only limited returns, the return of the balanced schemes is higher than that of the income schemes, while the growth schemes, which are fully equity-oriented, provide the highest returns. The return of the ELS schemes is mostly similar to that of the balanced schemes. This analysis however provides only the number of schemes, both sector-wise and category-wise in each of the return class. To understand more about the returns of the schemes, the mean score of the IRR is analysed below.

The mean score of IRR of the sample schemes and their standard deviation (SD) are computed both sector-wise and category-wise and presented in Table – 5.2.

Table – 5.2 Mean and Standard Deviation of IRR of the Sample Schemes

Sector	*Category*	*Mean*	*Std. Deviation*
Private	Income	8.81	3.0681
	Balance	18.79	5.7259
	Growth	27.44	13.4126
	ELSS	18.12	8.7984
Public	Income	6.06	2.3181
	Balance	7.03	2.3722
	Growth	9.90	6.7937
	ELSS	7.77	10.9159

Source: Computed from Appendix A-5.

The table indicates that the mean IRR scores of the private sector schemes in all categories are considerably higher than their counterparts in the public sector. For instance, the mean IRR score of the income schemes in the private sector is 8.81 as against 6.06 in the public sector. The balanced schemes in the private sector provide 18.79 as their mean IRR, while the public sector balanced schemes provide only 7.03 as mean IRR. In the case of growth schemes in the private sector, the mean IRR is 27.44 as against

9.90 in the case of public sector. Similarly, in the case of ELS schemes also, the mean IRR scores are 18.12 and 7.77 in the two sectors. The table also suggests that the mean IRR scores of the growth schemes are the highest followed by the balanced schemes and then the income schemes. As the mean IRR of the ELS schemes is mostly equal to that of balanced schemes, obviously the income schemes provide the least return. This pattern is discernible in both the sectors.

Standard deviation of the returns reveals that it is highest in the case of growth schemes, particularly in the private sector, followed by the ELS schemes, the balanced schemes and lastly the income schemes. However, in the case of public sector schemes, the standard deviation of ELSS is the highest, which is followed by the growth schemes, balanced schemes and then the income schemes. This indicates that the degree of deviation in the returns of the growth schemes is the highest compared to that of other schemes. This is the case in both the sectors, while the inter-sector comparison suggests that the deviation in the returns of the public sector schemes is lower than that of the private sector.

The sector-wise and category-wise analysis of the mean and standard deviation of IRR of the sample schemes indicates that the mean IRR of each category of the sample schemes in the private sector is notably higher than its corresponding category in the public sector. This signifies higher return of the private sector schemes. However, the private sector sample schemes are also associated with higher risk as indicated by higher standard deviation of all the four categories. Hence, the private sector schemes provide higher return with higher risk compared to that of the public sector schemes.

Sharpe Ratio

The analysis of performance evaluation of the managed portfolios has attracted the interest of many scholars and a number of models have been developed which could also be applied to evaluate the performance of mutual fund schemes. The more popular and important models are applied here on the selected sample schemes in order to assess their performance. Sharpe was the pioneer and his model known as Sharpe Ratio[1] is applied here. This ratio indicates the relationship between the portfolio's additional return over and above the risk-free return and the total risk of the scheme, measured in terms of standard deviation. Thus, the sample scheme's return is compared against the rate of return of the risk-free portfolio. The latter usually refers to the yield of the Government Treasury Bill, which is absolutely risk-free. In this study, the risk-free rate refers to the 91-day Treasury bill rate. The Sharpe ratio is also referred to as the reward to variability ratio ($RVAR_p$) and expressed as:

$$RVAR_p = \frac{AR_p - AR_f}{\sigma_p}$$

where AR_p is the average return of the scheme, AR_f is the average return of the risk-free portfolio and σ_p is the total risk of the scheme.

The calculation of AR_f is similar to that of AR_m. The benchmark comparison is done by:

$$RVOL = \frac{(AR_p - AR_f)}{\beta_p}$$

where AR_m is the average return of the market index and σ_m is the total risk of the market index.

The calculated Sharpe ratio and the benchmark ratios in terms of both indices are presented in Appendix A-6. The Sharpe ratio is compared with the benchmark ratio and is classified into two groups, viz., below benchmark and above benchmark to capture the relative performance of the additional return of the schemes.

Sharpe Ratio Returns of the Sample Schemes in Comparison with Sensex

Table – 5.3 provides the Sharpe ratio in terms of Sensex.

Table – 5.3 Sharpe Ratio Returns of the Sample Schemes in Comparison with Benchmark Sensex, April 2003 to March 2008

	SECTOR						*Total*		
	Private			*Public*					
Category	*Below Bench mark*	*Above Bench mark*	*All*	*Below Bench mark*	*Above Bench mark*	*All*	*Below Bench mark*	*Above Bench mark*	*All*
Income	29	Nil	**29**	14	Nil	**14**	**43**	**Nil**	**43**
Balance	3	17	**20**	5	3	**8**	**8**	**20**	**28**
Growth	7	21	**28**	4	8	**12**	**11**	**29**	**40**
ELSS	5	8	**13**	2	4	**6**	**7**	**12**	**19**
Total	**44**	**46**	**90**	**25**	**15**	**40**	**69**	**61**	**130**

Source: Computed from Appendix A-6.

Out of the 130 schemes, a total of 69 schemes are below benchmark (53.1 per cent) which includes 44 private sector schemes (out of 90, 48.9 per cent) and 25 public sector schemes (out of 40, 62.5 per cent). Thus, a greater proportion of public sector schemes underperform the market, as the additional returns of these schemes fall below that of the market. Category-wise, these 69 schemes consist of 43 income schemes (62.3 per cent), 8 balanced schemes (11.6 per cent), 11 growth schemes (15.9 per cent) and 7 ELS schemes (10.1 per cent). The underperformance of the income schemes vis-à-vis the market is understandable given their objective. But, in the case of balanced schemes, 40 per cent of the schemes (8 out of 20 schemes) underperform, which is 37.9 per cent among the growth schemes (11 from 29 schemes) and 36.8 per cent in the case of ELS schemes (7 out of 19 schemes). Thus, underperformance of the schemes is widespread among all the categories of the schemes, though the growth and ELS schemes perform marginally better.

Sector-wise, out of the 44 private sector schemes that underperform, all the 29 income schemes, 3 of the balanced schemes (15 per cent), 7 of the growth schemes (25 per cent) and 5 of the ELS schemes (38.5 per cent) come under this category. This clearly indicates that the proportion of schemes that underperform is quite less in all these categories, except the case of ELS, ignoring the income schemes. Moreover, the growth schemes perform better in comparison with the balanced schemes. This relatively less underperformance of the private sector schemes implies that underperformance among the public sector schemes is in general more. For instance, out of the 25 underperforming schemes in this sector, apart from the 14 income schemes, 5 out of the 8 balanced schemes (62.5 per cent), 4 out of 12 growth schemes (33.3 per cent) and 2 out of the 6 ELS schemes (33.3 per cent) underperform compared to the market return.

Sharpe Ratio Returns of the Sample Schemes in Comparison with Nifty

Table – 5.4 provides the Sharpe ratio in terms of Nifty.

TABLE – 5.4 Sharpe Ratio Returns of the Sample Schemes in Comparison with Benchmark Nifty, April 2003 to March 2008

	SECTOR						*Total*		
	Private			*Public*					
Category	*Below Bench mark*	*Above Bench mark*	*All*	*Below Bench mark*	*Above Bench mark*	*All*	*Below Bench mark*	*Above Bench mark*	*All*
Income	29	Nil	**29**	13	1	**14**	**42**	**1**	**43**
Balance	3	17	**20**	5	3	**8**	**8**	**20**	**28**
Growth	9	19	**28**	4	8	**12**	**13**	**27**	**40**
ELSS	5	8	**13**	2	4	**6**	**7**	**12**	**19**
Total	**46**	**44**	**90**	**24**	**16**	**40**	**70**	**60**	**130**

Source: Computed from Appendix A-6.

There is no great difference in the degree of schemes' underperformance both sector-wise and category-wise with two exceptions. One, in the case of private sector schemes, 2 more schemes underperform, which come from the growth category, while in the case of public sector, underperformance declines by one scheme in the income category. Thus, overall, 70 schemes underperform with Nifty as the benchmark and 69 schemes underperform as Sensex as the benchmark.

Treynor Ratio

Another measure of performance evaluation of the managed portfolios is the one devised by Treynor (1966).[2] His ratio measures the scheme's additional return with relation to its systematic risk (beta). Thus, the only difference between the Sharpe ratio and Treynor ratio is that the former measures the additional return in relation to the scheme's total risk (σ), while the latter does it with systematic risk. The ratio, which is called as reward to volatility ratio (RVOL) is expressed as:

$$RVOL_p = \frac{(AR_p - AR_f)}{\beta_p}$$

where βp is the systematic risk of the scheme. The benchmark for comparison with the Treynor ratio is measured by calculating the return of the market over and above the risk free-return in relation with the market beta. That is,

$$RVOL_m = \frac{(AR_m - AR_f)}{\beta_m}$$

where β_m is the systematic risk of the market index. But, for the market index, beta is equal to one and thus, the benchmark comparison is measured only through calculating the arithmetic difference between AR_m and AR_f. The $RVOL_p$ and $RVOL_m$ in terms of both Sensex and Nifty of all the sample schemes are presented in Appendix A-7.

Treynor Ratio Returns of the Sample Schemes in Comparison with Sensex

The Treynor ratio in terms of Sensex classified on the basis of sector and category are presented in Table – 5.5.

TABLE – 5.5 Treynor Ratio Returns of the Sample Schemes in Comparison with Benchmark Sensex, April 2003 to March 2008

Category	*SECTOR*						*Total*		
	Private			*Public*					
	Below Bench mark	*Above Bench mark*	*All*	*Below Bench mark*	*Above Bench mark*	*All*	*Below Bench mark*	*Above Bench mark*	*All*
Income	13	16	**29**	8	6	**14**	**21**	**22**	**43**
Balance	9	11	**20**	3	5	**8**	**12**	**16**	**28**
Growth	3	25	**28**	3	9	**12**	**6**	**34**	**40**
ELSS	3	10	**13**	2	4	**6**	**5**	**14**	**19**
Total	**28**	**62**	**90**	**16**	**24**	**40**	**44**	**86**	**130**

Source: Computed from Appendix A-7.

Under Treynor's measure, in terms of Sensex, out of the 130 schemes, 44 schemes (33.8 per cent) underperform which includes 28 private sector schemes (31.1 per cent within that sector) and 16 public sector schemes (40 per cent within that sector). Thus, under Treynor measure also, the proportion of underperformance of the sample scheme is higher in the public sector. Category-wise, these 44 schemes include 21 income schemes, which show that, unlike in the case of Sharpe measure, here the performance of some income schemes is above the benchmark. The proportion of underperformance is marginally higher in case of balanced schemes, while lower among the growth and ELS schemes. Out of the 28 balanced schemes, 12 schemes (42.9 per cent) underperform the market, which is 15 per cent among the growth schemes (6 out of the 40), and 26.3 per cent in the case of ELS schemes (5 out of 19). This reduced underperformance or conversely, greater above-performance of especially the growth and ELS schemes under Treynor measure is the outcome of the change in the risk component.

Sector-wise, 28 out of 90 private sector schemes (31.1 per cent) perform below the benchmark which also consists of 13 income schemes. Thus, as noted earlier, the remaining 16 income schemes perform better than the benchmark. In the case of 20 balanced schemes, underperformance is to the extent of 45 per cent (9 out of 20 schemes), while it is as low as 10.7 per cent among the growth schemes (3 out of 28 schemes) and 23.1 per cent in the case of ELS schemes (3 out of 13 schemes). This suggests that as in the case of overall trend, the degree of underperformance declines considerably among all the categories of the schemes in the private sector when compared to the Sharpe measure, except that of the balanced schemes, in which case it goes up marginally. Moreover, growth schemes are the best performing schemes among all the categories.

Among the public sector schemes, the rate of underperformance shrinks across the board. The 16 underperforming schemes include 8 income schemes (57.1 per cent), 3 balanced schemes (37.5 per cent), 3 growth schemes (25 per cent) and 2 ELS scheme (33.3 per cent). Thus, the degree of underperformance of the public sector under Treynor measure declines compared to that of Sharpe, while still the level of underperformance of these schemes is higher than that of the private sector.

Treynor Ratio Returns of the Sample Schemes in Comparison with Nifty

Table – 5.6 presents the Treynor's measure in terms of Nifty.

TABLE – 5.6 Treynor Ratio Returns of the Sample Schemes in Comparison with Benchmark Nifty, April 2003 to March 2008

Category	*SECTOR*						*Total*		
	Private			*Public*					
	Below Bench mark	*Above Bench mark*	*All*	*Below Bench mark*	*Above Bench mark*	*All*	*Below Bench mark*	*Above Bench mark*	*All*
Income	11	18	**29**	7	7	**14**	**18**	**25**	**43**
Balance	12	8	**20**	4	4	**8**	**16**	**12**	**28**
Growth	11	17	**28**	5	7	**12**	**16**	**24**	**40**
ELSS	8	5	**13**	4	2	**6**	**12**	**7**	**19**
Total	**42**	**48**	**90**	**20**	**20**	**40**	**62**	**68**	**130**

Source: Computed from Appendix A-7.

When it comes to the Nifty index, there is a marked increase in the rate of underperformance of the schemes from that of Sensex. Out of the130 schemes, 62 schemes (47.7 per cent) come under the below benchmark category, as against 44 in terms of Sensex. This greater underperformance has more to do with the private sector schemes than public sector schemes. These 62 schemes include 42 private sector schemes (46.7 per cent within that sector). Thus, the number of private sector schemes which underperform goes up from 28 (under Sensex) to 42 (under Nifty), while in the case of public sector schemes, the number increases from 16 to 20.

Category-wise, underperformance increases among all, but income schemes. The 58 underperforming schemes include 18 income schemes, 16 balanced, 16 growth and 12 ELS schemes. This shows that under Nifty, more growth schemes and ELS schemes are pushed into the underperformance category. Again, this occurs especially among the private sector schemes, as noted earlier.

Treynor ratio returns suggests that the systematic risk of the private sector schemes differs between Sensex and Nifty which results in the differing performances of the schemes under the two indices. However, private sector schemes outperform the public sector schemes in the overall analysis.

Jensen Measures

Another variation to the CAPM, in the lines of Sharpe differential measure was given by Jensen (1968)[3] who sought to recognise the efficiency of the fund manager in superior stock picking. Jensen's model provides a measure of the market return, which is an important constituent of systematic risk that is measured with beta. Segregating the return due to market variations or through the impact of systematic risk from that of risk premium (R_p-R_f), the alpha value is identified as the risk adjusted return on the scheme. As in the case of Sharpe differential measure, Jensen's alpha also suggests a positive stock selection for a positive value and *vice versa*. The model is expressed as:

$$R_p - R_f = \alpha + \beta (R_m - R_f)$$

Where, á is the differential return earned by the scheme out of the ability of fund manager in selecting correct stocks and â is the systematic risk of the scheme. The calculated alpha values for the sample schemes along with their 't' values are given in Appendix A- 8.

Jensen's Alpha in terms of Sensex

The sector-wise and category-wise number of alpha values with negative and positive signs in terms of Sensex is shown in Table – 5.7.

TABLE – 5.7 Sector-wise and Category-Wise Jensen's Alpha in Terms of Sensex, April 2003 to March 2008

	SECTOR						*Total*		
	Private			*Public*					
Category	*a* < 0	*a* > 0	*All*	*a* < 0	*a* > 0	*All*	*a* < 0	*a* > 0	*All*
Income	27	2	29	14	Nil	14	**41**	**2**	43
Balance	14	6	20	8	Nil	8	**22**	**6**	28
Growth	11	17	28	7	5	12	**18**	**22**	40
ELSS	5	8	13	4	2	6	**9**	**10**	19
Total	**57**	**33**	**90**	**33**	7	**40**	**90**	**40**	**130**

Source: Computed from Appendix A-8.

The table suggests that overall only 40 schemes (30.8 per cent) are positive thereby indicating superior performance. In other words, these schemes generate returns in excess of equilibrium return. The value of alpha is an absolute, which implies differential return of the scheme between equilibrium return and actual return. It should also be noted that the equilibrium return of a scheme is the return that it is expected to earn with the given level of systematic or market risk. Out of the 40 schemes, 33 schemes (82.5 per cent) are from the private sector and the remaining 7 schemes (17.5 per cent) are from the public sector. The proportion of schemes that have a positive alpha value in each sector is quite high in the private sector (33 out of 90 schemes, 36.7 per cent) than the public sector (7 out of 40 schemes, 17.5 per cent). Thus, under the Jensen's measure also, the private sector schemes outperform the public sector schemes. The 40 schemes consist of 2 income schemes, 6 balanced schemes, 22 growth schemes and 10 ELS schemes, which underscore the superior performance of the growth schemes.

Category-wise, 2 out of the 40 income schemes (4.7 per cent), 6 of the 28 balanced schemes (21.4 per cent), 22 out of 40 growth schemes (55 per cent) and 10 out of the 19 ELS schemes (52.6 per cent) notch up superior performance. Thus, proportion-wise, the growth schemes and the ELS schemes perform better than the equilibrium return.

Sector-wise, out of the 33 private sector schemes which have superior return due to better stock selecting ability, 17 schemes are from the growth category, which is 60.7 per cent in that category. From the 13 ELS schemes, 8 schemes (61.5 per cent) have better returns, while in the balanced scheme category, the proportion of better performing schemes is 30 per cent (6 out of 20 schemes).

Among the public sector schemes, out of the 7 schemes, there is no income or balanced schemes, which suggest poor stock selecting ability of the concerned fund managers of these categories. Out of 12 growth schemes, 5 schemes (41.7 per cent) perform better while it is 33.3 per cent in the case of ELS schemes (2 out of 6 schemes). This clearly underlines the superiority of the private sector in the efficient stock selecting and category-wise, growth schemes and ELS schemes perform better.

Jensen's Alpha in terms of Nifty

The Jensen's alpha in terms of Nifty is presented in Table – 5.8.

TABLE – 5.8 Sector-wise and Category-wise Jensen's Alpha in Terms of Nifty, April 2003 to March 2008

	SECTOR						*Total*		
	Private			*Public*					
Category	*a < 0*	*a > 0*	*All*	*a < 0*	*a > 0*	*All*	*a < 0*	*a > 0*	*All*
Income	27	2	29	13	1	14	40	3	43
Balance	10	10	20	4	4	8	14	14	28
Growth	8	20	28	6	6	12	14	26	40
ELSS	4	9	13	2	4	6	6	13	19
Total	**49**	**41**	**90**	**25**	**15**	**40**	**74**	**56**	**130**

Source: Computed from Appendix A-8.

There is a considerable increase in the number of schemes with positive values which beat the equilibrium return in the market. These positive values which are 40 in terms of Sensex now move up to 56 out of 130 schemes (43.1 per cent). This is made possible by the increase in the number of schemes from both sectors.

The schemes with positive alpha in the private sector go up from 33 to 41, while there is a big leap in the public sector which moves up to 15 from 7 under Sensex. Category-wise, the number of schemes that outperform the market from the balanced category is 14 out of 28 (50 per cent), 26 out of 40 from the growth category (65 per cent) and 13 out of 19 from the ELSS category (68.4 per cent).

Thus the trend witnessed under Sensex is repeated here too, with the growth schemes and the ELS schemes performing better than the others in overall scenario. The same trend could be seen in the case of intra-sector comparison as well. Overall, in terms of Nifty also, private sector schemes have superior performance compared to the public sector and scheme category-wise, the growth and ELS schemes have superior performance.

Sharpe Differential Measure

In performance evaluation, diversification plays a pivotal role as it is capable of reducing the degree of unique risk associated with the scheme. But, evidently, it is not the quantity of diversification that matters, but the quality of diversification. This underscores the significance of the nature of stock-picking rather than the number of stock-picking. Only by identifying and investing in right stocks, can the degree of risk be reduced and / or return is increased. This is known as the fund manager's stock selecting ability. Sharpe termed this as the 'Differential Return'. This differential return is measured as follows:

$$\alpha = AR_p - \left[AR_f + \frac{(AR_m - AR_f)\sigma_p}{\sigma_m} \right]$$

where σ_m is the total risk of the market and α is Sharpe's differential measure, which suggests better stock selecting ability of the fund manager, if its value is higher and *vice versa*.[4] The calculated Sharpe differential measure in terms of both the market indices is given in Appendix A - 9. The alpha values are classified into two groups, viz., below zero and above zero. The former points to negative stock selection and the latter imply positive stock selection on the part of the fund manager.

Sharpe Differential Measure in terms of Sensex

The classified alpha values in terms of Sensex are presented in Table –5.9.

TABLE – 5.9 Sector-wise and Category-wise Sharpe Differential Measure in Terms of Sensex, April 2003 to March 2008

	SECTOR						*Total*		
	Private			*Public*					
Category	*a < 0*	*a > 0*	*All*	*a < 0*	*a > 0*	*All*	*a < 0*	*a > 0*	*All*
Income	29	Nil	**29**	14	Nil	**14**	**43**	**Nil**	**43**
Balance	3	17	**20**	5	3	**8**	**8**	**20**	**28**
Growth	8	20	**28**	4	8	**12**	**12**	**28**	**40**
ELSS	5	8	**13**	2	4	**6**	**7**	**12**	**19**
Total	**45**	**45**	**90**	**25**	**15**	**40**	**70**	**60**	**130**

Source: Computed from Appendix A-9.

Out of the 130 sample schemes, only 60 schemes (46.2 per cent) show positive stock selecting ability which include 45 private sector schemes (50 per cent within that sector) and 15 public sector schemes (37.5 per cent within that sector). Hence, comparatively, private sector schemes exhibit a superior stock selecting ability. Category-wise, the 60 schemes consist of no income schemes, 20 balanced schemes (71.4 per cent within the category), 28 growth schemes (70 of that category) and 12 ELS schemes (63.2 per cent). This shows that in relative terms, balanced schemes and growth schemes portray better stock selecting ability, as a greater proportion of these two schemes come with positive alpha values.

Sector-wise, out of the 45 private sector schemes, 17 balanced schemes out of 20 (85 per cent) have a positive alpha value. This proportion is 71.4 per cent among the growth schemes (20 out of 28) and 61.5 per cent in the case of ELS schemes (8 out of 13 schemes). Among the private sector schemes also, the performance of balanced schemes is the best which is followed by the growth schemes and the ELS schemes in that order. Among the public sector schemes, of the 15 better performing ones, 3 schemes are from the balanced scheme category (37.5 per cent), 8 from the growth category (66.7 per cent) and 4 schemes from the ELSS category (66.7 per cent). When compared with the performance of the private sector schemes, in the public sector, only the ELS schemes perform better, while the intra-sector comparison suggests that growth schemes and ELS schemes have a greater proportion of positive alpha values.

Sharpe Differential Measure in terms of Nifty

Table – 5.10 presents the alpha values in terms of Nifty.

The table indicates that in the overall picture, there is no change from the earlier table, as again 60 schemes turn up with positive alpha values. But, among the 60 schemes, there is one income scheme, which comes from the public sector (SBI Magnum Income Fund-Growth) with a positive alpha value. This is compensated by one growth scheme that comes from the private sector, (DSP Merrill Lynch Equity Fund - Growth) which turns negative. In all other cases, the direction of stock selection under Nifty is similar to that of Sensex. Thus, the private sector fund managers' stock picking ability far outweighs the ability of their counterparts in the public sector.

Table – 5.10 Sector-wise and Category-wise Sharpe Differential Measure in Terms of Nifty, April 2003 to March 2008

	SECTOR						*Total*		
	Private			*Public*					
Category	*a < 0*	*a > 0*	*All*	*a < 0*	*a > 0*	*All*	*a < 0*	*a > 0*	*All*
Income	29	Nil	**29**	13	1	**14**	**42**	**1**	**43**
Balance	3	17	**20**	5	3	**8**	**8**	**20**	**28**
Growth	9	19	**28**	4	8	**12**	**13**	**27**	**40**
ELSS	5	8	**13**	2	4	**6**	**7**	**12**	**19**
Total	**46**	**44**	**90**	**24**	**16**	**40**	**70**	**60**	**130**

Source: Computed from Appendix A-9.

FAMA'S Break-up

Fama synthesised the findings of popular models and provided the break-up values of different types of risk. The components of risk and relevant return for the same are summarised by Fama as follows:

Impact of Beta: This is the systematic risk component explained by the beta of the scheme due to change in the uncontrollable market risk of the scheme. This is expressed as:

$$\beta\,(AR_m - AR_f)$$

Impact of Diversification: This explains the reward for the degree of diversification of the scheme that is derived by the fund manager. This is measured as:

$$(AR_m - AR_f)\ [(\sigma_p / \sigma_m) - \beta]$$

Impact of Selectivity: The degree of diversification alone is not sufficient to beat the market but more importantly the quality of diversification. This underscores the significance of picking up the correct stocks by the fund manager, which decides the effectiveness of diversification. This is expressed as:

$$(AR_p - AR_f) - [(\sigma_p / \sigma_m)\,(AR_m - AR_f)]$$

These three components are considered as the break-up values of the risk-premium, which is the reward for the additional risk involved in investing in the mutual fund schemes. Thus, according to Fama, effectively the reward for risk or risk premium equals the sum of impact of beta, diversification and selectivity. These three break-up values in terms of both the market indices are calculated for all the sample schemes and presented in Appendix A – 10.

IMPACT OF SYSTEMATIC RISK (β) ON MUTUAL FUND SCHEMES

Impact of Beta in terms of Sensex

The sector-wise and category-wise impact of beta in terms of Sensex is shown in Table – 5.11.

The impact of systematic risk assesses the returns which are being generated by the fund managers due to their decision to take risk. The table

Table – 5.11 Sector-wise and Category-wise Impact of beta in Terms of Sensex, April 2003 to March 2008

Category	*SECTOR*						*Total*		
	Private			*Public*					
	Negative	*Positive*	*All*	*Negative*	*Positive*	*All*	*Negative*	*Positive*	*All*
Income	9	20	**29**	7	7	**14**	**16**	**27**	**43**
Balance	15	5	**20**	1	7	**8**	**16**	**12**	**28**
Growth	17	11	**28**	9	3	**12**	**26**	**14**	**40**
ELSS	5	8	**13**	1	5	**6**	**6**	**13**	**19**
Total	**46**	**44**	**90**	**18**	**22**	**40**	**64**	**66**	**130**

Source: Computed from Appendix A – 10.

indicates that out of the 130 sample schemes, a little more than 50 per cent of the schemes (66 schemes) produce positive values which implies positive returns due to systematic risk. A little less than 50 per cent (49.2 per cent) of the sample schemes generate negative return due to the impact of beta. Sector-wise, these 66 positive schemes include 44 (out of 90) private sector schemes and 22 public sector schemes (out of 40). Hence, sector-wise too, the positive impact is more than 50 per cent in the case of public sector. But, category-wise, there is no such equality. The 66 schemes consist of 27 income schemes out of 43, (62.8 per cent), 12 balanced schemes out of 28, (42.9 per cent), 14 schemes from the growth category out of 40, (35 per cent) and 13 ELSS category out of 19, (68.4 per cent). Thus, category-wise, the ELS schemes provide the best impact due to systematic risk, which is followed by income, balanced and growth category schemes.

Taking the sectors individually, out of the 44 private sector schemes which have the positive impact, there are 20 income schemes from 29 schemes, (69 per cent), 5 balanced schemes out of 20, (25 per cent), 11 schemes from the growth category out of 28 schemes, (39.3 per cent) and 8 from the ELS category out of 13, (61.5 per cent). Thus, among the private sector schemes, the positive impact mainly comes from the income schemes, followed by the ELSS, growth and the balanced schemes in that order. This suggests that the trend in the public sector will be different from that of the private sector. For instance, out of the 22 positive return schemes in the public sector, there are 7 schemes from the income category out of 14, (50 per cent), another 7 schemes from the balanced category out of 8, (87.5 per cent), 3 growth schemes from 12 schemes, (25 per cent), and 5 schemes from the ELSS category out of 6, (83.3 per cent). Hence, among the public sector schemes, balanced schemes have the highest positive impact, followed by the ELSS, income and growth schemes. This suggests a mixed trend among the categories.

Impact of Beta in terms of Nifty

Table – 5.12 presents the impact of beta in terms of Nifty.

There is a marked difference in the performance of the schemes under Nifty as 82 schemes out of 130 (63.1 per cent) come with positive impact. This difference is mainly contributed by the private sector in which 58 schemes out of 90, (64.4 per cent) have the positive impact, while in the case

Table – 5.12 Sector-wise and Category-wise Impact of Beta in Terms of Nifty, April 2003 to March 2008

Category	*SECTOR*						*Total*		
	Private			*Public*					
	Negative	*Positive*	*All*	*Negative*	*Positive*	*All*	*Negative*	*Positive*	*All*
Income	7	22	**29**	7	7	**14**	**14**	**29**	**43**
Balance	14	6	**20**	1	7	**8**	**15**	**13**	**28**
Growth	9	19	**28**	7	5	**12**	**16**	**24**	**40**
ELSS	2	11	**13**	1	5	**6**	**3**	**16**	**19**
Total	**32**	**58**	**90**	**16**	**24**	**40**	**48**	**82**	**130**

Source: Computed from Appendix A – 10.

case of the public sector, it is 60 per cent (24 out of 40). Category-wise, out of the 82 schemes, there are 29 income schemes, 13 balanced schemes, 24 growth schemes and 16 ELS schemes.

Comparison with the result under Sensex indicates that there is a big jump in the growth category, since 24 (out of 40 schemes) come with positive impact under Nifty, as against 14 in terms of Sensex. At the sectoral level also, the major difference in the performance comes from the growth schemes, especially from the private sector and then from the ELSS category, though the positive impact increases in the case of other categories as well.

IMPACT OF DIVERSIFICATION ON THE SAMPLE SCHEMES

Diversification measures the additional return that compensates the fund manager for bearing diversifiable risk.

Impact of Diversification in terms of Sensex

Table – 5.13 provides the impact of diversification in the sample schemes in terms of Sensex.

Table – 5.13 Sector-wise and Category-wise Impact of Diversification in Terms of Sensex, April 2003 to March 2008

Category	*SECTOR*						*Total*		
	Private			*Public*					
	Negative	*Positive*	*All*	*Negative*	*Positive*	*All*	*Negative*	*Positive*	*All*
Income	5	24	**29**	6	8	**14**	**11**	**32**	**43**
Balance	15	5	**20**	1	7	**8**	**16**	**12**	**28**
Growth	17	11	**28**	9	3	**12**	**26**	**14**	**40**
ELSS	4	9	**13**	1	5	**6**	**5**	**14**	**19**
Total	**41**	**49**	**90**	**17**	**23**	**40**	**58**	**72**	**130**

Source: Computed from Appendix A – 10.

The table indicates that out of the 130 schemes, 72 (55.4 per cent) schemes have a positive impact due to diversification, which include 49 private sector schemes out of 90, (54.4 per cent) and 23 schemes out of 40, (57.5 per cent) from the public sector. Thus, the public sector schemes exhibit marginally better diversification than the private sector. Category-wise, these 72 schemes incorporate 32 income schemes (74.4 per cent within the category), 12 balanced schemes (42.9 per cent within the category), 14 schemes out of 40 (35 per cent) from the growth category and 14 schemes out of 19 ELSS category (73.7 per cent). Hence, income schemes contribute more towards better diversification followed by ELSS, balanced, and growth schemes.

Sector-wise, out of the 49 private sector schemes with better diversification, 24 schemes belong to the income category (out of 29 schemes, 82.8 per cent). But, there are only 5 balanced schemes (25 per cent), 11 growth schemes (39.3 per cent) and 9 schemes from the ELSS category (69.2 per cent), under the positive return class. This indicates that the best diversified schemes belong to the income category, ELS schemes come second, followed by the growth schemes and finally the balanced schemes. In the case of the public sector, the 23 schemes include 8 from the income category (57.1 per cent), 7 from the balanced category (87.5 per cent), 3 schemes from the growth category (25 per cent) and the ELSS category includes 5 schemes (83.3 per cent). Thus, in the public sector, balanced schemes are the best diversified followed by the growth schemes. Hence, the impact of diversification under

Sensex indicates a mixed trend between the two sectors, where the income schemes dominate the private sector, while it is the balanced category in the public sector.

Impact of Diversification in terms of Nifty

Table – 5.14 presents the impact of diversification in terms of Nifty.

The number of schemes with positive diversification is 78 under Nifty, a small increase over that of under Sensex. This change comes solely from the growth schemes of the private sector. Thus, more number of schemes in the private sector is positively diversified under Nifty. This pushes up the number of schemes with positive diversification in the private sector to 55 (49 under Sensex), while the number of growth schemes moves up from 11 to 16. Similarly, in the overall scenario too, the number of positively diversified growth schemes increases from 14 to 20.

Table – 5.14 Sector-wise and Category-wise Impact of Diversification in Terms of Nifty, April 2003 to March 2008

	SECTOR						*Total*		
	Private			*Public*					
Category	*Negative*	*Positive*	*All*	*Negative*	*Positive*	*All*	*Negative*	*Positive*	*All*
Income	5	24	**29**	6	8	**14**	**11**	**32**	**43**
Balance	15	5	**20**	1	7	**8**	**16**	**12**	**28**
Growth	12	16	**28**	8	4	**12**	**20**	**20**	**40**
ELSS	3	10	**13**	2	4	**6**	**5**	**14**	**19**
Total	**35**	**55**	**90**	**17**	**23**	**40**	**52**	**78**	**130**

Source: Computed from Appendix A – 10.

Impact of Selectivity

Impact of diversification and the impact of selectivity on the schemes mostly come from a single source, viz., stock-picking. The former can be said to emerge from the degree or extent of diversification, while the latter is the manifestation of the nature or quality of diversification. Thus, after accounting for diversification, the residual performance on selectivity is assigned to net selectivity. A positive net selectivity indicates superior performance and a negative one indicates the risk taken by the fund managers that has not been compensated by the additional returns.

Impact of Selectivity in terms of Sensex

The sample schemes were analysed for the impact of selectivity on the basis of both the indices. Table – 5.15 presents the impact of selectivity on the sample schemes in terms of Sensex.

Table – 5.15 Sector-wise and Category-wise Impact of Selectivity in Terms of Sensex, April 2003 to March 2008

	SECTOR						*Total*		
	Private			*Public*					
Category	*Negative*	*Positive*	*All*	*Negative*	*Positive*	*All*	*Negative*	*Positive*	*All*
Income	29	Nil	**29**	14	Nil	**14**	**43**	**Nil**	**43**
Balance	3	17	**20**	5	3	**8**	**8**	**20**	**28**
Growth	8	20	**28**	4	8	**12**	**12**	**28**	**40**
ELSS	5	8	**13**	2	4	**6**	7	**12**	**19**
Total	**45**	**45**	**90**	**25**	**15**	**40**	**70**	**60**	**130**

Source: Computed from Appendix A – 10.

The table shows that out of the 130 schemes, only 60 schemes (46.1 per cent) demonstrate superior performance which comprise of 45 private sector schemes (50 per cent of the sector) and 15 public sector schemes (37.5 per cent of the sector). Hence, the private sector fund managers exhibit better stock selecting ability *vis-à-vis* their counterparts in the public sector.

The 60 schemes with superior performance consists of no scheme from the income category, 20 schemes from the balanced category (71.4 per cent of the category), 28 schemes from the growth category (70 per cent of that category) and 12 from the ELSS category (63.2 per cent). Thus, net selectivity impact is much superior among the balanced and growth schemes, followed by the ELS schemes. In the case of income schemes, it suggests that the risk taken by the fund managers in stock-picking has not been rewarded by any additional return.

In the case of 45 private sector schemes with superior performance, again no income scheme turns positive, while there are 17 balanced schemes (85 per cent of the category), 20 growth schemes (71.4 per cent) and 8 ELS schemes (61.5 per cent). Thus, as in the case of overall trend, here too, balanced schemes and growth schemes reveal much better stock selection than the ELSS category. Among the 15 public sector schemes with positive performance, income schemes fail to provide any additional return, while there are 3 balanced schemes (37.5 per cent of the category), 8 growth schemes

(66.7 per cent) and 4 ELS schemes (66.7 per cent). Thus, in the case of public sector, the growth and the ELS schemes have superior performance than the balanced schemes.

The impact of selectivity in terms of Sensex implies that the private sector schemes have much superior stock selection compared to the public sector. The balanced and growth categories provide better reward for stock selection than the other categories.

Impact of Selectivity in Terms of Nifty

The impact of stock selection in terms of Nifty is shown in Table – 5.16.

The overall result indicates absolutely no difference from that of the earlier table. The difference occurs at the sectoral level, where in the private

Table – 5.16 Sector-wise and Category-wise Impact of Selectivity in Terms of Nifty, April 2003 to March 2008

Category	*SECTOR*						*Total*		
	Private			*Public*					
	Negative	*Positive*	*All*	*Negative*	*Positive*	*All*	*Negative*	*Positive*	*All*
Income	29	Nil	**29**	**13**	1	**14**	**42**	**1**	**43**
Balance	3	17	**20**	**5**	3	**8**	**8**	**20**	**28**
Growth	9	19	**28**	**4**	8	**12**	**13**	**27**	**40**
ELSS	5	8	**13**	**2**	4	**6**	**7**	**12**	**19**
Total	**46**	**44**	**90**	**24**	**16**	**40**	**70**	**60**	**130**

Source: Computed from Appendix A – 10.

sector, the number of schemes with superior performance comes down from 45 to 44, which is influenced by the decrease in the number of growth schemes, by the same margin. And, in the case of public sector, the number of schemes goes up from 15 to 16, contributed by the income category.

MARKET TIMING ABILITY – TREYNOR AND MAZUY MODEL

Mutual fund schemes attract investment as they are expected to beat not only the conventional financial products like provident fund, post office and bank savings, which they in fact do, but also the market. This is made possible by the fund managers who have the ability to sense the mood of the market in advance, and collect the required information about the impending market movements. This enables them to move their investment in such a way that they reduce the systematic risk, which is known as market timing ability. In other words, the fund managers can shift the overall risk composition of their portfolios in anticipation of broad price movements. Technically, market timing implies altering the beta of the portfolio return by balancing the portfolio mix of the scheme. This also implies that the differential return is generated not only by correct stock picking which is done at the individual stock level, but also by involving in market timing activities. This would suggest that the fund managers are capable of perfectly assessing the direction of change of market in the near future. Hence, by correctly timing the market, the fund managers could produce superior returns.

Treynor and Mazuy (1966)[5] developed a model to analyse the timing ability of the fund managers. This model used a quadratic equation to capture the relationship between the fund return and market return. The equation is:

$$(R_{pt} - R_{ft}) = \alpha + \beta (R_{mt} - R_{ft}) + \gamma (R_{mt} - R_{ft})^2 + e_{it}$$

where, α is the constant term and β and γ are the slope coefficients. According to Treynor and Mazuy, the coefficient of the squared term gamma (γ) captures the fund managers' market timing ability. A positive value indicates the existence of market timing and in the absence of market timing, γ will be zero. In extreme cases, γ can also be negative, which will suggest not only the absence of timing but the timing is such that it goes against the investors' interest by earning negative returns. The calculated γ values need not only be positive, but more importantly statistically significant also, to underscore the presence or absence of timing.

Market Timing Ability in Terms of Sensex

The γ values for all the sample schemes are calculated in terms of both Sensex and Nifty and presented along with the 't' values in Appendix A – 11. These γ values are classified sector and category-wise depending on whether they are significant or not and shown in terms of Sensex is given in Table – 5.17.

The table indicates that all the 130 sample schemes produce positive γ values, of which the values of 33 schemes (25.4 per cent) are insignificant. That is, though these schemes show the existence of market timing, the returns thus generated are not significant enough. In case of all the remaining 97 schemes, the γ values are significant up to 5 per cent level. These 97 schemes comprise of 38 income schemes out of 43, (88.4 per cent), 24 out of 28 balanced schemes (85.7 per cent), 22 from the 40 growth schemes (55 per cent) and 13 out of 19 ELS schemes

(68.4 per cent). Thus, among the different categories, the income and balanced category schemes show much superior timing ability, and the ELSS and growth category schemes follow in that order.

Table – 5.17 Sector-wise and Category-wise Market timing Ability in Terms of Sensex, April 2003 to March 2008

Sector	*Category*	*Significant* *	*Insignificant*	*Total*
Private	Income	27	2	29
	Balance	16	4	20
	Growth	16	12	28
	ELSS	10	3	13
	All	**69**	**21**	**90**
Public	Income	11	3	14
	Balance	8	Nil	8
	Growth	6	6	12
	ELSS	3	3	6
	All	**28**	**12**	**40**
Total	Income	38	5	43
	Balance	24	4	28
	Growth	22	18	40
	ELSS	13	6	19
	All	**97**	**33**	**130**

Note: *Significant up to 5 per cent level.

Source: Computed from Appendix A – 11.

Sector-wise, these 97 schemes consist of 69 private sector schemes out of 90 schemes, (76.7 per cent) and 28 public sector schemes out of 40, (70 per cent). This again underlines the superiority of the private sector schemes in better timing ability than the public sector schemes.

In the case of private sector schemes, in which 69 schemes are statistically significant, 27 schemes are from the income category (93.1 per cent of the category), 16 schemes belong to the balanced category (80 per cent), 16 from the growth category (57.1 per cent) and 10 from the ELSS category (76.9 per cent). Balanced and the ELS schemes stand second and third positions in the performance of timing ability. Among the 28 public sector schemes with significantly superior returns, 11 out of 14 income schemes (78.6 per cent) again show positively significant γ values, while all the balanced schemes have significant values. In the case of growth schemes and the ELS schemes in this sector, only 50 per cent of them turn positively significant. This indicates that the private sector shows better timing ability than the public sector, while the intra-sector comparison suggests that the income and balanced schemes are the better categories. This implies that the non-equity market (the bond market) plays a pivotal role in enabling the market timing ability of the income and balanced schemes in both the sectors.

Market Timing Ability in Terms of Nifty

Table – 5.18 presents the γ values in terms of Nifty.

Table – 5.18 Sector-wise and Category-wise Market Timing Ability in Terms of Nifty, April 2003 to March 2008

Sector	*Category*	*Significant* *	*Insignificant*	*Negative*	*Total*
Private	Income	27	2	Nil	29
	Balance	18	2	Nil	20
	Growth	17	11	Nil	28
	ELSS	8	4	1	13
	All	**70**	**19**	**1**	**90**
Public	Income	11	2	1	14
	Balance	7	1	Nil	8
	Growth	10	2	Nil	12
	ELSS	4	2	Nil	6
	All	**32**	**7**	**1**	**40**
Total	**Income**	**38**	**4**	**1**	**43**
	Balance	**25**	**3**	**Nil**	**28**
	Growth	**27**	**13**	**Nil**	**40**
	ELSS	**12**	**6**	**1**	**19**
	All	**102**	**26**	**2**	**130**

Note: *Significant up to 5 per cent level.

Source: Computed from Appendix A – 11.

The situation under Nifty is only marginally different from that of Sensex, as five more schemes (102 out of 130, 78.5 per cent) become statistically significant, while two schemes show negative γ values, though they are insignificant. These two schemes consist of one ELS scheme from the private sector (Escorts Tax Plan Dividend) and the other from the public sector income category (SBI Magnum Income Fund - Dividend). The 102 schemes comprise of 70 private sector schemes (77.8 per cent) and 32 public sector schemes (80 per cent). Thus, under Nifty, both the sectors display similar performance, though the public sector is marginally better.

The 102 schemes comprise of 38 from the income category out of 43, (88.4 per cent), 25 from the balanced category (89.3 per cent), 27 schemes from the growth category (67.5 per cent) and 12 from the ELSS category (63.2 per cent). Hence, under Nifty too, income and the balanced categories are the better performing categories compared to the other two categories. The table also indicates that this overall trend is replicated at the individual sector level as well. That is, the income and the balanced schemes produce better performance in timing the market followed by the ELSS and the growth schemes in both the sectors. The growth schemes being exposed totally to the equity market are struggling to time the market.

Overall Performance Ranking of Sample Schemes

The evaluation of performance of the sample schemes under various measures portrays differing results, as some schemes perform better under some measures, while other schemes turn better under some other measures. Hence, to locate the best performing scheme / schemes among all the 130 sample schemes, the overall performance ranking is done to pinpoint the best scheme. The schemes are ranked under the measures that include IRR, AR_p, SD_p, Sharpe, Treynor, Sharpe Differential measure, Jensen, Fama's impact of beta, diversification and selectivity and also market timing ability under both indices, and their final average ranks are arrived at, which is presented in Appendix A – 12. Schemes are ranked according to their performance, as the scheme with highest value under a measure is given the rank of 1, except under standard deviation, in which case the scheme with the least value is given the rank of 1. Schemes' ranks under the measures mentioned above are added and the average rank value is derived. Finally, the scheme with the lowest average rank value is given the rank of 1.

The average overall ranking of the individual schemes is presented in Table – 5.19. The table indicates that among the 130 sample schemes, all the top 5 performers hail from the private sector and moreover, all of them belong to the growth category, which underscores their relative dominance. However, in the top 10 schemes, there are two balanced schemes – from the private sector – at the 7th and 8th positions, though no public sector scheme could be found as yet. The five schemes that top the list are viz., the Sundaram BNP Paribas Capex Opportunities Fund-Growth, followed by the Birla Index Fund-Growth, Tata Pure Equity Fund-Growth, the ICICI Prudential Growth Plan-Growth and the Reliance Growth Fund-Growth. Thus, there is one scheme from each of the top performing AMCs among the best schemes.

Table– 5.19 Average Ranging of the Sample Schemes

Sl. No.	*Name of the Scheme*	*Average Rank*
1	Sundaram BNP Paribas Capex Opportunities Fund-Growth	36.056
2	Birla Index Fund – Growth	36.333
3	Tata Pure Equity Fund - Growth	38.000
4	ICICI Prudential Growth Plan - Growth Option	38.278
5	Reliance Growth Fund - Growth Plan	38.389
6	Sundaram BNP Paribas Growth Fund-Dividend	38.611
7	ING Balanced Portfolio (G)	38.944
8	HDFC Balanced Fund	40.222
9	Templeton India Growth Fund-Dividend Plan	40.222
10	Kotak 30 – Growth	40.444
11	Reliance Vision Fund - Dividend Plan	42.444
12	Taurus Libra Taxshield	43.611
13	Kotak Balance	44.389
14	ICICI Pru FMCG Plan – Dividend	45.056
15	ICICI Prudential Tax Plan-Growth Option	45.611
16	ICICI Prudential Balanced Fund (G)	46.000
17	HDFC Growth Fund	46.333
18	Reliance Income Fund - Growth Plan	46.667
19	Sundaram BNP Paribas Growth Fund-Growth	47.056
20	LICMF Growth Fund - Dividend Option	48.000
21	Escorts Growth Plan - Growth	48.167
22	Tata Income Fund - Qtrly	48.222
23	Sundaram PNB Paribas Tax Saver OE Fund	49.556
24	ING Balanced Portfolio (D)	49.611
25	Sundaram Taxsaver 98	50.056
26	Tata Pure Equity Fund - Dividend	50.167

Sl. No.	*Name of the Scheme*	*Average Rank*
27	Templeton India Growth Fund-Growth Plan	50.778
28	Birla Advantage Fund - Dividend/ Reinvestment	50.944
29	Sundaram BNP Balanced – Appreciation	51.278
30	DSP Merrill Lynch Opportunities Fund	51.611
31	ICICI Prudential Balanced Fund (D)	52.333
32	Reliance Growth Fund - Dividend Plan	53.722
33	Birla Sun Life Income Fund – G	53.778
34	Sundaram BNP Balanced – Dividend	54.000
35	ICICI Prudential Tax Plan-Dividend Option	54.111
36	Reliance Income Fund - Annual Dividend Plan	54.778
37	Bank of Baroda Balanced – Dividend	55.333
38	Tata Balanced Fund	55.833
39	DBS Chola Freedom Income -STF-Institutional	56.000
40	Escorts Tax Plan Growth	56.222
41	Tata Income Fund - Semi	57.389
42	ICICI Prudential Income Plan-Growth Option	57.722
43	Bob ELS 96	58.056
44	UTI Mahila Unit Scheme	58.167
45	ICICI Prudential Growth Plan - Dividend Option	58.611
46	DBS Chola Freedom Income -STF-DD	58.778
47	Birla Tax Plan 98	58.833
48	Canara Robeco Income Bonus	59.833
49	DBS Chola Growth Fund-Quarterly Dividend	60.056
50	Franklin India Taxshield – Growth	60.056
51	SBI Magnum Multiplier Plus Scheme-93–Dividend	60.389
52	ICICI Prudential MIP - Cumulative	60.444
53	JM Equity Fund - Growth	60.444
54	Sahara Income Fund-Growth	60.667

Sl. No.	*Name of the Scheme*	*Average Rank*
55	DSP Merrill Lynch Equity Fund	61.056
56	Franklin India Balanced Fund (G)	61.111
57	Tata Tax Saving	61.444
58	J M Balanced Fund (Growth)	61.611
59	Bank of Baroda Balanced – Growth	61.944
60	BOB Income Fund - Dividend	62.500
61	LIC Balanced – Plan C – Growth	62.889
62	Sundaram BNP Paribas Income Plus-Dividend	63.000
63	JM Income Fund - Growth	63.111
64	LICMF Taxplan-Growth	63.389
65	FT India MIP-Growth	64.167
66	FT India MIP-Monthly Bonus	64.556
67	SBI Magnum Taxgain Scheme 1993 – Dividend	64.667
68	ICICI Prudential Income Plan-Dividend Option	64.722
69	SBI Magnum Balanced Fund – Dividend	64.722
70	Principal Balanced Fund – Growth	64.778
71	Tata Income Fund - Monthly	64.944
72	UTI Balanced Fund – Growth	64.944
73	Canara Robeco Income – Income	65.444
74	Franklin Taxshield – Dividend	67.333
75	LICMF Growth Fund - Growth Option	67.444
76	SBI MSFU IT	67.778
77	Sahara Growth Fund-Growth	67.944
78	Canara Robeco Expo Growth Plan	68.056
79	Escorts Tax Plan Dividend	68.722
80	Sahara Growth Fund-Dividend	69.111
81	Canara Robeco Income – Growth	69.222
82	UTI-Master Equity Plan Unit Scheme	69.222

Sl. No.	*Name of the Scheme*	*Average Rank*
83	JM Income Fund – Dividend	69.444
84	Franklin India Balanced Fund (D)	70.333
85	SBI MSFU Contra – Dividend	70.500
86	Birla Balance (D)	70.611
87	Canara Robeco Equity Tax Saver	70.722
88	SBI Magnum Equity Fund	71.444
89	Principal Tax Saving fund	72.889
90	Birla Balance (G)	73.333
91	Sahara Income Fund-Dividend	73.889
92	SBI MSFU Contra- Growth	74.000
93	UTI Balanced Fund – Dividend	74.167
94	UTI Monthly Income Scheme – Dividend	74.444
95	Sundaram BNP Paribas Income Plus-Appreciation	74.889
96	BOB Income Fund -Growth	75.278
97	LIC Balanced – Plan A – Dividend	75.667
98	ING Income Fund- Dividend Option	75.889
99	Reliance Income Fund Retail Plan Half Yearly	75.944
100	DBS Chola Growth Fund-Cumulative	76.667
101	ING Income Fund-Growth Option	77.000
102	UTI Monthly Income Scheme – Growth	77.778
103	LIC MF Bond Fund - Growth	78.167
104	Taurus Star Share	78.611
105	Sundaram Balanced Fund	79.944
106	Kotak Income Plus - Monthly Dividend	80.611
107	J M Balanced Fund (Dividend)	80.833
108	Kotak Income Plus – Growth	81.222
109	DSP Merill Lynch Balanced Fund (D)	82.056
110	Escorts Growth Plan - Dividend	82.278

Sl. No.	*Name of the Scheme*	*Average Rank*
111	SBI Magnum Income Fund – Dividend	82.778
112	SBI Magnum Income Fund – Bonus	84.500
113	Templeton India Income Fund - Dividend	85.278
114	Canara Robeco Expo Income Plan	85.833
115	SBI Magnum Income Fund - Growth	86.389
116	LIC Unit Linked Insurance Scheme	86.556
117	Templeton India Income Fund - Growth	87.889
118	JM Equity Fund - Dividend	88.556
119	UTI - Equity Fund-Income Option	88.889
120	DSP Merill Lynch Balanced Fund (G)	89.333
121	Birla Sun Life Income Fund – D	89.556
122	Principal Balanced Fund – Dividend	92.056
123	LIC MF Bond Fund - Dividend	96.667
124	LICMF Taxplan-Dividend	98.000
125	SaharaTax Gain-Growth	99.111
126	HDFC Income Fund - Growth	100.056
127	HDFC Income Fund - Dividend	100.103
128	UTI - Equity Fund-Growth Option	100.222
129	Baroda Diversified Fund-Growth	102.722
130	SBI Magnum Monthly Income Fund – Bonus	106.722

Source: Computed from Appendix A – 12.

On the other extreme, among the least 5 performers, there are three public sector schemes, viz., the SBI Magnum Monthly Income Fund-Bonus, Baroda Diversified Fund-Growth and the UTI Equity Fund-Growth, beginning from the last. The other two schemes which are from the private sector belong to HDFC. The table also indicates that among the least performers, there are more number of income and balanced schemes. This one again brings out the superior performance of the private sector schemes and specifically the growth schemes in a categorical manner.

Descriptive Statistics related to Sample Schemes' Ranks

Further, to understand the relative performance of the schemes, both sector and category-wise, descriptive statistics of the schemes' ranks is shown in Table – 5.20.

Table – 5.20 Descriptive Statistics of Sector/Category-wise Performance Ranking of The Sample Schemes

Sector / Category	*Mean*	*Standard Deviation*	*Minimum*	*Maximum*	*Sum*	*Count*
Private	**61.79**	**16.32**	**36.06**	**108.83**	**5561.54**	**90**
Public	**73.84**	**13.88**	**48.00**	**106.72**	**2953.44**	**40**
Income	72.03	14.88	46.67	108.83	3097.34	43
Balanced	64.46	14.75	38.94	92.06	1804.81	28
Growth	60.03	18.24	36.06	102.72	2401.22	40
ELSS	63.77	14.86	43.61	99.11	1211.61	19

Source: Computed from Appendix A – 12.

The table provides the mean, standard deviation, minimum, maximum and sum of the ranking of the schemes grouped under sector and category. Mean score of the rankings indicates the average rank attained by that sector/ category, while standard deviation indicates the degree of deviation in the rankings. Lower value suggests lower deviation in the rankings from the mean score and thus consistent performance, while higher value means higher deviation and thus more fluctuations in the rankings.

Analysing the mean scores between the two sectors, the private sector stands first with lower mean score of rank with 61.79 as against 73.84 in the case of public sector. The ranks in the former ranges from a minimum of 36.06 to the maximum of 108.83, while that of the public sector ranges from 48.00 to 106.72. Among the different categories, the growth schemes become 'Numero Uno', followed by the ELS schemes, balanced and finally the income schemes. This clearly indicates that though the growth schemes do not perform better under measures like risk, impact of beta, impact of diversification and also market timing ability, still they become the top performers, as their relative performance is better in terms of other measures that include IRR, AR_p, R^2, Sharpe, Treynor, Sharpe differential, Jensen's alpha and Fama's impact of selectivity.

The overall standard deviation of the two sectors indicates that the private sector schemes, with a standard deviation of 16.32, are associated with higher risk compared to the public sector schemes, which have a standard deviation of 13.88. Category-wise, balanced schemes provide the least risk with a standard deviation of 14.75, which are followed by ELS schemes whose standard deviation is 14.86, income schemes which have a standard deviation of 14.88 and then the growth schemes which are linked with highest risk with a standard deviation of 18.24.

Table – 5.21 Descriptive Statistics of Category-wise Scheme's Ranking

Category	*Sector*	*Mean*	*SD*	*Min*	*Max*	*Sum*	*Count*
Income	Private	69.64	14.97	46.67	108.83	2019.45	29
	Public	76.99	13.90	58.17	106.72	1077.89	14
Balanced	Private	62.93	16.27	38.94	92.06	1258.59	20
	Public	68.28	9.89	55.33	86.56	546.22	8
Growth	Private	53.43	14.98	36.06	88.56	1495.95	28
	Public	75.44	16.09	48.00	102.72	905.27	12
ELSS	Private	60.58	14.60	43.61	99.11	787.55	13
	Public	70.68	14.12	58.06	98.00	424.06	6

Source: Computed from Appendix A – 12.

Table – 5.21 provides the descriptive statistics of the rank of schemes under sector specific categories. A cursory glance at the table tells that in each category, the private sector dominates the overall rankings. The mean score of the overall rank of the private sector growth scheme, 53.43 is the lowest among all the categories, while that of the public sector, 75.44 is substantially higher than the mean score of any other private sector category. But, in the case of public sector, balanced schemes are the best with the lowest mean score, followed by the ELS schemes, growth schemes and finally the income schemes. Among the private sector categories too, the income category stands the last as in the case of the public sector.

Category-wise standard deviation values indicate that the private sector schemes are riskier than the public sector schemes in all the categories. Sector-wise, in the public sector, balanced schemes are the least risky, while in the private sector, the ELS schemes bear the least risk. On the other hand, growth schemes are the riskiest in the public sector, while the balanced schemes are the riskiest in the private sector.

NORMALITY OF RETURNS OF THE SAMPLE SCHEMES

The returns of the mutual fund schemes depend largely on the stock market and to a lesser extent also on the bond market, both of which fluctuate considerably. Thus, the return of the schemes is also expected to be volatile. Hence, it is imperative to verify the normality of the returns. This will enable in ascertaining whether the returns produced by the schemes are normally distributed over the years or not. The normality of the returns of both the sample schemes and market indices can be tested with the application of the tools like the Kolmogorov-Smirnov (K-S) statistic and Kurtosis.[66] The K-S test is based on the largest absolute difference between the observed and the expected cumulative distributions of a given variable, while kurtosis is measured as:

$$\text{Kurtosis} = \frac{\mu_4}{\mu_2^2} - 3$$

where, μ_4 is the 4th moment about the mean and μ_2 is the second moment. 'Minus 3' is used to make the kurtosis of the normal distribution equal to zero. If the kurtosis measure is positive, the curve is leptokurtic (more peaked) and if it is negative, the curve is platykurtic (more flat).[7] The K-S statistic has been calculated for all the sample schemes along with the market indices for the study period 2003-2008 as a whole and the values along with the p-values are given in Appendix A-13.[8]

For a normal distribution, the calculated K-S values need to be equal to zero and also statistically significant. The calculated values are statistically highly significant for all the sample schemes, but none of them is equal to zero. This implies that during the study period, the returns of the sample schemes are not normally distributed. This is also the case with the market returns, where the calculated values are significantly different from zero.

Kurtosis is calculated for each of the five years (2003-04 to 2007-08) separately and also for the whole period, in order to find out the nature of return year-wise and presented in Appendix A – 14. Since none of the calculated value is equal to zero, the values are classified into less than -0.5, -0.5 to 0.5 and more then 0.5, where the second class is expected to provide the kurtosis values which are closer to zero and thus to form a normal distribution. The year-wise and sector-wise classification of the kurtosis values are presented in Table – 5.22.

The year-wise analysis shows that there is a lot of fluctuation in the number of schemes falling in the closer to zero class of -0.5 to 0.5. It ranges from a minimum of 16 in 2004-05 to the maximum of 36 in 2007-08. Thus, the number of schemes with considerable normal distribution has not gone beyond 27.8 per cent (36 schemes out of 130) which clearly indicates that the schemes' returns during the study period are not normally distributed.

Table – 5.22 Sector-wise and Year-wise Kurtosis Value Ranges of the Sample Schemes

Year	*Sector*	*Kurtosis Values*			*Total*
		Less than-0.5	*- 0.5 to 0.5*	*More than 0.5*	
2003-04	Private	31	17	42	90
	Public	7	16	17	40
	Total	**38**	**33**	**59**	**130**
2004-05	Private	13	10	67	90
	Public	2	6	32	40
	Total	**15**	**16**	**99**	**130**
2005-06	Private	12	17	61	90
	Public	4	7	29	40
	Total	**16**	**24**	**90**	**130**
2006-07	Private	9	14	67	90
	Public	4	5	31	40
	Total	**13**	**19**	**98**	**130**
2007-08	Private	4	28	58	90
	Public	10	8	22	40
	Total	**14**	**36**	**80**	**130**

Source: Computed from Appendix A-14.

Moreover, the sector-wise analysis shows that in three out of five years, (since 2005-06), the proportion of private schemes in the middle range is higher than the proportion of public sector schemes. Hence, overall the proportion of schemes with normal distribution is quite low in each year. The proportion of private sector schemes with normal distribution is marginally higher than that of public sector schemes in more number of years.

Table – 5.23 provides the sector and category-wise analysis of kurtosis values for the total period. This indicates that only 5 schemes out of 130 (3.8 per cent) fall in the middle range of closer to zero, which consists of 4 schemes from the private sector and one from the public sector. This again reiterates the point that the schemes' returns are not normally distributed,

Table – 5.23 Sector-wise and Category-wise Kurtosis Value Ranges during 2003-08

Year	*Sector*	*Kurtosis Values*			*Total*
		Less than-0.5	*- 0.5 to 0.5*	*More than 0.5*	
Private	Income	Nil	2	27	29
	Balance	Nil	1	19	20
	Growth	Nil	Nil	28	28
	ELSS	Nil	1	12	13
	All	Nil	**4**	**86**	**90**
Public	Income	Nil	Nil	14	14
	Balance	Nil	1	7	8
	Growth	Nil	Nil	12	12
	ELSS	Nil	Nil	6	6
	All	Nil	**1**	**39**	**40**
Total	**Income**	Nil	**2**	**41**	**43**
	Balance	Nil	**2**	**26**	**28**
	Growth	Nil	Nil	**40**	**40**
	ELSS	Nil	**1**	**18**	**19**
	All	Nil	**5**	**125**	**130**

Source: Computed from Appendix A-14.

while the overall picture shows that the proportion of private sector schemes is marginally higher than the public sector schemes. The table also indicates that as many as 125 schemes fall in the positively higher values, suggesting the fact that the returns are highly peaked in nature.

Category-wise, out of the 5 schemes which fall in the range closer to zero, there are 2 income schemes, one balanced scheme and one ELS scheme from the private sector. The lone public sector scheme which is in the middle range belongs to the balanced scheme category. Thus, no scheme from the growth category comes in the closer to zero class.

Kurtosis Values of the Market Indices

The returns of the schemes emanate from the market and thus, normality of the market returns too needs to be tested.

Table – 5.24 Year-wise Kurtosis Values of The Market Indices

Index	*2003-04*	*2004-05*	*2005-06*	*2006-07*	*2007-08*	*2003-08*
Sensex	-1.285	4.385	1.518	1.914	0.361	**1.107**
Nifty	-0.850	3.086	4.382	0.283	1.032	**1.560**

Source: Computed from Appendix A-14.

The kurtosis values given in the table suggests the market indices fall in the normal range of -0.5 to 0.5 in only one year each, Sensex in 2007-08 and Nifty in 2006-07. The values range from a low of -1.285 to the high of 4.385 in the case of Sensex and from -0.850 to 4.382 in the case of Nifty, signifying the point that the market returns themselves are not normally distributed over the years.

INVESTMENT SIZE AND PERFORMANCE OF THE SAMPLE SCHEMES

It is normally opined that those funds which boast of larger investment can afford more facilities and personnel and due to economies of scale, they can also reduce the average cost. This lower average cost enables the funds to charge lower expenses which pushes up their NAVs. Moreover, larger funds also tend to have more impact on the market through their buying and selling activities. This relationship is tested by taking the size of investment made in the concerned scheme and it's NAV. These two variables are taken for all sample schemes for the concluding year of the study period, that is 2007-08, since year-wise data on the size of investment for all the sample schemes is not available. The monthly NAVs of the schemes are annualised for estimation purposes. This is tested with the application of an uni-variate regression model, which is specified as:[9]

$$NAV_i = \alpha + \beta\, SIZE_i + e_i$$

where, NAV_i is the annualised NAV of the ith scheme pertaining to the year 2007-08 and $SIZE_i$ is the size of investment attracted by that scheme in the given year. α is the intercept term and β is the slope co-efficient, while 'e' is the normal error term. However, as both NAV and SIZE of the sample schemes are quite varying in their magnitude, both the variables are taken in their log form to reduce the impact of such magnitude. The equation to be estimated is:

$$\ln NAV_i = \alpha + \beta \ln SIZE_i + e_i$$

where 'ln' is the natural logarithm. This equation is applied on the collected data (given in Appendix A – 15) and the result is given below:

Table– 5.25 Linear Regression Estimate : Size of Investment and NAV

Variable	*Coefficient*	*t – value*	*p - value*
C	2.2730	9.1773***	0.000
SIZE	0.1306	4.4363***	0.000
Adjusted R^2	0.1265		
F-statistic	19.6814***		
Prob (F-statistic)	0.000		

Note: *** indicates 1 per cent level of significance.

Source: Computed from Appendix A-15.

The result shown Table – 5.25 indicates that the impact made by the size of the investment of the scheme is statistically highly significant and it is positive. That is larger the investment size, better the performance of the scheme. This implies that one unit increase in the size of investment of a scheme will increase its NAV by 0.13 units and *vice versa.* The value of adjusted R^2 (12.64 per cent) indicates that the investment size of the scheme alone is capable of accounting for more than 12 per cent of changes in the scheme's NAV and the F-value which is significant at 1 per cent level suggests that the model is a good fit. This suggests that the performance of the scheme is positively and strongly influenced by its size of investment.

Conclusion

The analysis shows that the IRR of the growth schemes are the highest followed by ELSS and balanced schemes, while sector-wise, private sector schemes provide higher IRR during the study period. The same trend could be seen in the case of average return as well. The Sharpe ratio which analyses the risk-adjusted returns of the sample schemes indicate that just around 50 per cent of the sample schemes could beat the market return during the study period, in terms of both indices. In the case of Treynor's measure, more (66.2 per cent) schemes outperform the market in terms of Sensex, though in terms of Nifty, only 50 per cent could do so. In terms of Jensen's alpha, the sample schemes' performance suffers even more as not even 50 per cent of them could outperform the market under both indices, though under Nifty, the underperformance is marginally less.

The analysis about the sample schemes' performance under Sharpe differential measure suggests that the private sector fund manager's stock picking ability far outweighs the ability of their counterparts in the public sector. Fama's break up indicates that just around 50 per cent of the schemes have positive impact of beta in which the proportion of ELS schemes is the highest followed by income, balanced and growth schemes in terms of Sensex. In terms of Nifty, positive impact increases to 63.1 per cent, though the category-wise trend is similar. The impact of selectivity shows that only 46 per cent of the schemes turn positive in terms of both indices. Growth schemes have the highest proportion of positive schemes followed by balanced and ELS schemes, while the private sector has more positive schemes under both indices.

The market timing ability measure suggests that all the sample schemes have positive γ values in terms of Sensex, while two schemes (SBI Magnum Income Fund-Dividend and Escorts Tax Plan-Dividend) have negative γ values in terms of Nifty. However, more than 75 per cent of the values are statistically significant under both indices in which the private sector schemes perform better under Sensex, while it is the public sector schemes under Nifty.

Ranking of the performance of the schemes suggests that the private sector growth schemes top the list, while public sector income schemes lie at the bottom. The private sector schemes clearly outcompete the public sector schemes in all categories.

The test for normality of returns of the sample schemes during the study period implies that the returns are not normally distributed, which is also the case with the market indices. Moreover, size of the scheme in terms of its investment has a positive and statistically significant relationship with its performance. This indicates that those schemes with higher investment perform better in terms of their NAV.

References

1. Sharpe, William F., (1966), op.cit.,
2. Treynor, Jack L., (1966), op.cit.,
3. Jensen, Michael C (1968), op.cit.,
4. Sharpe, William F., (1975), "Adjusting for Risk in Portfolio Performance Measurement." Journal of Portfolio Management, Winter, pp. 29-34.
5. Treynor, Jack l., and Mazuy, Kay K., (1966), op.cit.,
6. To study the nature of distribution of the returns, many tools like Kolkogorov-Smirnov test and Kurtosis among others are applied. Kurtosis as a tool to analyse the nature of distribution has been applied by many, of which the following studies can be mentioned: Banerjee, Ashok and Sahadeb Sarkar, (2006, "Modeling daily

volatilityof the Indian stock market using intra-day data", WPS No. 588/March, Indian Institute of Management, Kolkotta, p. 18; Raju M.T., and Anirban Ghosh, (2004, "Stock Market Volatility – An International Comparison", WPS No. 8, April, Securities and Exchange Boardof India, Mumbai, p. 16; Gali, Kanti Kumar (1995), "Mutual Funds Performance Appraisal and Organizational Factors: An Analysis based on Risk-adjusted Returns", unpublished Ph.D. Thesis, IIM Bangalore, p.63, while Kolmogorov-Smirnov test has been used by Gali (1995), p.62.

7. Gupta, S.P., (2006), Statistical Methods, sultan Chand and sons, New Delhi, pp.350-351.
8. The K-S test is done with the application of SPSS.
9. In order to study the impact of the size of the scheme on its performance, Gali has applied regression model. Gali, (1995), op.cit., p.73.

6

SUMMARY, CONCLUSION AND SUGGESTIONS

The present study evaluates the performance of mutual funds in the Indian mutual fund industry. It compares the risk and returns of 130 sample schemes taken from the public and private sector comprising of four different categories viz., income schemes, balanced schemes, growth schemes and ELS schemes and also evaluates their performance.

Evaluation of the performance of mutual funds was pioneered by Harry Markowitz and was developed and refined by Sharpe, Treynor, Jensen, Fama, Mazuy among others. Many researchers have evaluated the performance of mutual funds in India and other countries. Review of the important studies which have dealt with the performance evaluation of mutual funds indicates that most of the studies have analysed the schemes of either public sector or private sector exclusively and they have taken only two or three categories of schemes. The sample size was normally restricted to 100 and the length of the study period was also short – upto three years. Importantly, in most of the studies the number of observations for each of the sample schemes was not uniform, which renders intra-sector and inter-sector comparison meaningless and only one market index was used as the benchmark.

This study, thus makes an attempt to fill this void by taking the schemes belonging to both public sector and private sector, comprising of four popular categories, viz., income schemes, balanced schemes, growth schemes and ELS schemes. Totally, 130 schemes have been selected and monthly net asset value data for a period of 5 years, from April 2003 to March 2008 have been gathered and the performance of these schemes have been analysed in comparison with two market indices separately, viz, Sensex and Nifty.

The objectives of the study are to analyse the growth of household sector savings in India and its components since 1993-94. It examines the growth trends in the Indian mutual fund industry from 1993-94 in terms of amount mobilised. It analyses the sample schemes in terms of their risk and return, systematic risk and unique risk. It evaluates their performance on the basis of IRR, the methods developed by Sharpe, Treynor, Jensen, Fama, Treynor and Mazuy, among others. Moreover, the sample schemes have also been ranked based on their overall performance in order to identify the best scheme. The normality of returns of the schemes has also been verified with the application of Kurtosis. It also examines the relationship between size of investment of the scheme and its performance with the help of an uni-variate regression model.

The analysis is done for a sample of 130 schemes, which included 40 public sector schemes and 90 private sector schemes, comprising of four categories. The sample schemes have been selected on the basis of multi-stage purposive proportionate sampling technique. Only those schemes which had complete monthly net asset value during April 2003 to March 2008 have been purposively selected and an equal proportion of 25 per cent of the schemes from both public and private sector have been chosen as sample.

SUMMARY OF FINDINGS

The main findings of the study are summarised as follows:

Growth Trends of the Indian Mutual Fund Industry

The number of schemes launched fluctuated on a year-to-year basis, ranging from the lowest of 36 in 1998-99 to the highest of 413 in 2006-07. The sales volume of the new schemes also fluctuated, though not in the same manner. In 1998-99, when only 36 schemes were launched, it amassed Rs.5,736 crore, whereas double the number of the schemes in 2001-02, had accounted only for Rs.2,271 crore and 46 new schemes in 2003-04 were able to gather Rs.8,549 crore. When compared with the changes in the investments made in shares and debentures, its correlation with new schemes' sales volume is marginally closer than its correlation with the number of new schemes. This brings out the fact that the Indian investors are more cautious in investing as they are not attracted just by the number of schemes launched but by the performance of the stock market.

The growth schemes of the asset management companies show that among the public sector asset management companies, bank of Baroda has eroded in terms of its asset under management, as it declined from Rs. 242 crore in October 2003 to Rs.72 crore in March 2008. However, during the same period the asset under management of Life Insurance Corporation and State Bank of India had gone up quite remarkably. The asset under management of UTI too had grown but the rate of increase has left much to be desired. Thus, the total asset under management of the public sector funds has nearly quadrupled from Rs.24,552 crore to Rs.95,175 crore.

Among the private asset management companies too, not all the funds witnessed uniform growth. For instance, ABN AMRO which entered in 2005, had amassed asset worth of Rs.6,400 crore, while the asset of Escorts struck between Rs.117 crore and Rs.143 crore during October 2003 and March 2008. This kind of sluggish growth can be seen in the case of Quantum and Taurus as well. But, there are market toppers who had blown up the growth chart like Reliance, whose asset under management had galloped from Rs.6,714 crore in October 2003 to Rs.90,938 crore in March 2008. Similarly, the asset under management of Sundaram BNP Paribas went up from Rs.18 crore to Rs.12,564 crore and that of Tata from Rs.2,872 crore to Rs.19679 crore. This indicates that both public and private sectors had fluctuating growth in their asset under management, though the private asset management companies had amassed huge amount of investment in a very short span of time.

Average Return (AR)

The AR of the sample schemes indicates that as far as the income schemes are concerned, out of the 43 schemes, 31 schemes (72.1 per cent) generate 3 per cent return or less and the remaining 12 schemes (27.9 per cent) yield 3 per cent or more of average return. This clearly indicates that the level of average return of the income schemes is rather restricted. In the case of balanced and growth schemes, however, the monthly average returns are more widespread. Sector-wise, the returns of the private sector schemes are much more spread out than the returns of public sector schemes. Moreover, in the case of the latter, not many schemes yield more than 5 per cent return, while in the case of the former, considerable number of schemes produce not only more than 5 per cent, but also more than 8 per cent of average return. This occurs in all categories of schemes.

Total Risk

The analysis of the total risk of the schemes suggests that in the private sector, income schemes and growth schemes are less risky, while the other two categories viz., balanced schemes and ELS schemes are less risky in the public sector. Overall, there is a mixed trend between return and risk of the sample schemes and there is no clear evidence to believe that higher return is associated with higher risk or *vice versa*. This would have happened as the fund managers vying for better returns, increase the risk quotient, though they fail in attaining higher returns. The average return of the public sector schemes is less even in the higher risk classes, while in the case of private sector schemes, comparatively a greater proportion of schemes earn higher return in the higher risk categories.

Risk – Return Scenario

Depending on the degree of risk and return, the sample schemes are categorised under four different scenarios. This analysis indicates that there are more private sector schemes in the first scenario (higher return-less risk) which possesses greater proportion of balanced schemes. The second scenario (less return-less risk) has more schemes than the third, which is markedly influenced by the income schemes. In both private and public sectors, most of the growth schemes come under the third (higher return-higher risk) and fourth (less return-higher risk) scenarios. This shows the risky nature of the growth schemes.

Beta

The beta values which stand for systematic risk shows that out of the total of 130 sample schemes, 20 schemes (15.4 per cent) produce negative beta values underlining the fact that these schemes' returns are inversely correlated with the market return, in terms of Sensex. The proportion of public sector schemes is higher in the lower risk classes and *vice versa*, and this has happened in almost all the categories. Moreover, only less number of schemes falls in the higher risk classes, when beta is analysed in terms of Nifty, than when the same is done in terms of Sensex. This indicates that the sample schemes possess lesser degree of systematic risk in terms of Nifty, than under Sensex.

R^2 Value

The degree of diversification of the schemes suggests that under Sensex, income schemes show least diversification, while there is considerable degree of diversification in the case of balanced schemes. Out of the 40 growth schemes, as many as 65 per cent come in the more than 20 per cent degree of diversification, while the remaining 35 per cent schemes is diversified only up to 20 per cent, which also include 2 schemes with lowest degree of diversification. Also, the degree of diversification of the ELS schemes mostly resembles that of the growth schemes. The sample schemes which exhibited lower degree of systematic risk in terms of Nifty also show lower degree of diversification (and hence higher unique risk). Sector-wise, the public sector schemes' degree of diversification is less compared to that of private sector schemes. This discrepancy is quite pronounced in terms of Sensex than under Nifty.

PERFORMANCE EVALUATION OF SAMPLE SCHEMES

Internal Rate of Return

The IRR of the sample schemes over the study period ranges from below 0 per cent (negative) to above 50 per cent. Out of the 130 schemes, 9 schemes (6.9 per cent) provide sub-zero returns. Sector-wise, there are 3 private sector and 6 public sector schemes in this class. The category-wise analysis indicates that the income schemes, true to their objective, yield only limited returns, while the return of the balanced schemes is higher than that of the income schemes, and the growth schemes, which are fully equity-oriented, provide the highest returns. The return of the ELS schemes is mostly similar to that of the balanced schemes.

The mean IRR scores of the private sector schemes in all categories, is considerably higher than that of the public sector. The mean IRR scores of the growth schemes are the highest followed by the balanced schemes and then the income schemes. As the mean IRR of the ELS schemes is mostly equal to that of balanced schemes, obviously the income schemes provide the least return. This pattern is discernible in both sectors.

Sharpe Measure

In terms of Sensex, a greater proportion of public sector schemes (62.5 per cent) underperform the market. Underperformance is widespread among all the categories. Underperformance of the private sector is relatively less compared to that of the public sector schemes. However, in terms of Nifty, there is no much difference in the degree of schemes' underperformance, both sector-wise and category-wise.

Treynor Measure

Under Treynor's measure, in terms of Sensex, the proportion of underperformance of the sample scheme is higher in the public sector. Category-wise, the performance of some income schemes is above the benchmark; the proportion of underperformance is marginally higher in case of balanced schemes, while lower among the growth and ELS schemes. The reduced underperformance or conversely, greater above-performance of especially the growth and ELS schemes under Treynor measure (*vis-à-vis* Sharpe measure) is the outcome of the change in the risk component of these categories. Thus, the degree of underperformance of the public sector schemes under Treynor measure declines from that of Sharpe, while the level of underperformance of these schemes is still higher than that of the private sector.

Under Nifty, more growth schemes and ELS schemes are pushed into the underperformance category, which occurs especially among the private sector schemes. This suggests that the systematic risk of the private sector schemes differs between Sensex and Nifty which results in the differing performances of the schemes under the two indices. However, private sector schemes outperform the public sector schemes in the overall analysis.

Jensen's Alpha

Jensen's alpha identifies the risk adjusted return of the scheme which is derived by segregating the return due to market variations from that of risk free return.

Under Sensex, the proportion of schemes that have a positive alpha value is quite high in the private sector (36.7 per cent) than the public sector (17.5 per cent). Thus, under the Jensen's measure also, the private sector schemes outperform the public sector schemes. Category-wise, the growth schemes and the ELS schemes perform better compared to the equilibrium return. This clearly underlines the superiority of the private sector schemes in efficient stock selection and category-wise, growth schemes and ELS schemes outcompete the others.

The trend witnessed under Sensex is repeated under Nifty too, with the growth schemes and the ELS schemes performing better than the others in the overall scenario. Overall, in terms of Nifty also, private sector schemes have superior performance compared to the public sector and category-wise, the growth and ELS schemes have superior performance.

MEASURES BASED ON STOCK SELECTING ABILITY AND DIVERSIFICATION

Sharpe Differential Measure

Under Sensex, out of the 130 sample schemes, only 60 schemes show positive alpha values which include 45 private sector schemes and 15 public sector schemes. Hence, comparatively, private sector schemes exhibit a superior stock selecting ability. Category-wise, the 60 schemes consist of no income schemes, 20 balanced schemes, 28 growth schemes and 12 ELS schemes. This shows that in relative terms, balanced schemes and growth schemes portray better stock selecting ability, as a greater proportion of these two schemes come with positive alpha values.

Under Nifty also, a greater proportion of private sector schemes have positive alpha values than the public sector schemes, as in the case of Sensex. This underscores the fact that the private sector fund managers' stock picking ability far outweighs the ability of their counterparts in the public sector.

Fama's Beta

Fama's beta captures the return due to systematic risk which arises from the market dynamics. A positive beta implies positive returns due to systematic risk, while a negative beta suggests negative returns.

Out of the 130 sample schemes, in terms of Sensex, nearly 50 per cent of the schemes (66 schemes) produce positive values which imply positive returns due to systematic risk. Sector-wise too, the positive impact is close to 50 per cent (slightly better in the case of public sector). But, category-wise, there is no such equality, as the ELS schemes provide the best impact due to systematic risk, which is followed by income, balanced and growth categories. Among the public sector schemes, balanced schemes have the most positive impact, succeeded by the ELSS, income and growth schemes. This suggests a mixed trend among the categories, while overall around 50 per cent of the schemes have positive impact of beta.

The result under Sensex indicates that there is a marked increase in the number of growth schemes, since 24 (out of 40 schemes) come with positive impact under Nifty, as against 14 schemes in terms of Sensex. At the sectoral level also, the major difference in the performance comes from the private sector growth schemes and then from the ELSS category, though the positive impact increases in the case of other categories as well.

Fama's Diversification

Fama's diversification measure explains the return from the degree of diversification of the schemes, which is attained by the fund manager. In terms of Sensex, out of the 130 schemes, 55.4 per cent of the schemes have a positive impact due to diversification, which include 49 private sector schemes (54.4 per cent) and 23 schemes (57.5 per cent) from the public sector. Thus, the public sector schemes exhibit marginally better diversification than the private sector.

Category-wise, income schemes contribute more towards better diversification which is succeeded by ELSS, balanced, and growth schemes. The impact of diversification under Sensex indicates a mixed trend between the two sectors, where the income schemes dominate the private sector, while it is the balanced category in the public sector.

In terms of Nifty, the number of schemes with positive diversification goes up marginally, which comes solely from the growth schemes of the private sector. Thus, more number of schemes in the private sector becomes positively diversified under Nifty. This pushes up the number of schemes with positive diversification in the private sector to 55 (from 49 under Sensex), while the number of private sector growth schemes moves up from 11 to 16.

Similarly, in the overall scenario too, the number of positively diversified growth schemes increases from 14 to 20.

Fama's Selectivity

Fama's impact of selectivity measures the stock selecting ability of the fund manager. Positive impact of selectivity indicates positive return due to stock selecting ability of the fund manager, while a negative impact implies a negative return.

Under Sensex, out of the 130 schemes, 60 schemes demonstrate superior performance which comprise of 45 private sector schemes (50 per cent of the sector) and 15 public sector schemes (37.5 per cent of the sector). Hence, the private sector fund managers exhibit better stock selecting ability *vis-à-vis* their counterparts in the public sector.

Category-wise, the net selectivity impact is much superior among the balanced and growth schemes, followed by the ELS schemes. In the case of income schemes, it suggests that the risk taken by the fund mangers in stock-picking has not been rewarded by any additional return. In the case of public sector, the growth and the ELS schemes have superior performance than the balanced schemes. This implies that the private sector schemes have much superior stock selection compared to the public sector, while the balanced and growth categories provide positive reward for stock selection.

Under Nifty, the overall result indicates absolutely no difference from that of under Sensex. The difference occurs at the sectoral level, where in the private sector, the number of schemes with superior performance comes down from 45 to 44, which is influenced by the decrease in the number of growth schemes, by the same margin. And, in the case of public sector, the number of schemes goes up from 15 to 16, contributed by the income category.

Market Timing Ability – Treynor and Mazuy Model

The Treynor and Mazuy model brings out the market timing ability of the fund manager, which is measured by ã. The fund manager is expected to sense the mood of the market in advance, collect the required information about the impending market movements and act accordingly. A positive ã value indicates the presence of market timing and in the absence of market timing, ã will be zero. Moreover, ã values also need to be statistically significant.

In terms of Sensex, all the 130 schemes produce positive ã values, of which the values of 33 schemes (25.4 per cent) are insignificant. That is, though these schemes show the existence of market timing, the superior returns thus generated are not significant enough. In case of all the remaining 97 schemes, the ã values are statistically significant. Among the different categories, the income and balanced category schemes show much superior timing ability, while the ELSS and growth category schemes follow in that order. Sector-wise, the private sector shows better timing ability than the public sector, while the intra-sector comparison suggests that the income and balanced schemes are the better categories. This implies that the non-equity market (the bond market) plays a pivotal role in enabling better market timing by the income and balanced schemes in both the sectors.

The situation under Nifty is only marginally different from that of Sensex, as five more schemes become statistically significant, while two schemes show negative γ values, though both are insignificant. Thus, under Nifty, both the sectors display similar performance, though the public sector is marginally better. Under Nifty too, income and the balanced categories are the better performing ones compared to the other two categories. At the individual sector level also, the income and the balanced schemes produce better performance in timing the market followed by the ELSS and the growth schemes in both the sectors. The growth schemes being exposed totally to the equity market are struggling to time the market.

Overall Performance Ranking

Sector-wise and category-wise performance evaluation of the sample schemes portrays differing results. Some schemes perform better under some measures, while they perform poorly under some other measures, which make it difficult to select the best performing scheme. Thus, in order to identify the best performing scheme from the sample of 130 schemes, they are ranked under all measures and their averages are derived. The scheme with a highest value under a measure is given the rank of 1, except under standard deviation, in which the scheme with the least value takes the rank of 1. The ranks of the schemes under all measures are added and the average is worked out. The scheme with the lowest average rank value is given the rank of 1.

Between the two sectors, the private sector stands first with lower mean score of rank with 61.79 as against 73.84 in the case of public sector. Among the different categories, the growth schemes become the 'Numero Uno', followed by the ELS schemes, balanced and finally the income schemes. This clearly shows that though the growth schemes do not perform better under some measures, still they become the top performers in the overall ranking, as they out-compete other categories in terms of other measures. Moreover, in each category, the private sector schemes dominate the overall rankings.

The mean overall rank score of the private sector growth scheme is the lowest among all the categories, whereas, in the case of public sector, balanced schemes are the best with the lowest mean score, followed by the ELS, growth and finally the income schemes. Among the private sector categories too, the income category stands at the last in the overall ranking.

At the individual scheme level, all the top 5 performers hail from the private sector and moreover, all of them belong to the growth category, which underscores their relative dominance. The five schemes that top the list are viz., the Sundaram BNP Paribas Capex Opportunities Fund-Growth, the Birla Index Fund-Growth, Tata Pure Equity Fund-Growth, the ICICI Prudential Growth Plan-Growth and the Reliance Growth Fund-Growth.

On the other extreme, among the least 5 performers, there are three public sector schemes, viz., the SBI Magnum Monthly Income Fund-Bonus, Baroda Diversified Fund-Growth and the UTI Equity Fund-Growth, beginning from the last. The other two schemes which are from the private sector belong to the HDFC. Among the least performers, there is more number of income and balanced schemes. This once again brings out the superiority the private sector schemes and specifically the growth schemes in a categorical manner.

Normality of Returns

The nature of distribution of the schemes' returns clearly indicates that during the study period the returns are not normally distributed. Moreover, the sector-wise analysis shows that in three out of five years, (since 2005-06), the proportion of private schemes in the 'closer to zero' range is higher than the proportion of public sector schemes. Hence, overall the proportion of schemes with normal distribution is quite low in each year, while the proportion of private sector schemes is marginally higher than that of public sector schemes in more number of years. Highly positive kurtosis values of the schemes indicate that the returns are highly peaked in nature. The kurtosis values of the market indices signify the point that the market returns themselves are not normally distributed during the study period.

Impact of Investment Size

It is usually held that the funds with larger investment can spend more on personnel and can reduce the average cost, which will help the fund to push up its net asset value. This indicates a positive relationship between size of investment of a scheme and its performance. This relationship is tested by applying an uni-variate regression model in which the net asset value of a scheme is taken as the dependent variable and size of investment is taken as the independent variable.

Analysis shows that the impact made by the size of investment of the scheme is statistically highly significant and it is positive in influencing the performance of the scheme. This implies that one unit increase in the size of investment of a scheme will increase its NAV by 0.13 units and *vice versa.* Hence it can be concluded that the performance of the scheme is influenced by the size of its investment.

Conclusion

The overall picture shows that most of the schemes fail to provide better risk-adjusted returns under both market indices, while sector-wise, underperformance is more among the public sector schemes. However, the degree of underperformance is less among the private sector schemes. Similarly, the risk quotient of the public sector schemes is also higher. In terms of diversification and stock selection too, most of the sample schemes fail to post additional return. The measure of market timing ability is the only exception, where most of the schemes are able to generate not only positive but also statistically significant returns.

At the individual category level, growth schemes are the best performers under many of the measures and thus become the top five performers among the 130 sample schemes and all the five belong to the private sector. On the other, out of the five least performers, the bottom three belongs to the income category of the public sector. Hence, it can be concluded that during the study period, the private sector schemes performed better, of which the growth schemes are the best schemes.

Suggestions

- Investors who want to earn more, need to invest in growth schemes, though these schemes are the riskiest among all categories.
- Risk-averters, obviously can invest in income schemes, while balanced schemes are as riskier as ELS schemes.
- The public sector schemes provide relatively less returns, but not without risk.
- Private sector schemes outperform the public sector schemes in all categories.
- Majority of the public sector schemes produce positive return from market risk, better diversification and also better market timing, though they lack in stock selecting ability.
- ELS schemes, which are more popular among the investors for their tax saving nature, produce considerably high return, but they are riskier too.

- In general, the degree of diversification of the sample schemes needed to be increased, as only around 50 per cent of them provide additional return due to diversification.
- Similarly, stock selecting ability of the sample schemes too needed to be improved as positive stock selection is restricted to only 60 schemes, of which the share of the public sector schemes is less.
- Asset management companies should try to provide normalised or stable returns to their investors, which will help them in planning their income and investment.
- Asset management companies should also seek to improve their record in earning better risk-adjusted returns, since only 40 schemes in all provide positive alphas.
- Asset management companies should divulge more details regarding their portfolio construction for all schemes at regular intervals to assist investors who want to know about the same.
- Asset management companies can also come forward to publish measures of various performance indicators, by which the investors can compare the performances of different asset management companies before investing.
- Public sector asset management companies in particular, should try to improve their performances in terms of better risk-adjusted returns, diversification and stock selection, since their performance is very poor when compared to the private sector schemes under these measures.

Scope for Further Research

- This study has taken only open-ended schemes for its consideration and thus, a similar study can be done on close-ended schemes.
- The present study has evaluated the performance of only four categories of schemes, while categories like liquid funds, fund of funds, index funds, sector-oriented funds, gilt funds can also be considered.
- The number of sample schemes too can be increased, which might provide some more variations in the results.
- A longer study period (upto 10 years) can throw more light on the qualities of the funds, since such longer time period would involve ups and downs in the market.
- Comparison of the performance of the Indian mutual fund industry with, preferably with a similar developing country's mutual fund industry can also be considered, as it will bring in the dynamics of that country into consideration.

APPENDIX

Sample Scheme
Income - Private

Birla Sun Life Income Fund - D
Birla Sun Life Income Fund - G
DBS Chola Freedom Income -STF-Institutional
DBS Chola Freedom Income -STF-DD
FT India MIP-Growth
FT India MIP-Monthly Bonus
HDFC Income Fund - Dividend
HDFC Income Fund - Growth
ICICI Prudential Income Plan-Dividend Option
ICICI Prudential Income Plan-Growth Option
ICICI Prudential MIP - Cumulative
ING Income Fund- Dividend Option
ING Income Fund-Growth Option
JM Income Fund - Dividend
JM Income Fund - Growth
Kotak Income Plus - Growth
Kotak Income Plus - Monthly Dividend
Reliance Income Fund - Annual Dividend Plan
Reliance Income Fund - Growth Plan
Reliance Income Fund Retail Plan Half Yearly
Sahara Income Fund-Dividend
Sahara Income Fund-Growth
Sundaram BNP Paribas Income Plus-Appreciation
Sundaram BNP Paribas Income Plus-Dividend
Tata Income Fund - Monthly
Tata Income Fund - Qtrly
Tata Income Fund - Semi
Templeton India Income Fund - Dividend
Templeton India Income Fund - Growth

Income – Public

BOB Income Fund - Dividend
BOB Income Fund -Growth
Canara Robeco Income – Bonus
Canara Robeco Income – Growth
Canara Robeco Income – Income
LIC MF Bond Fund - Dividend
LIC MF Bond Fund - Growth
SBI Magnum Monthly Income Fund – Bonus
SBI Magnum Income Fund – Bonus
SBI Magnum Income Fund – Dividend
SBI Magnum Income Fund - Growth
UTI Mahila Unit Scheme
UTI Monthly Income Scheme – Growth
UTI Monthly Income Scheme - Income

Balance – Private

Birla Balance (D)
Birla Balance (G)
DSP Merill Lynch Balanced Fund (D)
DSP Merill Lynch Balanced Fund (G)
Franklin India Balanced Fund (D)
Franklin India Balanced Fund (G)
HDFC Balanced Fund – Dividend
ICICI Prudential Balanced Fund (D)
ICICI Prudential Balanced Fund (G)
ING Balanced Fund (D)
ING Balanced Fund (G)
J M Balanced Fund (Dividend)
J M Balanced Fund (Growth)
Kotak Balance
Principal Balanced Fund – Dividend
Principal Balanced Fund – Growth
Sundaram Balanced Fund
Sundaram BNP Balanced – Appreciation
Sundaram BNP Balanced – Dividend
Tata Balanced Fund – Dividend

Balance – Public

Bank of Baroda Balanced – Dividend
Bank of Baroda Balanced – Growth
LIC Balanced – Plan A – Dividend
LIC Balanced – Plan C – Growth
LIC Unit Linked Insurance Scheme
SBI Magnum Balanced Fund – Dividend
UTI Balanced Fund – Dividend
UTI Balanced Fund – Growth

ELSS-Private

Birla Advantage Fund - Dividend/ Reinvestment
Birla Index Fund – Growth
DBS Chola Growth Fund-Cumulative
DBS Chola Growth Fund-Quarterly Dividend
DSP Merrill Lynch Equity Fund – Growth
DSP Merrill Lynch Opportunities Fund – Growth
Escorts Growth Plan - Dividend
Escorts Growth Plan - Growth
HDFC Growth Fund – Growth
ICICI Pru FMCG Plan – Dividend
ICICI Prudential Growth Plan - Dividend Option
ICICI Prudential Growth Plan - Growth Option
JM Equity Fund - Dividend
JM Equity Fund - Growth
Kotak 30 – Growth
Reliance Growth Fund - Dividend Plan
Reliance Growth Fund - Growth Plan
Reliance Vision Fund - Dividend Plan
Sahara Growth Fund-Dividend
Sahara Growth Fund-Growth
Sundaram BNP Paribas Capex Opportunities Fund-Growth
Sundaram BNP Paribas Growth Fund-Dividend
Sundaram BNP Paribas Growth Fund-Growth
Tata Pure Equity Fund - Dividend
Tata Pure Equity Fund - Growth
Taurus Star Share
Templeton India Growth Fund-Dividend Plan
Templeton India Growth Fund-Growth Plan

Growth – Public

Baroda Diversified Fund – Growth
Canara Robeco Expo Growth Plan
Canara Robeco Expo Income Plan
LICMF Growth Fund - Dividend Option
LICMF Growth Fund - Growth Option
SBI Magnum Equity Fund – Growth
SBI Magnum Multiplier Plus Scheme - 93 –Dividend
SBI MSFU Contra – Dividend
SBI MSFU Contra- Growth
SBI MSFU IT
UTI - Equity Fund-Growth Option
UTI - Equity Fund-Income Option

ELSS – Private

Birla Tax Plan 98
Escorts Tax Plan Dividend
Escorts Tax Plan Growth
Franklin Taxshield – Dividend
Franklin India Taxshield – Growth
ICICI Prudential Tax Plan-Dividend Option
ICICI Prudential Tax Plan-Growth Option
Principal Tax Saving fund
SaharaTax Gain-Growth
Sundaram PNB Paribas Tax Saver OE Fund
Sundaram Taxsaver 98
Tata Tax Saving
Taurus Libra Taxshield 96

ELSS – Public

Bob ELSS 96
Canara Robeco Equity Tax Saver
LICMF Taxplan-Dividend
LICMF Taxplan-Growth
SBI Magnum Taxgain Scheme 1993 – Dividend
UTI-Master Equity Plan Unit Scheme
Birla Sun Life Income Fund – D

Source: www.amfiindia.com

A- 2 RISK AND RETURN - I

Income - Private	AR_p	SD_p	SENSEX	
			AR_m	SD_m
Birla Sun Life Income Fund - D	0.0121	0.0040	0.0205	0.0282
Birla Sun Life Income Fund - G	0.0191	0.0224	0.0335	0.0296
DBS Chola Freedom Income -STF-Institutional	0.0422	0.0333	0.0548	0.0422
DBS Chola Freedom Income -STF-DD	0.0319	0.0093	0.0920	0.0288
FT India MIP-Growth	0.0033	0.0020	0.0726	0.0286
FT India MIP-Monthly Bonus	0.0251	0.0317	0.0605	0.0484
HDFC Income Fund - Dividend	0.0032	0.0396	0.0128	0.0584
HDFC Income Fund - Growth	0.0216	0.0336	0.0410	0.0684
ICICI Prudential Income Plan-Dividend Option	0.0246	0.0330	0.0827	0.0494
ICICI Prudential Income Plan-Growth Option	0.0220	0.0243	0.0406	0.0286
ICICI Prudential MIP - Cumulative	0.0136	0.0059	0.0790	0.0269
ING Income Fund- Dividend Option	0.0014	0.0145	0.0117	0.0292
ING Income Fund-Growth Option	0.0164	0.0133	0.0612	0.0292
JM Income Fund - Dividend	0.0060	0.0103	0.0136	0.0300
JM Income Fund - Growth	0.0070	0.0015	0.1006	0.0291
Kotak Income Plus - Growth	0.0402	0.0382	0.0626	0.0489
Kotak Income Plus - Monthly Dividend	0.0290	0.0355	0.0506	0.0489
Reliance Income Fund - Annual Dividend	0.0318	0.0262	0.0408	0.0288
Reliance Income Fund - Growth Plan	0.0382	0.0568	0.0757	0.0685
Reliance Income Fund Retail Plan Half Yea	0.0296	0.0249	0.0519	0.0298
Sahara Income Fund-Dividend	0.0079	0.0055	0.0817	0.0296
Sahara Income Fund-Growth	0.0052	0.0038	0.0510	0.0291
Sundaram BNP Paribas Income Plus-Appre	0.0313	0.0218	0.0423	0.0286
Sundaram BNP Paribas Income Plus-D	0.0411	0.0207	0.0625	0.0288
Tata Income Fund - Monthly	0.0163	0.0249	0.0320	0.0299
Tata Income Fund - Qtrly	0.0211	0.0097	0.0815	0.0294
Tata Income Fund - Semi	0.0157	0.0134	0.0519	0.0313
Templeton India Income Fund - Dividend	0.0021	0.0291	0.0127	0.1351
Templeton India Income Fund - Growth	0.0042	0.0338	0.0306	0.0289

	AR_p	SD_p	SENSEX	
			AR_m	SD_m
BOB Income Fund - Dividend	0.0516	0.0217	0.0610	0.0288
BOB Income Fund -Growth	0.0616	0.0327	0.0910	0.0490
Canara Robeco Income - Bonus	0.0466	0.0283	0.0609	0.0332
Canara Robeco Income - Growth	0.0321	0.0340	0.0605	0.0498
Canara Robeco Income - Income	0.0416	0.0147	0.0981	0.0363
LIC MF Bond Fund - Dividend	0.0026	0.0339	0.0132	0.0287
LIC MF Bond Fund - Growth	0.0189	0.0325	0.0207	0.0385
SBI Magnum Monthly Income Fund-Bonus	0.0139	0.0304	0.0217	0.0385
SBI Magnum Income Fund - Bonus	0.0158	0.0560	0.0218	0.0700
SBI Magnum Income Fund - Dividend	0.0067	0.0584	0.0363	0.0429
SBI Magnum Income Fund - Growth	0.0070	0.0372	0.0296	0.0328
UTI Mahila Unit Scheme	0.0169	0.0385	0.0257	0.0464
UTI Monthly Income Scheme - Growth	0.0026	0.0193	0.0120	0.0325
UTI Monthly Income Scheme - Income	0.0057	0.0323	0.0133	0.0495
Balance - Private				
Birla Balance (D)	0.0231	0.0268	0.0065	0.0219
Birla Balance (G)	0.0491	0.0324	0.0035	0.0296
DSP Merill Lynch Balanced Fund (D)	0.0640	0.0397	0.0686	0.0472
DSP Merill Lynch Balanced Fund (G)	0.0283	0.0514	0.0343	0.0693
Franklin India Balanced Fund (D)	0.0574	0.0357	0.0052	0.0290
Franklin India Balanced Fund (G)	0.3092	0.0346	0.0034	0.0257
HDFC Balanced Fund - Dividend	0.0839	0.0603	0.0087	0.0398
ICICI Prudential Balanced Fund (D)	0.0931	0.0596	0.0095	0.0379
ICICI Prudential Balanced Fund (G)	0.0804	0.0750	0.0022	0.0281
ING Balanced Fund (D)	0.0471	0.0298	0.0055	0.0195
ING Balanced Fund (G)	0.0565	0.0296	0.0061	0.0139
J M Balanced Fund (Dividend)	0.0357	0.0358	0.0069	0.0304
J M Balanced Fund (Growth)	0.0737	0.0341	0.0089	0.0389
Kotak Balance	0.0673	0.0453	0.0053	0.0318
Principal Balanced Fund – Dividend	0.0140	0.0434	0.0086	0.0490
Principal Balanced Fund – Growth	0.0958	0.0370	0.0067	0.0417
Sundaram Balanced Fund	0.0435	0.0355	0.0091	0.0375

	AR_p	SD_p	SENSEX	
			AR_m	SD_m
Sundaram BNP Balanced - Appreciation	0.0999	0.0253	0.0027	0.0306
Sundaram BNP Balanced - Dividend	0.2035	0.0336	0.0091	0.0358
Tata Balanced Fund - Dividend	0.0162	0.0234	0.0014	0.0271
Balance - Public				
Bank of Baroda Balanced - Dividend	0.0265	0.0307	0.0361	0.0336
Bank of Baroda Balanced – Growth	0.0164	0.0293	0.0262	0.0228
LIC Balanced – Plan A - Dividend	0.0013	0.0282	0.0100	0.0283
LIC Balanced – Plan C - Growth	0.0183	0.0267	0.0043	0.0197
LIC Unit Linked Insurance Scheme	-0.0305	0.0301	0.0131	0.0348
SBI Magnum Balanced Fund - Dividend	0.0281	0.0301	0.0045	0.0298
UTI Balanced Fund - Dividend	-0.0012	0.0189	0.0114	0.0288
UTI Balanced Fund - Growth	0.0090	0.0197	0.0036	0.0255
Growth - Private				
Birla Advantage Fund-Dividend/ Reinvest	0.0450	0.0431	0.0076	0.0414
Birla Index Fund –Growth	0.0715	0.0287	0.0011	0.0276
DBS Chola Growth Fund-Cumulative	0.0099	0.0492	0.0047	0.0487
DBS Chola Growth Fund-Quarterly Dividend	0.0209	0.0462	0.0117	0.0428
DSP Merrill Lynch Equity Fund - Growth	0.0444	0.0497	0.0012	0.0419
DSP Merrill Lynch Opportunities Fund - G	0.0587	0.0362	0.0639	0.0225
Escorts Growth Plan - Dividend	-0.0335	0.0673	0.0091	0.0664
Escorts Growth Plan - Growth	0.0735	0.0612	0.0009	0.0310
HDFC Growth Fund - Growth	0.0832	0.0371	0.0006	0.0217
ICICI Pru FMCG Plan – Dividend	0.0916	0.0372	0.0010	0.0376
ICICI Prudential Growth Plan - Dividend Option	0.0665	0.0666	0.0061	0.0642
ICICI Prudential Growth Plan-Growth Option	0.0627	0.0327	0.0001	0.0320
JM Equity Fund - Dividend	-0.0165	0.0381	0.0060	0.0374
JM Equity Fund - Growth	0.0129	0.0310	0.0003	0.0303
Kotak 30 - Growth	0.0949	0.0289	0.0024	0.0193

	AR_p	SD_p	SENSEX	
			AR_m	SD_m
Reliance Growth Fund - Dividend Plan	0.0381	0.0345	0.0444	0.0257
Reliance Growth Fund - Growth Plan	0.0882	0.0668	0.0057	0.0685
Reliance Vision Fund - Dividend Plan	0.0755	0.0309	0.0029	0.0295
Sahara Growth Fund-Dividend	0.0041	0.0465	0.0085	0.0561
Sahara Growth Fund-Growth	0.0097	0.0405	0.0029	0.0336
Sundaram BNP Paribas Capex Oppor Fund-G	0.0943	0.0375	0.0018	0.0360
Sundaram BNP Paribas Growth Fund-Dividend	0.0843	0.0374	0.0018	0.0362
Sundaram BNP Paribas Growth Fund-Growth	0.1514	0.1275	0.0018	0.0360
Tata Pure Equity Fund - Dividend	0.0657	0.0448	0.0731	0.0359
Tata Pure Equity Fund - Growth	0.0932	0.0287	0.0094	0.0275
Taurus Star Share	0.0017	0.0473	0.0042	0.0463
Templeton India Growth Fund-Dividend Plan	0.0807	0.0325	0.0019	0.0322
Templeton India Growth Fund-Growth Plan	0.0820	0.0386	0.0906	0.0346
Growth - Public				
Baroda Diversified Fund - Growth	-0.0319	0.0717	0.0000	0.0252
Canara Robeco Expo Growth Plan	0.0205	0.0729	0.0006	0.0324
Canara Robeco Expo Income Plan	0.0125	0.0936	-0.0091	0.0479
LICMF Growth Fund - Dividend Option	0.0281	0.0790	0.0019	0.0349
LICMF Growth Fund - Growth Option	0.0037	0.0275	0.0110	0.0282
SBI Magnum Equity Fund - Growth	0.0163	0.0832	0.0028	0.0372
SBI Magnum Multiplier Plus Scheme-93-D	0.0375	0.0784	0.0021	0.0331
SBI MSFU Contra - Dividend	0.0225	0.0808	0.0044	0.0373
SBI MSFU Contra- Growth	0.0191	0.0738	0.0052	0.0359
SBI MSFU IT	0.0320	0.0738	0.0052	0.0359
UTI - Equity Fund-Growth Option	-0.0305	0.0729	0.0006	0.0324
UTI - Equity Fund-Income Option	0.0029	0.0926	0.0133	0.0496
ELSS - Private				
Birla Tax Plan 98	0.0148	0.0419	0.0222	0.0426

	AR_p	SD_p	SENSEX	
			AR_m	SD_m
Escorts Tax Plan Dividend	0.0240	0.0503	0.0086	0.0459
Escorts Tax Plan Growth	0.0127	0.0314	0.0201	0.0318
Franklin Taxshield - Dividend	0.0130	0.0243	0.0004	0.0176
Franklin India Taxshield - Growth	0.0104	0.0248	0.0122	0.0268
ICICI Prudential Tax Plan-Dividend Option	0.0562	0.0446	0.0064	0.0440
ICICI Prudential Tax Plan-Growth Option	0.0357	0.0385	0.0031	0.0387
Principal Tax Saving fund	0.0143	0.0285	0.0217	0.0407
SaharaTax Gain-Growth	-0.0060	0.1217	0.0186	0.1264
Sundaram PNB Paribas Tax Saver OE Fund	0.0940	0.0454	0.0086	0.0350
Sundaram Taxsaver 98	0.0628	0.0732	0.0002	0.0318
Tata Tax Saving	0.0111	0.0460	0.0015	0.0506
Taurus Libra Taxshield 96	0.0186	0.0436	0.0040	0.0430
ELSS - Public				
Bob ELSS 96	0.0271	0.0409	0.0055	0.0379
Canara Robeco Equity Tax Saver	0.0157	0.0397	0.0069	0.0375
LICMF Taxplan-Dividend	-0.0610	0.0371	0.0136	0.0427
LICMF Taxplan-Growth	0.0154	0.0332	0.0072	0.0392
SBI Magnum Taxgain Scheme 1993 - D	0.0160	0.0521	0.0026	0.0534
UTI-Master Equity Plan Unit Scheme	-0.0109	0.0310	0.0017	0.0391

Source: Computed from Secondary data.

A- 2 RISK AND RETURN - II

Income - Private	Nifty		
	AR_m	SD_m	AR_m
Birla Sun Life Income Fund - D	0.0235	0.0256	0.0425
Birla Sun Life Income Fund - G	0.0305	0.0296	0.0007
DBS Chola Freedom Income -STF-Institutional	0.0611	0.0456	0.0143
DBS Chola Freedom Income -STF-DD	0.0646	0.0215	0.0143
FT India MIP-Growth	0.0378	0.0297	0.0011
FT India MIP-Monthly Bonus	0.0554	0.0450	0.0001
HDFC Income Fund - Dividend	0.0108	0.0536	0.1023
HDFC Income Fund - Growth	0.0459	0.0466	0.1024
ICICI Prudential Income Plan-Dividend Option	0.0603	0.0422	0.0021
ICICI Prudential Income Plan-Growth Option	0.0469	0.0299	0.0020
ICICI Prudential MIP - Cumulative	0.0588	0.0219	0.0020
ING Income Fund- Dividend Option	0.0143	0.0269	0.0012
ING Income Fund-Growth Option	0.0513	0.0256	0.0007
JM Income Fund - Dividend	0.0272	0.0316	0.0031
JM Income Fund - Growth	0.0901	0.0258	0.0030
Kotak Income Plus - Growth	0.0542	0.0436	0.0221
Kotak Income Plus - Monthly Dividend	0.0359	0.0439	0.0221
Reliance Income Fund - Annual Dividend	0.0461	0.0297	0.0003
Reliance Income Fund - Growth Plan	0.0444	0.0644	0.0004
Reliance Income Fund Retail Plan Half Yea	0.0433	0.0299	0.0014
Sahara Income Fund-Dividend	0.0466	0.0215	-0.0007
Sahara Income Fund-Growth	0.0341	0.0159	-0.0005
Sundaram BNP Paribas Income Plus-Appre	0.0461	0.0269	0.0318
Sundaram BNP Paribas Income Plus-D	0.0625	0.0259	0.0320
Tata Income Fund - Monthly	0.0322	0.0267	0.0002
Tata Income Fund - Qtrly	0.0724	0.0349	0.0019
Tata Income Fund - Semi	0.0442	0.0369	0.0014
Templeton India Income Fund - Dividend	0.0134	0.0989	0.1002
Templeton India Income Fund - Growth	0.0311	0.0289	0.1001
Income - Public			
BOB Income Fund - Dividend	0.0610	0.0288	0.0305
BOB Income Fund -Growth	0.0873	0.0444	0.0305

	Nifty		
	AR_m	SD_m	AR_m
Canara Robeco Income - Bonus	0.0601	0.0359	0.0064
Canara Robeco Income - Growth	0.0455	0.0469	0.0063
Canara Robeco Income - Income	0.0872	0.0316	0.0064
LIC MF Bond Fund - Dividend	0.0125	0.0222	0.0227
LIC MF Bond Fund - Growth	0.0211	0.0397	0.0226
SBI Magnum Monthly Income Fund - Bonus	0.0217	0.0459	0.1012
SBI Magnum Income Fund - Bonus	0.0258	0.0738	0.1012
SBI Magnum Income Fund - Dividend	0.0314	0.0439	0.1013
SBI Magnum Income Fund - Growth	0.0069	0.0346	0.1010
UTI Mahila Unit Scheme	0.0257	0.0460	-0.0028
UTI Monthly Income Scheme - Growth	0.0120	0.0333	-0.0025
UTI Monthly Income Scheme - Income	0.0133	0.0469	-0.0027
Balance - Private			
Birla Balance (D)	0.0165	0.0220	0.0804
Birla Balance (G)	0.0126	0.0296	0.0804
DSP Merill Lynch Balanced Fund (D)	0.0645	0.0427	0.1062
DSP Merill Lynch Balanced Fund (G)	0.0351	0.0666	0.1062
Franklin India Balanced Fund (D)	0.0025	0.0239	0.7062
Franklin India Balanced Fund (G)	0.0068	0.0257	0.7062
HDFC Balanced Fund - Dividend	0.0265	0.0333	0.0019
ICICI Prudential Balanced Fund (D)	0.0059	0.0397	0.0080
ICICI Prudential Balanced Fund (G)	0.0022	0.0249	0.0083
ING Balanced Fund (D)	0.0068	0.0195	0.0050
ING Balanced Fund (G)	0.0156	0.0128	0.0044
J M Balanced Fund (Dividend)	0.0096	0.0326	0.0604
J M Balanced Fund (Growth)	0.0089	0.0369	0.0604
Kotak Balance	0.0146	0.0349	0.0052
Principal Balanced Fund – Dividend	0.0096	0.0499	0.0802
Principal Balanced Fund – Growth	0.0658	0.0444	0.0819
Sundaram Balanced Fund	0.0249	0.0398	0.0819
Sundaram BNP Balanced - Appreciation	0.0368	0.0306	0.0819
Sundaram BNP Balanced - Dividend	0.0340	0.0379	0.0814
Tata Balanced Fund - Dividend	0.0126	0.0299	0.0091
Bank of Baroda Balanced - Dividend	0.0123	0.0399	0.0044

	Nifty		
Balance Public	AR_m	SD_m	AR_m
Bank of Baroda Balanced – Growth	0.0235	0.0228	0.0044
LIC Balanced – Plan A - Dividend	0.0100	0.0389	0.0006
LIC Balanced – Plan C - Growth	0.0169	0.0139	0.0006
LIC Unit Linked Insurance Scheme	0.0113	0.0346	0.0026
SBI Magnum Balanced Fund - Dividend	0.0045	0.0246	0.0060
UTI Balanced Fund - Dividend	0.0109	0.0249	-0.0009
UTI Balanced Fund - Growth	0.0026	0.0290	-0.0009
Growth - Private			
Birla Advantage Fund - Dividend/ Reinvest	0.0236	0.0414	0.0030
Birla Index Fund – Growth	0.0168	0.0213	0.0029
DBS Chola Growth Fund-Cumulative	0.0056	0.0456	0.0059
DBS Chola Growth Fund-Quarterly Dividend	0.0136	0.0411	0.0059
DSP Merrill Lynch Equity Fund - Growth	0.0345	0.0359	0.0059
DSP Merrill Lynch Opportunities Fund - G	0.0649	0.0269	0.0059
Escorts Growth Plan - Dividend	0.0045	0.0613	0.0014
Escorts Growth Plan - Growth	0.0007	0.0333	0.0014
HDFC Growth Fund - Growth	0.0006	0.0217	0.0012
ICICI Pru FMCG Plan – Dividend	0.0010	0.0389	0.0096
ICICI Prudential Growth Plan - Dividend Option	0.0126	0.0623	0.0094
ICICI Prudential Growth Plan - Growth Option	0.0235	0.0310	0.0095
JM Equity Fund - Dividend	0.0060	0.0379	0.0045
JM Equity Fund - Growth	0.0003	0.0269	0.0045
Kotak 30 - Growth 0.0123	0.0139	0.0129	
Reliance Growth Fund - Dividend Plan	0.0425	0.0269	0.0061
Reliance Growth Fund - Growth Plan	0.0046	0.0728	0.0062
Reliance Vision Fund - Dividend Plan	0.0023	0.0202	0.0061
Sahara Growth Fund-Dividend	0.0085	0.0561	0.0020
Sahara Growth Fund-Growth	0.0026	0.0316	0.0021
Sundaram BNP Paribas Capex Oppor Fund-G	0.0018	0.0329	0.0123
Sundaram BNP Paribas Growth Fund-Dividend	0.0016	0.0329	0.0123
Sundaram BNP Paribas Growth Fund-Growth	0.0013	0.0360	0.0123
Tata Pure Equity Fund - Dividend	0.0726	0.0330	0.0011
Tata Pure Equity Fund - Growth	0.0093	0.0249	0.0011
Taurus Star Share	0.0045	0.0437	0.0147
Templeton India Growth Fund-Dividend Plan	0.0125	0.0313	0.0087
Templeton India Growth Fund-Growth Plan	0.0965	0.0329	0.0087

Growth - Public	Nifty		
	AR_m	SD_m	AR_m
Baroda Diversified Fund - Growth	0.0002	0.0359	0.0105
Canara Robeco Expo Growth Plan	0.0016	0.0349	0.0099
Canara Robeco Expo Income Plan	-0.0091	0.0439	0.0099
LICMF Growth Fund - Dividend Option	0.0029	0.0333	0.0005
LICMF Growth Fund - Growth Option	0.0125	0.0282	0.0005
SBI Magnum Equity Fund - Growth	0.0086	0.0372	0.0078
SBI Magnum Multiplier Plus Scheme - 93 -D	0.0064	0.0303	0.0078
SBI MSFU Contra - Dividend	0.0067	0.0458	0.0076
SBI MSFU Contra- Growth	0.0052	0.0327	0.0078
SBI MSFU IT	0.0050	0.0359	0.0078
UTI - Equity Fund-Growth Option	0.0016	0.0342	0.0028
UTI - Equity Fund-Income Option	0.0159	0.0399	0.0028
ELSS - Private			
Birla Tax Plan 98	0.0237	0.0458	0.0127
Escorts Tax Plan Dividend	0.0097	0.0459	0.0019
Escorts Tax Plan Growth	0.0246	0.0349	0.0019
Franklin Taxshield - Dividend	0.0016	0.0189	0.0083
Franklin India Taxshield - Growth	0.0144	0.0289	0.0083
ICICI Prudential Tax Plan-Dividend Option	0.0046	0.0420	0.0041
ICICI Prudential Tax Plan-Growth Option	0.0085	0.0397	0.0042
Principal Tax Saving fund	0.0269	0.0489	0.0123
SaharaTax Gain-Growth	0.0159	0.1289	-0.0081
Sundaram PNB Paribas Tax Saver OE Fund	0.0086	0.0350	0.0019
Sundaram Taxsaver 98	0.0002	0.0378	0.0019
Tata Tax Saving	0.0056	0.0589	0.0090
Taurus Libra Taxshield 96	0.0040	0.0427	-0.0066
ELSS - Public			
Bob ELSS 96	0.0036	0.0329	0.0050
Canara Robeco Equity Tax Saver	0.0049	0.0331	0.0037
LICMF Taxplan-Dividend	0.0146	0.0467	-0.0031
LICMF Taxplan-Growth	0.0089	0.0392	-0.0034
SBI Magnum Taxgain Scheme 1993 - D	0.0035	0.0567	0.0079
UTI-Master Equity Plan Unit Scheme	0.0014	0.0349	-0.0088

Source: Computed from Secondary data.

A - 3 RETURN AND RISK GROUPS

Income - Private	*Groups based on*	
	Sensex	*Nifty*
Birla Sun Life Income Fund - D	2	2
Birla Sun Life Income Fund - G	2	2
DBS Chola Freedom Income -STF-Institutional	2	2
DBS Chola Freedom Income -STF-DD	2	2
FT India MIP-Growth	2	2
FT India MIP-Monthly Bonus	2	2
HDFC Income Fund - Dividend	2	2
HDFC Income Fund - Growth	2	2
ICICI Prudential Income Plan-Dividend Option	2	2
ICICI Prudential Income Plan-Growth Option	2	2
ICICI Prudential MIP - Cumulative	2	2
ING Income Fund- Dividend Option	2	2
ING Income Fund-Growth Option	2	2
JM Income Fund - Dividend	2	2
JM Income Fund - Growth	2	2
Kotak Income Plus - Growth	2	2
Kotak Income Plus - Monthly Dividend	2	2
Reliance Income Fund - Annual Dividend Plan	2	2
Reliance Income Fund - Growth Plan	2	2
Reliance Income Fund Retail Plan Half Yearly	2	2
Sahara Income Fund-Dividend	2	2
Sahara Income Fund-Growth	2	2
Sundaram BNP Paribas Income Plus-Appreci	2	2
Sundaram BNP Paribas Income Plus-Dividend	2	2
Tata Income Fund - Monthly	2	2
Tata Income Fund - Qtrly	2	2
Tata Income Fund - Semi	2	2
Templeton India Income Fund - Dividend	2	2
Templeton India Income Fund - Growth	4	4
Income - Public		
BOB Income Fund - Dividend	2	2
BOB Income Fund -Growth	2	2

	Groups based on	
	Sensex	*Nifty*
Canara Robeco Income - Bonus	2	2
Canara Robeco Income - Growth	2	2
Canara Robeco Income - Income	2	2
LIC MF Bond Fund - Dividend	4	4
LIC MF Bond Fund - Growth	2	2
SBI Magnum Monthly Income Fund - Bonus	2	2
SBI Magnum Income Fund - Bonus	2	2
SBI Magnum Income Fund - Dividend	4	4
SBI Magnum Income Fund - Growth	4	3
UTI Mahila Unit Scheme	2	2
UTI Monthly Income Scheme - Growth	2	2
UTI Monthly Income Scheme - Income	2	2
Balance - Private		
Birla Balance (D)	3	3
Birla Balance (G)	3	3
DSP Merill Lynch Balanced Fund (D)	2	2
DSP Merill Lynch Balanced Fund (G)	2	2
Franklin India Balanced Fund (D)	3	3
Franklin India Balanced Fund (G)	3	3
HDFC Balanced Fund - Dividend	3	3
ICICI Prudential Balanced Fund (D)	3	3
ICICI Prudential Balanced Fund (G)	3	3
ING Balanced Fund (D)	3	3
ING Balanced Fund (G)	3	3
J M Balanced Fund (Dividend)	3	3
J M Balanced Fund (Growth)	1	1
Kotak Balance	3	3
Principal Balanced Fund – Dividend	1	1
Principal Balanced Fund – Growth	1	1
Sundaram Balanced Fund 1	1	
Sundaram BNP Balanced - Appreciation	1	1
Sundaram BNP Balanced - Dividend	1	1
Tata Balanced Fund - Dividend	1	1

Balance - Public	Groups based on	
	Sensex	Nifty
Bank of Baroda Balanced - Dividend	2	1
Bank of Baroda Balanced – Growth	4	4
LIC Balanced – Plan A - Dividend	2	2
LIC Balanced – Plan C - Growth	3	3
LIC Unit Linked Insurance Scheme	2	2
SBI Magnum Balanced Fund - Dividend	3	3
UTI Balanced Fund - Dividend	2	2
UTI Balanced Fund - Growth	1	1
Growth - Private		
Birla Advantage Fund - Dividend/ Reinvest	3	3
Birla Index Fund – Growth	3	3
DBS Chola Growth Fund-Cumulative	3	3
DBS Chola Growth Fund-Quarterly Dividend	3	3
DSP Merrill Lynch Equity Fund - Growth	3	3
DSP Merrill Lynch Opportunities Fund - Growth	4	4
Escorts Growth Plan - Dividend	4	4
Escorts Growth Plan - Growth	3	3
HDFC Growth Fund - Growth	3	3
ICICI Pru FMCG Plan – Dividend	1	1
ICICI Prudential Growth Plan - Dividend Option	3	3
ICICI Prudential Growth Plan - Growth Option	3	3
JM Equity Fund - Dividend	4	4
JM Equity Fund - Growth	3	3
Kotak 30 - Growth	3	3
Reliance Growth Fund - Dividend Plan	4	4
Reliance Growth Fund - Growth Plan	1	1
Reliance Vision Fund - Dividend Plan	3	3
Sahara Growth Fund-Dividend	2	2
Sahara Growth Fund-Growth	3	3
Sundaram BNP Paribas Capex Oppor Fund-G	3	3
Sundaram BNP Paribas Growth Fund-Dividend	3	3
Sundaram BNP Paribas Growth Fund-Growth	3	3

	Groups based on	
	Sensex	Nifty
Tata Pure Equity Fund - Dividend	4	4
Tata Pure Equity Fund - Growth	3	3
Taurus Star Share	4	4
Templeton India Growth Fund-Dividend Plan	3	3
Templeton India Growth Fund-Growth Plan	4	4
Growth - Public		
Baroda Diversified Fund - Growth	4	4
Canara Robeco Expo Growth Plan	3	3
Canara Robeco Expo Income Plan	3	3
LICMF Growth Fund - Dividend Option	3	3
LICMF Growth Fund - Growth Option	2	2
SBI Magnum Equity Fund - Growth	3	3
SBI Magnum Multiplier Plus Scheme - 93 -Div	3	3
SBI MSFU Contra - Dividend	3	3
SBI MSFU Contra- Growth	3	3
SBI MSFU IT	3	3
UTI - Equity Fund-Growth Option	4	4
UTI - Equity Fund-Income Option	4	4
ELSS - Private		
Birla Tax Plan 98	2	2
Escorts Tax Plan Dividend	3	3
Escorts Tax Plan Growth	2	2
Franklin Taxshield - Dividend	3	3
Franklin India Taxshield - Growth	2	2
ICICI Prudential Tax Plan-Dividend Option	3	3
ICICI Prudential Tax Plan-Growth Option	1	1
Principal Tax Saving fund	1	2
SaharaTax Gain-Growth	2	2
Sundaram PNB Paribas Tax Saver OE Fund	3	3
Sundaram Taxsaver 98	3	3
Tata Tax Saving	1	1
Taurus Libra Taxshield 96	3	3

	Groups based on	
	Sensex	Nifty
ELSS - Public		
Bob ELSS 96	3	3
Canara Robeco Equity Tax Saver	3	3
LICMF Taxplan-Dividend	2	2
LICMF Taxplan-Growth	1	1
SBI Magnum Taxgain Scheme 1993 - Dividend	1	1
UTI-Master Equity Plan Unit Scheme	2	2

Note: ONE: $AR_p > AR_m$; $\sigma_p < \sigma_m$; **TWO:** $AR_p < AR_m$; $\sigma_p < \sigma_m$;
THREE: $AR_p > AR_m$; $\sigma_p > \sigma_m$; **FOUR:** $AR_p < AR_m$; $\sigma_p > \sigma_m$

Source: Computed from Secondary data.

A - 4 BETA AND R^2

Income - Private	Beta		R^2	
	Sensex	Nifty	Sensex	Nifty
Birla Sun Life Income Fund - D	0.0309	0.0147	0.0510	0.0135
Birla Sun Life Income Fund - G	0.0177**	0.0244	0.1270	0.0018
DBS Chola Freedom Income -STF-Institutional	0.0975	0.0246	0.0070	0.0011
DBS Chola Freedom Income -STF-DD	0.0039	0.0009	0.0070	0.0000
FT India MIP-Growth	0.0115	0.0071	0.0270	0.0122
FT India MIP-Monthly Bonus	0.0168*	0.0026	0.0780	0.0021
HDFC Income Fund - Dividend	0.0254	0.0085	0.0410	0.0000
HDFC Income Fund - Growth	0.0237	0.0158	0.0350	0.0001
ICICI Prudential Income Plan-Dividend Option	0.1460	0.1027	0.0090	0.0148
ICICI Prudential Income Plan-Growth Option	0.0213	0.0192	0.0200	0.0196
ICICI Prudential MIP - Cumulative	0.0849**	-0.0024	0.0175	0.0002
ING Income Fund- Dividend Option	-0.0014	0.0001	0.0008	0.0000
ING Income Fund-Growth Option	-0.0042	-0.0233	0.0013	0.0490
JM Income Fund - Dividend	0.0251	0.0012	0.0048	0.0000
JM Income Fund - Growth	-0.0058	0.0016	0.0132	0.0011
Kotak Income Plus - Growth	-0.0001	-0.0008	0.0003	0.0000
Kotak Income Plus - Monthly Dividend	-0.0002	-0.0021	0.0134	0.0000
Reliance Income Fund-Annual Dividend	0.0236	0.0392	0.0121	0.0361
Reliance Income Fund-Growth Plan	0.3661	0.0114	0.0249	0.0002
Reliance Income Fund Retail Plan Half Year	-0.0187	-0.0009	0.0119	0.0000
Sahara Income Fund-Dividend	-0.0093	-0.0148	0.0024	0.0073
Sahara Income Fund-Growth	0.0013	0.0073	0.0000	0.0036
Sundaram BNP Paribas Income Plus-Appre	0.0115	0.0107	0.0342	0.0002
Sundaram BNP Paribas Income Plus-D	0.0024	0.0028	0.0111	0.0000
Tata Income Fund - Monthly	-0.0227	0.0153	0.0177	0.0091
Tata Income Fund - Qtrly	0.0385	0.0899*	0.0131	0.0744
Tata Income Fund - Semi	0.0183	0.0518	0.0015	0.0154
Templeton India Income Fund-Dividend	-0.4541	0.1868	0.0103	0.0361
Templeton India Income Fund-Growth	0.0065	-0.0166	0.0025	0.0000

Income - Public	*Beta*		R^2	
	Sensex	*Nifty*	*Sensex*	*Nifty*
BOB Income Fund - Dividend	0.0048	-0.0026	0.0067	0.0000
BOB Income Fund -Growth	-0.0026	-0.0164	0.0021	0.0000
Canara Robeco Income - Bonus	-0.1182**	0.0026	0.0007	0.0001
Canara Robeco Income - Growth	-0.0225	0.0096	0.0258	0.0053
Canara Robeco Income - Income	-0.1592*	-0.1179	0.0978	0.0887
LIC MF Bond Fund - Dividend	0.0155	0.0058	0.0131	0.0000
LIC MF Bond Fund - Growth	0.0167	0.0024	0.0368	0.0000
SBI Magnum Monthly Income Fund - Bonus	0.0768	0.1403**	0.0452	0.0024
SBI Magnum Income Fund - Bonus	-0.0172	-0.0362	0.0068	0.0001
SBI Magnum Income Fund - Dividend	-0.1228	-0.0742	0.0156	0.0030
SBI Magnum Income Fund - Growth	0.0319	-0.0544	0.0021	0.0005
UTI Mahila Unit Scheme	0.0998	0.0003	0.0056	0.0000
UTI Monthly Income Scheme - Growth	0.0889	-0.0438	0.0176	0.0072
UTI Monthly Income Scheme - Income	0.0998	-0.1658	0.0046	0.0468
Balance - Private				
Birla Balance (D)	0.3221**	0.0013	0.1199	0.0000
Birla Balance (G)	0.2771**	0.0244	0.1273	0.0000
DSP Merill Lynch Balanced Fund (D)	0.1081	0.1041	0.1262	0.0052
DSP Merill Lynch Balanced Fund (G)	0.1665	0.0578	0.3234	0.0016
Franklin India Balanced Fund (D)	0.3508*	0.1643	0.0806	0.0002
Franklin India Balanced Fund (G)	0.0994	0.1201	0.0136	0.0000
HDFC Balanced Fund - Dividend	0.1028	0.0814	0.2395	0.0123
ICICI Prudential Balanced Fund (D)	0.5783**	0.0724	0.1777	0.0079
ICICI Prudential Balanced Fund (G)	0.4001**	0.0585	0.2138	0.0080
ING Balanced Fund (D)	0.0937	0.1470	0.2683	0.0513
ING Balanced Fund (G)	0.3331**	0.0435	0.1058	0.0038
J M Balanced Fund (Dividend)	0.3462**	0.0496	0.1500	0.0033
J M Balanced Fund (Growth)	0.2876	0.0031	0.0593	0.0000
Kotak Balance	0.2777**	0.0025	0.0998	0.0000
Principal Balanced Fund – Dividend	0.1869	0.0211	0.0154	0.0007
Principal Balanced Fund – Growth	0.2816	0.1633	0.0481	0.0390
Sundaram Balanced Fund	0.4110**	0.0413	0.1118	0.0031

	Beta		R^2	
	Sensex	*Nifty*	*Sensex*	*Nifty*
Sundaram BNP Balanced - Appreciation	0.3219**	0.1568	0.1353	0.0494
Sundaram BNP Balanced - Dividend	0.4109**	-0.0464	0.1242	0.0041
Tata Balanced Fund - Dividend	0.3892**	0.0812	0.2295	0.0160
Balance - Public				
Bank of Baroda Balanced - Dividend	0.3865**	0.0661	0.1321	0.0082
Bank of Baroda Balanced – Growth	0.3706**	0.0538	0.1333	0.0057
LIC Balanced – Plan A - Dividend	0.4972**	0.0574	0.2581	0.0067
LIC Balanced – Plan C - Growth	0.3992**	0.0413	0.1859	0.0038
LIC Unit Linked Insurance Scheme	0.3173*	0.0905	0.0926	0.0152
SBI Magnum Balanced Fund - Dividend	0.5112**	0.1155	0.2400	0.0240
UTI Balanced Fund - Dividend	0.2174**	0.2013**	0.1093	0.1040
UTI Balanced Fund - Growth	0.3409**	0.1042	0.2502	0.0317
Growth - Private				
Birla Advantage Fund - Dividend/ Reinvest	0.5851**	0.0158	0.4335	0.0004
Birla Index Fund – Growth	0.5378**	0.1455	0.2671	0.0383
DBS Chola Growth Fund-Cumulative	0.5320*	0.6369**	0.2675	0.3624
DBS Chola Growth Fund-Quarterly Dividend	0.1042	0.0255	0.5604	0.0009
DSP Merrill Lynch Equity Fund - Growth	0.3676	0.3536	0.8199	0.1389
DSP Merrill Lynch Opportunities Fund-G	0.1984	0.0420	0.8823	0.0029
Escorts Growth Plan - Dividend	0.5796	0.3110	0.3261	0.1043
Escorts Growth Plan - Growth	0.5070**	0.0592	0.2539	0.0065
HDFC Growth Fund - Growth	0.2809	0.2897	0.5869	0.1081
ICICI Pru FMCG Plan – Dividend	0.4806**	0.1702	0.7934	0.0420
ICICI Prudential Growth Plan - Dividend Option	0.6876*	0.4132	0.8171	0.1770
ICICI Prudential Growth Plan-Growth Option	0.5258**	0.1516	0.2653	0.0371
JM Equity Fund - Dividend	0.5323**	0.0269	0.0520	0.0012
JM Equity Fund - Growth	0.5260**	0.0707	0.2642	0.0092
Kotak 30 - Growth	0.4846**	0.0454	0.2421	0.0042
Reliance Growth Fund - Dividend Plan	0.4487**	0.2133	0.2158	0.0662
Reliance Growth Fund - Growth Plan	0.3661	-0.0114	0.7349	0.0002
Reliance Vision Fund - Dividend Plan	0.5503**	0.1097	0.3858	0.0213
Sahara Growth Fund-Dividend	0.0896	0.2772	0.0117	0.0917
Sahara Growth Fund-Growth	0.3448	0.0766	0.1376	0.0087

	Beta		R^2	
	Sensex	Nifty	Sensex	Nifty
Sundaram BNP Paribas Capex Oppor Fund-G	0.5651**	0.1613	0.5142	0.0378
Sundaram BNP Paribas Growth Fund-Dividend	0.5522**	0.1705	0.4237	0.0420
Sundaram BNP Paribas Growth Fund-Growth	0.5651**	0.1613	0.2947	0.0378
Tata Pure Equity Fund - Dividend	0.4425*	0.0306	0.2051	0.0013
Tata Pure Equity Fund - Growth	0.1519	0.2791*	0.2109	0.1171
Taurus Star Share	0.5562**	0.0891	0.2964	0.0107
Templeton India Growth Fund-Dividend Plan	0.5100**	0.0905	0.2560	0.0142
Templeton India Growth Fund-Growth Plan	0.2019	0.6731**	0.0543	0.3541
Growth - Public				
Baroda Diversified Fund - Growth	0.6937**	0.4849**	0.0988	0.0452
Canara Robeco Expo Growth Plan	0.4432**	0.0652	0.4103	0.0014
Canara Robeco Expo Income Plan	0.1504	0.2269	0.1891	0.0131
LICMF Growth Fund - Dividend Option	0.4937**	0.0274	**0.1680**	0.0003
LICMF Growth Fund - Growth Option	0.0279	0.0067	0.7327	0.0008
SBI Magnum Equity Fund - Growth	0.4584**	0.0731	0.0867	0.0016
SBI Magnum Multiplier Plus Scheme-93D	0.5527**	0.1242	0.1010	0.0047
SBI MSFU Contra - Dividend	0.4524**	0.0177	0.1932	0.0001
SBI MSFU Contra- Growth	0.3808**	0.3669**	0.1100	0.0332
SBI MSFU IT	0.3808**	0.0652	0.0800	0.0010
UTI - Equity Fund-Growth Option	0.4432**	0.0652	**0.1719**	0.0091
UTI - Equity Fund-Income Option	0.0980	0.1655	0.0138	0.0019
ELSS - Private				
Birla Tax Plan 98	0.4642**	0.0730*	0.2228	0.3362
Escorts Tax Plan Dividend	0.7505**	0.4562*	0.4702	0.0080
Escorts Tax Plan Growth	0.4841**	0.0881	0.4806	0.0092
Franklin Taxshield - Dividend	0.6682**	0.0717	0.2340	0.0181
Franklin India Taxshield - Growth	0.4402**	0.0874	0.2251	0.1600
ICICI Prudential Tax Plan-Dividend Option	0.5284**	0.2662	0.2726	0.0012
ICICI Prudential Tax Plan-Growth Option	0.4898**	0.0317	0.3885	0.0000

	Beta		*R^2*	
	Sensex	*Nifty*	*Sensex*	*Nifty*
Principal Tax Saving fund	-0.0034	-0.0008	0.1303	1.6480
SaharaTax Gain-Growth	-0.2003	0.8741	0.0433	0.1639
Sundaram PNB Paribas Tax Saver OE Fund	0.9978**	0.4148*	0.5943	0.0541
Sundaram Taxsaver 98	0.5564**	0.2241	0.2833	0.0003
Tata Tax Saving	0.2293	0.0136	0.6454	0.0001
Taurus Libra Taxshield 96	0.5317**	0.0064	0.2749	0.0015
ELSS - Public				
Bob ELSS 96	0.6401**	0.0314	0.3525	0.0120
Canara Robeco Equity Tax Saver	0.6014**	0.0450	0.3229	0.0031
LICMF Taxplan-Dividend	0.2349	0.0096	0.0728	0.0002
LICMF Taxplan-Growth	0.2416	0.1547	0.0811	0.0506
SBI Magnum Taxgain Scheme 1993 - D	0.4153**	0.2859	0.1814	0.0939
UTI-Master Equity Plan Unit Scheme	0.1595	0.4309**	0.0405	0.2108

Note: * and ** indicate 5 and 1 per cent levels of significance respectively.

Source: Computed from Secondary data.

A- 5 IRR

Income – Private

Birla Sun Life Income Fund - D	11.26
Birla Sun Life Income Fund - G	10.58
DBS Chola Freedom Income -STF-Institutional	3.56
DBS Chola Freedom Income -STF-DD	4.78
FT India MIP-Growth	3.89
FT India MIP-Monthly Bonus	4.87
HDFC Income Fund - Dividend	6.78
HDFC Income Fund - Growth	7.33
ICICI Prudential Income Plan-Dividend Option	10.25
ICICI Prudential Income Plan-Growth Option	11.32
ICICI Prudential MIP - Cumulative	9.45
ING Income Fund- Dividend Option	5.78
ING Income Fund-Growth Option	6.87
JM Income Fund - Dividend	6.45
JM Income Fund - Growth	7.14
Kotak Income Plus - Growth	8.77
Kotak Income Plus - Monthly Dividend	7.41
Reliance Income Fund - Annual Dividend Plan	12.56
Reliance Income Fund - Growth Plan	13.58
Reliance Income Fund Retail Plan Half Yearly	12.82
Sahara Income Fund-Dividend	7.45
Sahara Income Fund-Growth	7.02
Sundaram BNP Paribas Income Plus-Appreciation	13.58
Sundaram BNP Paribas Income Plus-Dividend	12.98
Tata Income Fund - Monthly	14.42
Tata Income Fund - Qtrly	9.89
Tata Income Fund - Semi	8.79

Templeton India Income Fund - Dividend	7.58
Templeton India Income Fund - Growth	8.24

Income – Public

BOB Income Fund - Dividend	2.33
BOB Income Fund -Growth	4.58
Canara Robeco Income Bonus	5.22
Canara Robeco Income - Growth	7.06
Canara Robeco Income - Income	5.11
LIC MF Bond Fund - Dividend	3.96
LIC MF Bond Fund - Growth	9.92
SBI Magnum Monthly Income Fund - Bonus	4.56
SBI Magnum Income Fund - Bonus	7.28
SBI Magnum Income Fund - Dividend	6.49
SBI Magnum Income Fund - Growth	10.25
UTI Mahila Unit Scheme	8.59
UTI Monthly Income Scheme - Dividend	4.25
UTI Monthly Income Scheme - Growth	5.26

Balance - Private

Birla Balance (D)	14.02
Birla Balance (G)	13.48
DSP Merill Lynch Balanced Fund (D)	18.47
DSP Merill Lynch Balanced Fund (G)	26.20
Franklin India Balanced Fund (D)	22.59
Franklin India Balanced Fund (G)	25.64
HDFC Balanced Fund	15.92
ICICI Prudential Balanced Fund (D)	9.32
ICICI Prudential Balanced Fund (G)	21.02
ING Balanced Portfolio (D)	20.98
ING Balanced Portfolio (G)	18.32
J M Balanced Fund (Dividend)	8.98
J M Balanced Fund (Growth)	9.58
Kotak Balance	16.58
Principal Balanced Fund – Dividend	14.72
Principal Balanced Fund – Growth	24.70
Sundaram Balanced Fund	24.56
Sundaram BNP Balanced - Appreciation	23.45

Sundaram BNP Balanced - Dividend	21.58
Tata Balanced Fund	25.68

Balance – Public

Bank of Baroda Balanced - Dividend	4.58
Bank of Baroda Balanced – Growth	8.92
LIC Balanced – Plan A - Dividend	4.26
LIC Balanced – Plan C - Growth	7.89
LIC Unit Linked Insurance Scheme	6.89
SBI Magnum Balanced Fund - Dividend	11.45
UTI Balanced Fund - Dividend	6.45
UTI Balanced Fund - Growth	5.80

Growth – Private

Birla Advantage Fund - Dividend/ Reinvestment	19.30
Birla Index Fund – Growth	18.62
DBS Chola Growth Fund-Cumulative	22.45
DBS Chola Growth Fund-Quarterly Dividend	24.19
DSP Merrill Lynch Equity Fund	21.47
DSP Merrill Lynch Opportunities Fund	26.48
Escorts Growth Plan - Dividend	13.67
Escorts Growth Plan - Growth	17.48
HDFC Growth Fund	19.87
ICICI Pru FMCG Plan – Dividend	34.78
ICICI Prudential Growth Plan - Dividend Option	30.59
ICICI Prudential Growth Plan - Growth Option	34.59
JM Equity Fund - Dividend	8.98
JM Equity Fund - Growth	9.48
Kotak 30 - Growth	21.49
Reliance Growth Fund - Dividend Plan	32.49
Reliance Growth Fund - Growth Plan	51.25
Reliance Vision Fund - Dividend Plan	42.37
Sahara Growth Fund-Dividend	21.01
Sahara Growth Fund-Growth	19.58
Sundaram BNP Paribas Capex Opportunities Fund-Growth	45.65
Sundaram BNP Paribas Growth Fund-Dividend	56.65
Sundaram BNP Paribas Growth Fund-Growth	58.70
Tata Pure Equity Fund - Dividend	32.23
Tata Pure Equity Fund - Growth	26.58

Taurus Star Share	8.45
Templeton India Growth Fund-Dividend Plan	26.49
Templeton India Growth Fund-Growth Plan	23.47
Growth – Public	
Baroda Diversified Fund	-2.59
Canara Robeco Expo Growth Plan	16.75
Canara Robeco Expo Income Plan	13.10
LICMF Growth Fund - Dividend Option	15.40
LICMF Growth Fund - Growth Option	7.82
SBI Magnum Equity Fund	15.48
SBI Magnum Multiplier Plus Scheme - 93 -Dividend	16.59
SBI MSFU Contra - Dividend	13.40
SBI MSFU Contra- Growth	9.42
SBI MSFU IT	8.56
UTI - Equity Fund-Growth Option	7.85
UTI - Equity Fund-Income Option	-2.97
ELSS – Private	
Birla Tax Plan 98	18.49
Escorts Tax Plan Dividend	16.47
Escorts Tax Plan Growth	19.08
Franklin Taxshield - Dividend	13.60
Franklin India Taxshield - Growth	16.43
ICICI Prudential Tax Plan-Dividend Option	23.16
ICICI Prudential Tax Plan-Growth Option	21.56
Principal Tax Saving fund	15.48
SaharaTax Gain-Growth	-6.48
Sundaram PNB Paribas Tax Saver OE Fund	26.39
Sundaram Taxsaver 98	20.45
Tata Tax Saving	31.42
Taurus Libra Taxshield	19.46
ELSS – Public	
Bob ELSS 96	8.65
Canara Robeco Equity Tax Saver	9.50
LICMF Taxplan-Dividend	-3.08
LICMF Taxplan-Growth	-6.58
SBI Magnum Taxgain Scheme 1993 - Dividend	16.58
UTI-Master Equity Plan Unit Scheme	21.58

Source: Computed from Secondary data.

A - 6 SHARPE RATIO

Income-Private	*Sharpe*	*Benchmark*	
		Sensex	*Nifty*
Birla Sun Life Income Fund - D	-7.6672	-0.7786	-0.7416
Birla Sun Life Income Fund - G	0.8197	1.1088	1.0073
DBS Chola Freedom Income -STF-Institutional	0.8396	0.9612	1.0266
DBS Chola Freedom Income -STF-DD	1.8869	2.7003	2.3407
FT India MIP-Growth	1.1038	2.5008	1.2362
FT India MIP-Monthly Bonus	0.7896	1.2473	1.2296
HDFC Income Fund - Dividend	-2.5008	-1.5336	-1.7075
HDFC Income Fund - Growth	-2.4038	-0.8989	-1.2132
ICICI Prudential Income Plan-Dividend Option	0.6803	1.6315	1.3780
ICICI Prudential Income Plan-Growth Option	0.8211	1.3517	1.5017
ICICI Prudential MIP - Cumulative	1.9761	2.8596	2.5943
ING Income Fund- Dividend Option	0.0119	0.3595	0.4865
ING Income Fund-Growth Option	1.1764	2.0743	1.9781
JM Income Fund - Dividend	0.2829	0.3509	0.7629
JM Income Fund - Growth	2.7377	3.3574	3.3772
Kotak Income Plus - Growth	0.4743	0.8291	0.7356
Kotak Income Plus - Monthly Dividend	0.1925	0.5828	0.3139
Reliance Income Fund - Annual Dividend	1.2014	1.4045	1.5422
Reliance Income Fund - Growth Plan	0.6655	1.0985	0.6830
Reliance Income Fund Retail Plan Half Yea	1.1313	1.6946	1.3990
Sahara Income Fund-Dividend	1.5600	2.7789	2.1974
Sahara Income Fund-Growth	1.5003	1.7737	2.1784
Sundaram BNP Paribas Income Plus-Appre	-0.0212	0.3678	0.5328
Sundaram BNP Paribas Income Plus-D	0.4431	1.0595	1.1782
Tata Income Fund - Monthly	0.6452	1.0648	1.1993
Tata Income Fund - Qtrly	1.9801	2.7071	2.0195
Tata Income Fund - Semi	1.0669	1.6128	1.1608
Templeton India Income Fund - Dividend	-3.3736	-0.6476	-0.8776
Templeton India Income Fund - Growth	-2.8418	-2.4027	-2.3882

	Sharpe	Benchmark	
		Sensex	Nifty
Income - Public			
BOB Income Fund - Dividend	0.9715	1.0605	1.0605
BOB Income Fund -Growth	0.9515	1.2354	1.2781
Canara Robeco Income - Bonus	1.4191	1.6444	1.4954
Canara Robeco Income - Growth	0.7572	1.0876	0.8350
Canara Robeco Income - Income	2.3933	2.5279	2.5564
LIC MF Bond Fund - Dividend	-0.5921	-0.3307	-0.4586
LIC MF Bond Fund - Growth	-0.1136	-0.0490	-0.0374
SBI Magnum Monthly Income Fund - Bonus	-2.8700	-2.0632	-1.7317
SBI Magnum Income Fund - Bonus	-1.5250	-1.1361	-1.0223
SBI Magnum Income Fund - Dividend	-1.6215	-1.5158	-1.5944
SBI Magnum Income Fund - Growth	-2.5276	-2.1781	-2.7183
UTI Mahila Unit Scheme	0.5115	0.6130	0.6177
UTI Monthly Income Scheme - Growth	0.2680	0.4455	0.4350
UTI Monthly Income Scheme - Income	0.2604	0.3229	0.3409
Balance - Private			
Birla Balance (D)	-2.1351	-3.3764	-2.9046
Birla Balance (G)	-0.9658	-2.6016	-2.2936
DSP Merill Lynch Balanced Fund (D)	-1.0625	-0.7946	-0.9761
DSP Merill Lynch Balanced Fund (G)	-1.5157	-1.0381	-1.0678
Franklin India Balanced Fund (D)	-18.1884	-24.1729	-29.4441
Franklin India Balanced Fund (G)	-11.4810	-27.3954	-27.2612
HDFC Balanced Fund - Dividend	1.3609	0.1708	0.7399
ICICI Prudential Balanced Fund (D)	1.4273	0.0379	-0.0539
ICICI Prudential Balanced Fund (G)	0.9613	-0.2177	-0.2457
ING Balanced Fund (D)	1.4131	0.0274	0.0926
ING Balanced Fund (G)	1.7621	0.1245	0.8757
J M Balanced Fund (Dividend)	-0.6881	-1.7625	-1.5572
J M Balanced Fund (Growth)	0.3900	-1.3216	-1.3938
Kotak Balance	1.3711	0.0011	0.2671
Principal Balanced Fund – Dividend	-1.5263	-1.4598	-1.4146
Principal Balanced Fund – Growth	0.3773	-1.8030	-0.3619
Sundaram Balanced Fund	-1.0835	-1.9436	-1.4333

	Sharpe	Benchmark	
		Sensex	Nifty
Sundaram BNP Balanced - Appreciation	0.7116	-2.5885	-1.4744
Sundaram BNP Balanced - Dividend	3.6279	-2.0225	-1.2519
Tata Balanced Fund - Dividend	0.3018	-0.2870	0.1155
Balance - Public			
Bank of Baroda Balanced - Dividend	0.7191	0.9442	0.1985
Bank of Baroda Balanced – Growth	0.4122	0.9580	0.8410
LIC Balanced – Plan A - Dividend	0.0248	0.3315	0.2414
LIC Balanced – Plan C - Growth	0.6615	0.1880	1.1722
LIC Unit Linked Insurance Scheme	-1.0996	0.3023	0.2519
SBI Magnum Balanced Fund - Dividend	0.7330	-0.0497	-0.0602
UTI Balanced Fund - Dividend	-0.0151	0.4272	0.4737
UTI Balanced Fund - Growth	0.5033	0.1729	0.1194
Growth - Private			
Birla Advantage Fund - Dividend/ Reinvest	0.9765	0.1114	0.4986
Birla Index Fund – Growth	2.3865	-0.0668	0.6506
DBS Chola Growth Fund-Cumulative	0.0828	-0.0245	-0.0056
DBS Chola Growth Fund-Quarterly Dividend	0.3252	0.1357	0.1879
DSP Merrill Lynch Equity Fund - Growth	0.7757	-0.1114	0.7976
DSP Merrill Lynch Opportunities Fund - G	1.4593	2.5722	2.1930
Escorts Growth Plan - Dividend	-0.5178	0.1163	0.0506
Escorts Growth Plan - Growth	1.1777	-0.0166	-0.0220
HDFC Growth Fund - Growth	2.2148	-0.0237	-0.0237
ICICI Pru FMCG Plan – Dividend	2.2066	-0.2289	-0.2214
ICICI Prudential Growth Plan - Dividend Option	0.8575	-0.0516	0.0512
ICICI Prudential Growth Plan - Growth Option	1.6313	-0.2911	0.4528
JM Equity Fund - Dividend	-0.5513	0.0419	0.0414
JM Equity Fund - Growth	0.2701	-0.1391	-0.1567
Kotak 30 - Growth	2.8434	-0.5447	-0.0413
Reliance Growth Fund - Dividend Plan	0.9309	1.4947	1.3542
Reliance Growth Fund - Growth Plan	1.2278	-0.0075	-0.0216
Reliance Vision Fund - Dividend Plan	2.2446	-0.1089	-0.1895
Sahara Growth Fund-Dividend	0.0446	0.1169	0.1169
Sahara Growth Fund-Growth	0.1870	0.0253	0.0164
Sundaram BNP Paribas Capex Oppor Fund-G	2.1910	-0.2922	-0.3196
Sundaram BNP Paribas Growth Fund-Dividend	1.9289	-0.2906	-0.3242
Sundaram BNP Paribas Growth Fund-Growth	1.0919	-0.2922	-0.3048
Tata Pure Equity Fund - Dividend	1.4403	2.0057	2.1658
Tata Pure Equity Fund - Growth	3.2069	0.3013	0.3286
Taurus Star Share	-0.2759	-0.2270	-0.2342

	Sharpe	*Benchmark*	
		Sensex	*Nifty*
Templeton India Growth Fund-Dividend Plan	2.2196	-0.2112	0.1227
Templeton India Growth Fund-Growth Plan	1.8970	2.3662	2.6678
Growth - Public			
Baroda Diversified Fund - Growth	-0.5912	-0.4171	-0.2866
Canara Robeco Expo Growth Plan	0.1452	-0.2864	-0.2375
Canara Robeco Expo Income Plan	0.0275	-0.3973	-0.4331
LICMF Growth Fund - Dividend Option	0.3490	0.0387	0.0711
LICMF Growth Fund - Growth Option	0.1159	0.3725	0.4254
SBI Magnum Equity Fund - Growth	0.1032	-0.1346	0.0225
SBI Magnum Multiplier Plus Scheme - 93 -D	0.3792	-0.1727	-0.0474
SBI MSFU Contra - Dividend	0.1843	-0.0875	-0.0200
SBI MSFU Contra- Growth	0.0172	-0.0739	-0.0812
SBI MSFU IT	0.3274	-0.0739	-0.0789
UTI - Equity Fund-Growth Option	-0.4564	-0.0669	-0.0348
UTI - Equity Fund-Income Option	0.0012	0.2122	0.3295
ELSS - Private			
Birla Tax Plan 98	0.0496	0.2229	0.2402
Escorts Tax Plan Dividend	0.4391	0.1456	0.1695
Escorts Tax Plan Growth	0.3457	0.5739	0.6514
Franklin Taxshield - Dividend	0.1927	-0.4506	-0.3549
Franklin India Taxshield - Growth	0.0836	0.1443	0.2101
ICICI Prudential Tax Plan-Dividend Option	1.1681	0.0518	0.0115
ICICI Prudential Tax Plan-Growth Option	0.8171	-0.0288	0.1086
Principal Tax Saving fund	0.0727	0.2333	0.2996
SaharaTax Gain-Growth	0.0171	0.2111	0.1861
Sundaram PNB Paribas Tax Saver OE Fund	2.0299	0.1890	0.1890
Sundaram Taxsaver 98	0.8312	-0.0539	-0.0454
Tata Tax Saving	0.0451	-0.1489	-0.0582
Taurus Libra Taxshield 96	0.5774	0.2443	0.2462
ELSS - Public			
Bob ELSS 96	0.5397	0.0136	-0.0425
Canara Robeco Equity Tax Saver	0.3042	0.0855	0.0377
LICMF Taxplan-Dividend	-1.5599	0.3906	0.3785
LICMF Taxplan-Growth	0.5656	0.2684	0.3130
SBI Magnum Taxgain Scheme 1993 - D	0.1549	-0.1001	-0.0782
UTI-Master Equity Plan Unit Scheme	-0.0670	0.2692	0.2935

Source: Computed from Secondary data.

A - 7 TREYNOR RATIO

Income - Private	*Treynor Ratio*		*Benchmark*	
	Sensex	*Nifty*	*Sensex*	*Nifty*
Birla Sun Life Income Fund - D	-0.9862	-2.0731	-0.0220	0.0147
Birla Sun Life Income Fund - G	1.0376	0.7531	0.0328	0.0244
DBS Chola Freedom Income -STF-Institutional	0.2864	1.1351	0.0405	0.0246
DBS Chola Freedom Income -STF-DD	4.5194	19.5840	0.0777	0.0009
FT India MIP-Growth	0.1909	0.3092	0.0715	0.0071
FT India MIP-Monthly Bonus	1.4914	9.6367	0.0604	0.0026
HDFC Income Fund - Dividend	-3.9006	-1.6559	-0.0895	0.0085
HDFC Income Fund - Growth	-3.4092	-5.1138	-0.0615	0.0158
ICICI Prudential Income Plan-Dividend Option	0.1536	0.2184	0.0805	0.1027
ICICI Prudential Income Plan-Growth Option	0.9378	1.0404	0.0386	0.0192
ICICI Prudential MIP - Cumulative	0.1363	-4.8231	0.0770	-0.0024
ING Income Fund- Dividend Option	-0.1232	1.7254	0.0105	0.0001
ING Income Fund-Growth Option	-3.7315	-0.6726	0.0605	-0.0233
JM Income Fund - Dividend	0.1165	2.4372	0.0105	0.0012
JM Income Fund - Growth	-0.6872	2.4911	0.0976	0.0016
Kotak Income Plus - Growth	-1.2461	-2.6558	0.0405	-0.0008
Kotak Income Plus - Monthly Dividend	-2.5487	-3.2549	0.0285	-0.0021
Reliance Income Fund-Annual Dividend	1.3329	0.8031	0.0405	0.0392
Reliance Income Fund -Growth Plan	0.1033	3.3184	0.0752	0.0114
Reliance Income Fund Retail Plan Half Year	-1.5089	-1.3525	0.0505	-0.0009
Sahara Income Fund-Dividend	-0.9205	-0.5784	0.0824	-0.0148
Sahara Income Fund-Growth	4.3706	0.7783	0.0516	0.0073
Sundaram BNP Paribas Income Plus-Appre	-0.0402	-0.0432	0.0105	0.0107
Sundaram BNP Paribas Income Plus-D	3.8128	3.2681	0.0305	0.0028
Tata Income Fund - Monthly	-0.7088	1.0507	0.0319	0.0153
Tata Income Fund - Qtrly	0.4984	0.2135	0.0795	0.0899
Tata Income Fund - Semi	0.7787	0.2751	0.0505	0.0518
Templeton India Income Fund-Dividend	0.2160	-0.5250	-0.0875	0.1868
Templeton India Income Fund-Growth	-14.7597	5.7794	-0.0695	-0.0166

	Treynor Ratio		Benchmark	
	Sensex	Nifty	Sensex	Nifty
Income - Public				
BOB Income Fund - Dividend	4.3892	-8.1032	0.0305	-0.0026
BOB Income Fund -Growth	-11.9497	-1.8945	0.0605	-0.0164
Canara Robeco Income - Bonus	-0.3399	15.4517	0.0545	0.0026
Canara Robeco Income - Growth	-1.1461	2.6849	0.0541	0.0096
Canara Robeco Income - Income	-0.2210	-0.2984	0.0916	-0.1179
LIC MF Bond Fund - Dividend	-1.2952	-3.4613	-0.0095	0.0058
LIC MF Bond Fund - Growth	-0.2212	-1.5394	-0.0019	0.0024
SBI Magnum Monthly Income Fund-Bonus	-1.1371	-0.6224	-0.0795	0.1403
SBI Magnum Income Fund - Bonus	4.9657	2.3594	-0.0795	-0.0362
SBI Magnum Income Fund - Dividend	0.7710	1.2759	-0.0651	-0.0742
SBI Magnum Income Fund - Growth	-2.9443	1.7266	-0.0714	-0.0544
UTI Mahila Unit Scheme	0.1973	5.6287	0.0284	0.0003
UTI Monthly Income Scheme - Growth	0.0582	-0.1182	0.0145	-0.0438
UTI Monthly Income Scheme - Income	0.0842	-0.0507	0.0160	-0.1658
Balance - Private				
Birla Balance (D)	-0.1779	-4.0860	-0.0739	0.0013
Birla Balance (G)	-0.1130	-1.2831	-0.0769	0.0244
DSP Merill Lynch Balanced Fund (D)	-0.3906	-0.4056	-0.0375	0.1041
DSP Merill Lynch Balanced Fund (G)	-0.4680	-1.3482	-0.0719	0.0578
Franklin India Balanced Fund (D)	-1.8496	-3.9490	-0.7010	0.1643
Franklin India Balanced Fund (G)	-3.9938	-3.3054	-0.7029	0.1201
HDFC Balanced Fund - Dividend	0.7984	1.0083	0.0068	0.0814
ICICI Prudential Balanced Fund (D)	0.1471	1.1751	0.0014	0.0724
ICICI Prudential Balanced Fund (G)	0.1801	1.2321	-0.0061	0.0585
ING Balanced Fund (D)	0.4490	0.2862	0.0005	0.1470
ING Balanced Fund (G)	0.1563	1.1971	0.0017	0.0435
J M Balanced Fund (Dividend)	-0.0712	-0.4966	-0.0535	0.0496
J M Balanced Fund (Growth)	0.0462	4.2855	-0.0514	0.0031
Kotak Balance	0.2236	2.8302	0.0000	0.0025
Principal Balanced Fund – Dividend	-0.3543	-3.1383	-0.0716	0.0211
Principal Balanced Fund – Growth	0.0496	0.0856	-0.0751	0.1633
Sundaram Balanced Fund	-0.0935	-0.9304	-0.0729	0.0413

	Treynor Ratio		*Benchmark*	
	Sensex	*Nifty*	*Sensex*	*Nifty*
Sundaram BNP Balanced - Appreciation	0.0558	0.1146	-0.0791	0.1568
Sundaram BNP Balanced - Dividend	0.2971	-2.6309	-0.0724	-0.0464
Tata Balanced Fund - Dividend	0.0182	0.0871	-0.0078	0.0812
Balance - Public				
Bank of Baroda Balanced - Dividend	0.0571	0.3340	0.0318	0.0661
Bank of Baroda Balanced – Growth	0.0326	0.2244	0.0218	0.0538
LIC Balanced – Plan A - Dividend	0.0014	0.0122	0.0094	0.0574
LIC Balanced – Plan C - Growth	0.0443	0.4280	0.0037	0.0413
LIC Unit Linked Insurance Scheme	-0.1043	-0.3656	0.0105	0.0905
SBI Magnum Balanced Fund - Dividend	0.0432	0.1911	-0.0015	0.1155
UTI Balanced Fund - Dividend	-0.0013	-0.0014	0.0123	0.2013
UTI Balanced Fund - Growth	0.0290	0.0950	0.0044	0.1042
Growth - Private				
Birla Advantage Fun-Dividend/ Reinvest	0.0719	2.6630	0.0046	0.0158
Birla Index Fund – Growth	0.1275	0.4711	-0.0018	0.1455
DBS Chola Growth Fund-Cumulative	0.0077	0.0064	-0.0012	0.6369
DBS Chola Growth Fund-Quarterly Dividend	0.1442	0.5891	0.0058	0.0255
DSP Merrill Lynch Equity Fund - Growth	0.1049	0.1091	-0.0047	0.3536
DSP Merrill Lynch Opportunities Fund-G	0.2660	1.2566	0.0580	0.0420
Escorts Growth Plan - Dividend	-0.0602	-0.1121	0.0077	0.3110
Escorts Growth Plan - Growth	0.1422	1.2175	-0.0005	0.0592
HDFC Growth Fund - Growth	0.2922	0.2833	-0.0005	0.2897
ICICI Pru FMCG Plan–Dividend	0.1708	0.4822	-0.0086	0.1702
ICICI Prudential Growth Plan-Dividend Option	0.0830	0.1381	-0.0033	0.4132
ICICI Prudential Growth Plan-Growth Option	0.1013	0.3514	-0.0093	0.1516
JM Equity Fund - Dividend	-0.0395	-0.7814	0.0016	0.0269
JM Equity Fund - Growth	0.0159	0.1184	-0.0042	0.0707
Kotak 30 - Growth	0.1694	1.8078	-0.0105	0.0454
Reliance Growth Fund - Dividend Plan	0.0715	0.1504	0.0384	0.2133
Reliance Growth Fund - Growth Plan	0.2242	-7.1996	-0.0005	-0.0114
Reliance Vision Fund - Dividend Plan	0.1261	0.6324	-0.0032	0.1097
Sahara Growth Fund-Dividend	0.0232	0.0075	0.0066	0.2772
Sahara Growth Fund-Growth	0.0220	0.0989	0.0008	0.0766

	Treynor Ratio		Benchmark	
	Sensex	Nifty	Sensex	Nifty
Sundaram BNP Paribas Capex Oppor Fund-G	0.1452	0.5088	-0.0105	0.1613
Sundaram BNP Paribas Growth Fund-Dividend	0.1305	0.4227	-0.0105	0.1705
Sundaram BNP Paribas Growth Fund-Growth	0.2463	0.8628	-0.0105	0.1613
Tata Pure Equity Fund - Dividend	0.1459	2.1103	0.0720	0.0306
Tata Pure Equity Fund - Growth	0.6062	0.3299	0.0083	0.2791
Taurus Star Share	-0.0235	-0.1465	-0.0105	0.0891
Templeton India Growth Fund-Dividend Plan	0.1413	0.7964	-0.0068	0.0905
Templeton India Growth Fund-Growth Plan	0.3629	0.1089	0.0819	0.6731
Growth - Public				
Baroda Diversified Fund - Growth	-0.0611	-0.0874	-0.0105	0.4849
Canara Robeco Expo Growth Plan	0.0239	0.1624	-0.0093	0.0652
Canara Robeco Expo Income Plan	0.0171	0.0113	-0.0190	0.2269
LICMF Growth Fund - Dividend Option	0.0558	1.0062	0.0014	0.0274
LICMF Growth Fund - Growth Option	0.1143	0.4760	0.0105	0.0067
SBI Magnum Equity Fund - Growth	0.0187	0.1175	-0.0050	0.0731
SBI Magnum Multiplier Plus Scheme-93-D	0.0538	0.2392	-0.0057	0.1242
SBI MSFU Contra - Dividend	0.0329	0.8410	-0.0033	0.0177
SBI MSFU Contra- Growth	0.0296	0.0307	-0.0027	0.3669
SBI MSFU IT	0.0635	0.3706	-0.0027	0.0652
UTI - Equity Fund-Growth Option	-0.0751	-0.5102	-0.0022	0.0652
UTI - Equity Fund-Income Option	0.0011	0.0007	0.0105	0.1655
ELSS - Private				
Birla Tax Plan 98	0.0045	0.0284	0.0095	0.0730
Escorts Tax Plan Dividend	0.0294	0.0484	0.0067	0.4562
Escorts Tax Plan Growth	0.0224	0.1233	0.0183	0.0881
Franklin Taxshield - Dividend	0.0070	0.0652	-0.0079	0.0717
Franklin India Taxshield - Growth	0.0047	0.0237	0.0039	0.0874
ICICI Prudential Tax Plan-Dividend Option	0.0986	0.1956	0.0023	0.2662

	Treynor Ratio		Benchmark	
	Sensex	Nifty	Sensex	Nifty
ICICI Prudential Tax Plan-Growth Option	0.0643	0.9929	-0.0011	0.0317
Principal Tax Saving fund	-0.6104	-2.5942	0.0095	-0.0008
SaharaTax Gain-Growth	-0.0104	0.0024	0.0267	0.8741
Sundaram PNB Paribas Tax Saver OE Fund	0.0923	0.2220	0.0066	0.4148
Sundaram Taxsaver 98	0.1094	0.2716	-0.0017	0.2241
Tata Tax Saving	0.0091	0.1526	-0.0075	0.0136
Taurus Libra Taxshield 96	0.0474	3.9374	0.0105	0.0064
ELSS - Public				
Bob ELSS 96	0.0345	0.7030	0.0005	0.0314
Canara Robeco Equity Tax Saver	0.0201	0.2683	0.0032	0.0450
LICMF Taxplan-Dividend	-0.2466	-6.0338	0.0167	0.0096
LICMF Taxplan-Growth	0.0778	0.1215	0.0105	0.1547
SBI Magnum Taxgain Scheme 1993 - D	0.0194	0.0282	-0.0053	0.2859
UTI-Master Equity Plan Unit Scheme	-0.0130	-0.0048	0.0105	0.4309

Source: Computed from Secondary data.

A – 8 JENSEN MEASURE

Income - Private	*Sensex*	*Nifty*		
	Alpha	*t-value*	*Alpha*	*t-value*
Birla Sun Life Income Fund - D	-0.0053	-2.010*	-0.0044	-1.384
Birla Sun Life Income Fund - G	0.0921	0.326	0.0034	0.810
DBS Chola Freedom Income -STF-Institutional	-0.0094	-1.904	-0.0084	-1.580
DBS Chola Freedom Income -STF-DD	-0.0063	-2.538**	-0.0056	-1.904
FT India MIP-Growth	-0.0071	-2.783**	-0.0064	-2.087*
FT India MIP-Monthly Bonus	-0.0305	-1.967*	-0.0109	-1.396
HDFC Income Fund - Dividend	-0.0075	-2.881**	-0.0067	-2.134*
HDFC Income Fund - Growth	-0.0057	-2.145*	-0.0048	-1.512
ICICI Prudential Income Plan-Dividend Option	-0.0075	-1.226	-0.0068	-1.059
ICICI Prudential Income Plan-Growth Option	-0.0053	-1.989*	-0.0045	-1.393
ICICI Prudential MIP - Cumulative	-0.0040	-1.597	-0.0029	-0.910
ING Income Fund- Dividend Option	-0.0061	-2.238*	-0.0055	-1.791
ING Income Fund-Growth Option	-0.0055	-2.151*	-0.0048	-1.553
JM Income Fund - Dividend	-0.0081	-2.836**	-0.0074	-2.213*
JM Income Fund - Growth	-0.0047	-1.946	-0.0041	-1.428
Kotak Income Plus - Growth	-0.0068	-2.786**	-0.0062	-2.117*
Kotak Income Plus - Monthly Dividend	-0.0049	-1.977*	-0.0042	-1.437
Reliance Income Fund - Annual Dividend	-0.0052	-2.038*	-0.0047	-1.595
Reliance Income Fund - Growth Plan	0.0045	0.488	0.0061	0.608
Reliance Income Fund Retail Plan Half Yea	-0.0059	-2.384*	-0.0053	-1.838
Sahara Income Fund-Dividend	-0.0061	-2.244*	-0.0055	-1.718
Sahara Income Fund-Growth	-0.0052	-2.124*	-0.0045	-1.527
Sundaram BNP Paribas Income Plus-Appre	-0.0066	-2.706**	-0.0057	-1.961*
Sundaram BNP Paribas Income Plus-D	-0.0067	-2.745**	-0.0061	-2.089*
Tata Income Fund - Monthly	-0.0046	-1.710	-0.0042	-1.385
Tata Income Fund - Qtrly	-0.0074	-2.511**	-0.0072	-2.258*
Tata Income Fund - Semi	-0.0069	-2.085*	-0.0067	-1.841
Templeton India Income Fund - Dividend	-0.0016	-0.092	-0.0040	-0.229
Templeton India Income Fund - Growth	-0.0052	-1.956	-0.0044	-1.409
Income - Public				
BOB Income Fund - Dividend	-0.0053	-2.148*	-0.0046	-1.567
BOB Income Fund -Growth	-0.0053	-2.120*	-0.0045	-1.513
Canara Robeco Income - Bonus	-0.0046	-1.534	-0.0045	-1.452
Canara Robeco Income - Growth	-0.0746	-1.787	-0.0041	-1.402
Canara Robeco Income - Income	-0.0043	-1.261	-0.0037	-0.987

	Sensex		Nifty	
	Alpha	t-value	Alpha	t-value
LIC MF Bond Fund - Dividend	-0.0076	-3.004**	-0.0070	-2.306*
LIC MF Bond Fund - Growth	-0.0052	-2.047*	-0.0045	-1.488
SBI Magnum Monthly Income Fund-Bonus	-0.0064	-2.414*	-0.0063	-2.185*
SBI Magnum Income Fund - Bonus	-0.1501	-2.229*	-0.0052	-1.644
SBI Magnum Income Fund - Dividend	-0.0581	-2.075*	-0.0072	-1.764
SBI Magnum Income Fund - Growth	-0.2039	-1.185	-0.0026	-0.697
UTI Mahila Unit Scheme	-0.0106	-0.105	0.0005	0.089
UTI Monthly Income Scheme - Growth	-0.0067	-1.958	-0.0053	-1.313
UTI Monthly Income Scheme - Income	-0.0262	-1.107	-0.0034	-0.577
Balance - Private				
Birla Balance (D)	-0.0039	-0.947	-0.0019	-0.362
Birla Balance (G)	0.0014	0.326	0.0034	0.810
DSP Merill Lynch Balanced Fund (D)	-0.1044	-0.735	-0.0041	-0.662
DSP Merill Lynch Balanced Fund (G)	0.0702	0.040	0.0012	0.234
Franklin India Balanced Fund (D)	-0.0124	-0.471	0.0010	0.163
Franklin India Balanced Fund (G)	0.1008	0.188	0.0026	0.521
HDFC Balanced Fund - Dividend	-0.0264	-0.903	-0.0040	-0.772
ICICI Prudential Balanced Fund (D)	-0.0256	-1.529	-0.0048	-0.764
ICICI Prudential Balanced Fund (G)	1.2456	0.248	0.0031	0.663
ING Balanced Fund (D)	-1.3684	-0.347	0.0002	0.029
ING Balanced Fund (G)	-0.0026	-0.611	-0.0006	-0.113
J M Balanced Fund (Dividend)	-1.0032	-0.876	-0.0004	-0.089
J M Balanced Fund (Growth)	-0.4147	-0.984	-0.0026	-0.468
Kotak Balance	-1.0012	-0.328	0.0008	0.173
Principal Balanced Fund – Dividend	-0.8048	-0.757	-0.7923	-0.398
Principal Balanced Fund – Growth	-0.3131	-0.587	-0.0035	-0.304
Sundaram Balanced Fund	-0.4849	-1.067	0.4123	0.543
Sundaram BNP Balanced - Appreciation	0.1011	0.320	-0.0017	-0.353
Sundaram BNP Balanced - Dividend	-0.0951	-1.165	0.0023	0.968
Tata Balanced Fund - Dividend	0.6210	0.657	0.6301	0.022
Balance - Public				
Bank of Baroda Balanced - Dividend	-0.0621	-0.531	0.0041	0.968
Bank of Baroda Balanced – Growth	-0.4528	-0.686	0.0001	0.022
LIC Balanced – Plan A - Dividend	-0.9071	-2.007*	-0.0007	-0.137
LIC Balanced – Plan C - Growth	-1.2007	-0.200	-0.0042	-0.889
LIC Unit Linked Insurance Scheme	-1.0095	-2.203*	0.0018	0.132

	Sensex		Nifty	
	Alpha	*t-value*	*Alpha*	*t-value*
SBI Magnum Balanced Fund - Dividend	-0.0918	-0.480	-0.0767	-1.575
UTI Balanced Fund - Dividend	-0.6547	-2.230*	0.4514	0.356
UTI Balanced Fund - Growth	-0.9102	-0.052	-0.9133	-1.893
Growth - Private				
Birla Advantage Fund - Dividend/ Reinvest	-1.2564	-1.166	0.0041	0.881
Birla Index Fund – Growth	1.4417	0.504	-0.0033	-0.546
DBS Chola Growth Fund-Cumulative	-0.9845	-0.345	-0.0041	-0.759
DBS Chola Growth Fund-QuarterlyDividend	-0.4963	-0.956	-0.0035	-0.710
DSP Merrill Lynch Equity Fund - Growth	-1.0049	-0.719	0.0052	0.162
DSP Merrill Lynch Opportunities Fund - G	-1.0002	-0.038	-0.0050	-0.438
Escorts Growth Plan - Dividend	-1.0957	-0.643	1.2165	1.247
Escorts Growth Plan - Growth	0.2137	0.931	0.2553	0.998
HDFC Growth Fund - Growth	0.6552	1.016	0.5831	0.539
ICICI Pru FMCG Plan – Dividend	0.4814	0.279	-0.3615	-0.169
ICICI Prudential Growth Plan-Dividend Option	-0.9543	-0.356	0.4846	0.877
ICICI Prudential Growth Plan-Growth Option	0.6025	0.591	0.5301	0.019
JM Equity Fund - Dividend	-1.0031	-0.644	0.9553	1.005
JM Equity Fund - Growth	2.0825	0.648	1.4178	1.570
Kotak 30 - Growth	1.4851	1.375	-1.3521	-0.189
Reliance Growth Fund - Dividend Plan	-0.6122	-0.479	0.7561	0.608
Reliance Growth Fund - Growth Plan	0.7045	0.488	0.6875	1.410
Reliance Vision Fund - Dividend Plan	2.3048	1.247	-1.4002	-0.318
Sahara Growth Fund-Dividend	-1.0006	-0.091	2.5045	0.899
Sahara Growth Fund-Growth	1.0527	0.539	1.1266	1.156
Sundaram BNP Paribas Capex Oppor Fund-G	2.4043	0.905	2.5066	1.157
Sundaram BNP Paribas Growth Fund-Dividend	2.0643	0.921	1.9648	1.445
Sundaram BNP Paribas Growth Fund-Growth	1.0043	0.905	-0.3843	-1.031
Tata Pure Equity Fund - Dividend	1.0768	1.158	0.8583	1.145
Tata Pure Equity Fund - Growth	-1.9104	-0.936	2.6034	0.641
Taurus Star Share	1.0057	0.911	1.6021	0.456
Templeton India Growth Fund-Dividend Plan	0.4808	0.198	0.9036	0.890
Templeton India Growth Fund-Growth Plan	0.0949	0.938	0.0854	1.090
Growth - Public				
Baroda Diversified Fund - Growth	0.1526	0.838	-0.1106	-0.905
Canara Robeco Expo Growth Plan	0.6429	0.738	0.5637	0.648
Canara Robeco Expo Income Plan	-0.3952	-0.851	-0.4248	-1.558

	Sensex		Nifty	
	Alpha	t-value	Alpha	t-value
LICMF Growth Fund - Dividend Option	1.0211	0.169	1.0811	0.184
LICMF Growth Fund - Growth Option	-1.0056	-2.196*	0.8168	1.242
SBI Magnum Equity Fund - Growth	-1.3011	-0.212	1.2548	0.338
SBI Magnum Multiplier Plus Scheme-93 -D	2.0043	1.002	-1.8456	-0.195
SBI MSFU Contra - Dividend	-0.8109	-0.201	-0.7209	-0.195
SBI MSFU Contra- Growth	-0.4500	-0.233	0.3054	1.092
SBI MSFU IT	-1.0310	-0.233	-0.8956	-0.851
UTI - Equity Fund-Growth Option	1.0030	0.738	-0.4434	-0.578
UTI - Equity Fund-Income Option	-0.0962	-1.105	0.0825	0.483
ELSS - Private				
Birla Tax Plan 98	0.2100	0.699	0.2272	1.055
Escorts Tax Plan Dividend	-0.3601	-1.093	-0.3354	-0.791
Escorts Tax Plan Growth	0.4700	0.719	0.2153	1.036
Franklin Taxshield - Dividend	0.5825	1.201	0.5061	1.407
Franklin India Taxshield - Growth	1.0015	0.505	1.0039	0.930
ICICI Prudential Tax Plan-Dividend Option	-1.4500	-0.793	-1.0034	-0.523
ICICI Prudential Tax Plan-Growth Option	0.0719	0.949	0.0875	1.196
Principal Tax Saving fund	0.0367	1.384	0.0472	1.403
SaharaTax Gain-Growth	-0.5087	-0.531	-0.2015	-0.906
Sundaram PNB Paribas Tax Saver OE Fund	-1.0089	-1.866	-0.3062	-0.972
Sundaram Taxsaver 98	1.0616	0.621	1.0044	0.857
Tata Tax Saving	0.6922	0.339	0.6604	0.537
Taurus Libra Taxshield 96	-0.0024	-0.412	0.0107	0.100
ELSS - Public				
Bob ELSS 96	-0.4837	-0.727	1.2640	-0.006
Canara Robeco Equity Tax Saver	-0.3652	-1.036	-0.2819	-0.303
LICMF Taxplan-Dividend	-0.0983	-1.636	-0.8161	-1.100
LICMF Taxplan-Growth	-0.0816	-0.356	0.0917	0.331
SBI Magnum Taxgain Scheme 1993 - D	0.0450	0.056	0.0411	0.142
UTI-Master Equity Plan Unit Scheme	0.0042	0.979	0.0229	0.706

Note: * and ** indicate 5 and 1 per cent levels of significance respectively.

Source: Computed from Secondary data.

A – 9 SHAPRE DIFFERENTIAL MEASURE

Income - Private	*Sharpe Differential*	
	Sensex	*Nifty*
Birla Sun Life Income Fund - D	-0.0274	-0.0275
Birla Sun Life Income Fund - G	-0.0065	-0.0042
DBS Chola Freedom Income -STF-Institutional	-0.0040	-0.0062
DBS Chola Freedom Income -STF-DD	-0.0076	-0.0042
FT India MIP-Growth	-0.0028	-0.0003
FT India MIP-Monthly Bonus	-0.0145	-0.0140
HDFC Income Fund - Dividend	-0.0383	-0.0314
HDFC Income Fund - Growth	-0.0506	-0.0400
ICICI Prudential Income Plan-Dividend Option	-0.0314	-0.0230
ICICI Prudential Income Plan-Growth Option	-0.0129	-0.0166
ICICI Prudential MIP - Cumulative	-0.0052	-0.0036
ING Income Fund- Dividend Option	-0.0050	-0.0069
ING Income Fund-Growth Option	-0.0120	-0.0107
JM Income Fund - Dividend	-0.0007	-0.0050
JM Income Fund - Growth	-0.0009	-0.0009
Kotak Income Plus - Growth	-0.0136	-0.0100
Kotak Income Plus - Monthly Dividend	-0.0139	-0.0043
Reliance Income Fund - Annual Dividend	-0.0053	-0.0089
Reliance Income Fund - Growth Plan	-0.0246	-0.0010
Reliance Income Fund Retail Plan Half Yea	-0.0140	-0.0067
Sahara Income Fund-Dividend	-0.0067	-0.0035
Sahara Income Fund-Growth	-0.0010	-0.0026
Sundaram BNP Paribas Income Plus-Appre	-0.0085	-0.0121
Sundaram BNP Paribas Income Plus-D	-0.0127	-0.0152
Tata Income Fund - Monthly	-0.0105	-0.0138
Tata Income Fund - Qtrly	-0.0070	-0.0004
Tata Income Fund - Semi	-0.0073	-0.0013
Templeton India Income Fund - Dividend	-0.0792	-0.0726
Templeton India Income Fund - Growth	-0.0148	-0.0153
Income - Public		
BOB Income Fund - Dividend	-0.0019	-0.0019
BOB Income Fund -Growth	-0.0093	-0.0107

	Sharpe Differential	
	Sensex	Nifty
Canara Robeco Income - Bonus	-0.0064	-0.0022
Canara Robeco Income - Growth	-0.0112	-0.0027
Canara Robeco Income - Income	-0.0020	-0.0024
LIC MF Bond Fund - Dividend	-0.0089	-0.0045
LIC MF Bond Fund - Growth	-0.0021	-0.0025
SBI Magnum Monthly Income Fund - Bonus	-0.0245	-0.0346
SBI Magnum Income Fund - Bonus	-0.0218	-0.0282
SBI Magnum Income Fund - Dividend	-0.0062	-0.0016
SBI Magnum Income Fund - Growth	-0.0130	0.0071
UTI Mahila Unit Scheme	-0.0039	-0.0041
UTI Monthly Income Scheme - Growth	-0.0034	-0.0032
UTI Monthly Income Scheme - Income	-0.0020	-0.0026
Balance - Private		
Birla Balance (D)	0.0333	0.0207
Birla Balance (G)	0.0530	0.0430
DSP Merill Lynch Balanced Fund (D)	-0.0106	-0.0034
DSP Merill Lynch Balanced Fund (G)	-0.0246	-0.0230
Franklin India Balanced Fund (D)	0.2135	0.4015
Franklin India Balanced Fund (G)	0.5503	0.5456
HDFC Balanced Fund - Dividend	0.0718	0.0375
ICICI Prudential Balanced Fund (D)	0.0828	0.0883
ICICI Prudential Balanced Fund (G)	0.0884	0.0905
ING Balanced Fund (D)	0.0413	0.0393
ING Balanced Fund (G)	0.0484	0.0262
J M Balanced Fund (Dividend)	0.0385	0.0311
J M Balanced Fund (Growth)	0.0583	0.0608
Kotak Balance	0.0620	0.0500
Principal Balanced Fund – Dividend	-0.0029	-0.0048
Principal Balanced Fund – Growth	0.0808	0.0274
Sundaram Balanced Fund	0.0305	0.0124
Sundaram BNP Balanced - Appreciation	0.0834	0.0552
Sundaram BNP Balanced - Dividend	0.1901	0.1642
Tata Balanced Fund - Dividend	0.0138	0.0044

	Sharpe Differential	
	Sensex	*Nifty*
Balance - Public		
Bank of Baroda Balanced - Dividend	-0.0069	0.0160
Bank of Baroda Balanced – Growth	-0.0160	-0.0126
LIC Balanced – Plan A - Dividend	-0.0087	-0.0061
LIC Balanced – Plan C - Growth	0.0127	-0.0136
LIC Unit Linked Insurance Scheme	-0.0422	-0.0407
SBI Magnum Balanced Fund - Dividend	0.0236	0.0239
UTI Balanced Fund - Dividend	-0.0084	-0.0093
UTI Balanced Fund - Growth	0.0065	0.0076
Growth - Private		
Birla Advantage Fund - Dividend/ Reinvest	0.0373	0.0206
Birla Index Fund – Growth	0.0705	0.0499
DBS Chola Growth Fund-Cumulative	0.0053	0.0044
DBS Chola Growth Fund-Quarterly Dividend	0.0088	0.0063
DSP Merrill Lynch Equity Fund - Growth	0.0441	-0.0011
DSP Merrill Lynch Opportunities Fund - G	-0.0402	-0.0265
Escorts Growth Plan - Dividend	-0.0427	-0.0383
Escorts Growth Plan - Growth	0.0731	0.0734
HDFC Growth Fund - Growth	0.0830	0.0830
ICICI Pru FMCG Plan – Dividend	0.0906	0.0903
ICICI Prudential Growth Plan - Dividend Option	0.0605	0.0537
ICICI Prudential Growth Plan - Growth Option	0.0628	0.0385
JM Equity Fund - Dividend	-0.0226	-0.0226
JM Equity Fund - Growth	0.0127	0.0132
Kotak 30 - Growth	0.0978	0.0833
Reliance Growth Fund - Dividend Plan	-0.0194	-0.0146
Reliance Growth Fund - Growth Plan	0.0826	0.0835
Reliance Vision Fund - Dividend Plan	0.0727	0.0752
Sahara Growth Fund-Dividend	-0.0034	-0.0034
Sahara Growth Fund-Growth	0.0066	0.0069
Sundaram BNP Paribas Capex Oppor Fund-G	0.0930	0.0940
Sundaram BNP Paribas Growth Fund-Dividend	0.0829	0.0842
Sundaram BNP Paribas Growth Fund-Growth	0.1764	0.1780

	Sharpe Differential	
	Sensex	Nifty
Tata Pure Equity Fund - Dividend	-0.0253	-0.0325
Tata Pure Equity Fund - Growth	0.0834	0.0826
Taurus Star Share	-0.0023	-0.0020
Templeton India Growth Fund-Dividend Plan	0.0789	0.0681
Templeton India Growth Fund-Growth Plan	-0.0181	-0.0298
Growth - Public		
Baroda Diversified Fund - Growth	-0.0125	-0.0218
Canara Robeco Expo Growth Plan	0.0315	0.0279
Canara Robeco Expo Income Plan	0.0398	0.0431
LICMF Growth Fund - Dividend Option	0.0245	0.0220
LICMF Growth Fund - Growth Option	-0.0071	-0.0085
SBI Magnum Equity Fund - Growth	0.0198	0.0067
SBI Magnum Multiplier Plus Scheme - 93 -D	0.0432	0.0334
SBI MSFU Contra - Dividend	0.0220	0.0165
SBI MSFU Contra- Growth	0.0167	0.0173
SBI MSFU IT	0.0296	0.0300
UTI - Equity Fund-Growth Option	-0.0284	-0.0307
UTI - Equity Fund-Income Option	-0.0195	-0.0304
ELSS - Private		
Birla Tax Plan 98	-0.0073	-0.0080
Escorts Tax Plan Dividend	0.0148	0.0136
Escorts Tax Plan Growth	-0.0072	-0.0096
Franklin Taxshield - Dividend	0.0156	0.0133
Franklin India Taxshield - Growth	-0.0015	-0.0031
ICICI Prudential Tax Plan-Dividend Option	0.0498	0.0516
ICICI Prudential Tax Plan-Growth Option	0.0326	0.0273
Principal Tax Saving fund	-0.0046	-0.0065
SaharaTax Gain-Growth	-0.0236	-0.0206
Sundaram PNB Paribas Tax Saver OE Fund	0.0835	0.0835
Sundaram Taxsaver 98	0.0648	0.0642
Tata Tax Saving	0.0089	0.0048
Taurus Libra Taxshield 96	0.0145	0.0145

	Sharpe Differential	
	Sensex	*Nifty*
ELSS - Public		
Bob ELSS 96	0.0215	0.0238
Canara Robeco Equity Tax Saver	0.0087	0.0106
LICMF Taxplan-Dividend	-0.0724	-0.0720
LICMF Taxplan-Growth	0.0099	0.0084
SBI Magnum Taxgain Scheme 1993 - D	0.0133	0.0121
UTI-Master Equity Plan Unit Scheme	-0.0104	-0.0112

Source: Computed from Secondary data.

A – 10 FAMA'S BREAKUP

Income - Private	*Impact of Beta*		*Impact of Diversification*		*Impact of Selectivity*	
	Sensex	*Nifty*	*Sensex*	*Nifty*	*Sensex*	*Nifty*
Birla Sun Life Income Fund - D	-0.0007	-0.0003	-0.0024	-0.0027	-0.0274	-0.0275
Birla Sun Life Income Fund - G	0.0006	0.0007	0.0243	0.0219	-0.0065	-0.0042
DBS Chola Freedom Incom -STF-Insti	0.0040	0.0012	0.0280	0.0330	-0.0040	-0.0062
DBS Chola Freedom Income -STF-DD	0.0003	0.0000	0.0249	0.0218	-0.0076	-0.0042
FT India MIP-Growth	0.0008	0.0003	0.0042	0.0022	-0.0028	-0.0003
FT India MIP-Monthly Bonus	0.0010	0.0001	0.0386	0.0389	-0.0145	-0.0140
HDFC Income Fund - Dividend	-0.0023	-0.0008	-0.0585	-0.0669	-0.0383	-0.0314
HDFC Income Fund - Growth	-0.0015	-0.0009	-0.0288	-0.0399	-0.0506	-0.0400
ICICI Prudential Income Plan-Dividend	0.0118	0.0060	0.0420	0.0394	-0.0314	-0.0230
ICICI Prudential Income Plan-Growth	0.0008	0.0009	0.0321	0.0357	-0.0129	-0.0166
ICICI Prudential MIP - Cumulative	0.0065	-0.0001	0.0102	0.0153	-0.0052	-0.0036
ING Income Fund- Dividend Option	0.0000	0.0000	0.0052	0.0070	-0.0050	-0.0069
ING Income Fund-Growth Option	-0.0003	-0.0012	0.0279	0.0275	-0.0120	-0.0107
JM Income Fund - Dividend	0.0003	0.0000	0.0034	0.0079	-0.0007	-0.0050
JM Income Fund - Growth	-0.0006	0.0001	0.0055	0.0048	-0.0009	-0.0009
Kotak Income Plus - Growth	0.0000	0.0000	0.0317	0.0281	-0.0136	-0.0100
Kotak Income Plus - Monthly Dividend	0.0000	0.0000	0.0207	0.0112	-0.0139	-0.0043

	Impact of Beta		Impact of Diversification		Impact of Selectivity	
	Sensex	Nifty	Sensex	Nifty	Sensex	Nifty
Reliance Income Fund - Annual Divid	0.0010	0.0018	0.0358	0.0386	-0.0053	-0.0089
Reliance Income Fund - Growth Plan	0.0275	0.0005	0.0349	0.0383	-0.0246	-0.0010
Reliance In Fund Reta Plan Half Year	-0.0009	0.0000	0.0432	0.0349	-0.0140	-0.0067
Sahara Income Fund-Dividend	-0.0008	-0.0007	0.0160	0.0128	-0.0067	-0.0035
Sahara Income Fund-Growth	0.0001	0.0003	0.0067	0.0080	-0.0010	-0.0026
Sundaram BNP Par Income Plus-Appr	0.0001	0.0002	0.0079	0.0115	-0.0085	-0.0121
Sundaram BNP Parib Income Plus-D	0.0001	0.0001	0.0218	0.0242	-0.0127	-0.0152
Tata Income Fund - Monthly	-0.0007	0.0005	0.0273	0.0294	-0.0105	-0.0138
Tata Income Fund - Qtrly	0.0031	0.0063	0.0232	0.0132	-0.0070	-0.0004
Tata Income Fund - Semi	0.0009	0.0022	0.0206	0.0133	-0.0073	-0.0013
Templeton India Income Fund - Divi	0.0397	-0.0162	-0.0586	-0.0093	-0.0792	-0.0726
Templeton India Income Fund - Grow	-0.0005	0.0011	-0.0807	-0.0818	-0.0148	-0.0153
Income - Public						
BOB Income Fund - Dividend	0.0001	-0.0001	0.0229	0.0231	-0.0019	-0.0019
BOB Income Fund -Growth	-0.0002	-0.0009	0.0405	0.0427	-0.0093	-0.0107
Canara Robeco Income - Bonus	-0.0064	0.0001	0.0530	0.0422	-0.0064	-0.0022
Canara Robeco Income - Growth	-0.0012	0.0004	0.0382	0.0280	-0.0112	-0.0027

	Impact of Beta		Impact of Diversification		Impact of Selectivity	
	Sensex	Nifty	Sensex	Nifty	Sensex	Nifty
Canara Robeco Income - Income	-0.0146	-0.0095	0.0517	0.0471	-0.0020	-0.0024
LIC MF Bond Fund - Dividend	-0.0001	-0.0001	-0.0111	-0.0155	-0.0089	-0.0045
LIC MF Bond Fund - Growth	0.0000	0.0000	-0.0016	-0.0012	-0.0021	-0.0025
SBI Magnum Month Inc Fund - Bonus	-0.0061	-0.0112	-0.0567	-0.0415	-0.0245	-0.0346
SBI Magnum Income Fund - Bonus	0.0014	0.0027	-0.0650	-0.0600	-0.0218	-0.0282
SBI Magnum Income Fund - Dividend	0.0080	0.0052	-0.0965	-0.0983	-0.0062	-0.0016
SBI Magnum Income Fund - Growth	-0.0023	0.0051	-0.0787	-0.1061	-0.0130	0.0071
UTI Mahila Unit Scheme	0.0028	0.0000	0.0208	0.0238	-0.0039	-0.0041
UTI Monthly Income Scheme - Growth	0.0013	-0.0006	0.0073	0.0090	-0.0034	-0.0032
UTI Monthly Income Scheme - Income	0.0016	-0.0027	0.0088	0.0137	-0.0020	-0.0026
Balance - Private						
Birla Balance (D)	-0.0238	-0.0001	-0.0668	-0.0779	0.0333	0.0207
Birla Balance (G)	-0.0213	-0.0017	-0.0630	-0.0727	0.0530	0.0430
DSP Merill Lynch Balanced Fund (D)	-0.0041	-0.0043	-0.0275	-0.0345	-0.0106	-0.0034
DSP Merill Lynch Balanced Fund (G)	-0.0120	-0.0041	-0.0414	-0.0508	-0.0246	-0.0230
Franklin India Balanced Fund (D)	-0.2459	-0.1156	-0.6164	-0.9347	0.2135	0.4015
Franklin India Balanced Fund (G)	-0.0699	-0.0840	-0.8774	-0.8586	0.5503	0.5456

	Impact of Beta		*Impact of Diversification*		*Impact of Selectivity*	
	Sensex	*Nifty*	*Sensex*	*Nifty*	*Sensex*	*Nifty*
HDFC Balanced Fund - Dividend	0.0007	0.0020	0.0096	0.0426	0.0718	0.0375
ICICI Prudential Balanced Fund (D)	0.0008	-0.0002	0.0014	-0.0031	0.0828	0.0883
ICICI Prudential Balanced Fund (G)	-0.0024	-0.0004	-0.0139	-0.0181	0.0884	0.0905
ING Balanced Fund (D)	0.0001	0.0003	0.0008	0.0025	0.0413	0.0393
ING Balanced Fund (G)	0.0006	0.0005	0.0031	0.0254	0.0484	0.0262
J M Balanced Fund (Dividend)	-0.0185	-0.0025	-0.0446	-0.0532	0.0385	0.0311
J M Balanced Fund (Growth)	-0.0148	-0.0002	-0.0302	-0.0473	0.0583	0.0608
Kotak Balance	0.0000	0.0000	0.0000	0.0121	0.0620	0.0500
Principal Balanced Fund – Dividend	-0.0134	-0.0015	-0.0500	-0.0599	-0.0029	-0.0048
Principal Balanced Fund – Growth	-0.0212	-0.0026	-0.0456	-0.0108	0.0808	0.0274
Sundaram Balanced Fund	-0.0300	-0.0024	-0.0390	-0.0485	0.0305	0.0124
Sundaram BNP Balanced - Apprecia	-0.0255	-0.0071	-0.0399	-0.0302	0.0834	0.0552
Sundaram BNP Balanced - Dividend	-0.0297	0.0022	-0.0383	-0.0443	0.1901	0.1642
Tata Balanced Fund - Dividend	-0.0030	0.0003	-0.0037	0.0024	0.0138	0.0044
Balance - Public						
Bank of Baroda Balanced - Dividend	0.0123	0.0005	0.0167	0.0056	-0.0069	0.0160
Bank of Baroda Balanced – Growth	0.0081	0.0010	0.0200	0.0236	-0.0160	-0.0126
LIC Balanced – Plan A - Dividend	0.0047	0.0005	0.0047	0.0063	-0.0087	-0.0061

	Impact of Beta		*Impact of Diversification*		*Impact of Selectivity*	
	Sensex	*Nifty*	*Sensex*	*Nifty*	*Sensex*	*Nifty*
Growth - Public						
Baroda Diversified Fund - Growth	-0.0073	-0.0050	-0.0226	-0.0156	-0.0125	-0.0218
Canara Robeco Expo Growth Plan	-0.0041	-0.0005	-0.0168	-0.0168	0.0315	0.0279
Canara Robeco Expo Income Plan	-0.0029	-0.0043	-0.0343	-0.0362	0.0398	0.0431
LICMF Growth Fund – Dividen Option	0.0007	0.0001	0.0024	0.0056	0.0245	0.0220
LICMF Growth Fund - Growth Option	0.0003	0.0001	0.0100	0.0116	-0.0071	-0.0085
SBI Magnum Equity Fund - Growth	-0.0023	0.0001	-0.0089	0.0018	0.0198	0.0067
SBI Magnum Multipli Plus Sch - 93 -D	-0.0032	-0.0002	-0.0104	-0.0035	0.0432	0.0334
SBI MSFU Contra - Dividend	-0.0015	0.0000	-0.0056	-0.0016	0.0220	0.0165
SBI MSFU Contra- Growth	-0.0010	-0.0010	-0.0044	-0.0050	0.0167	0.0173
SBI MSFU IT	-0.0010	-0.0002	-0.0044	-0.0056	0.0296	0.0300
UTI - Equity Fund-Growth Option	-0.0010	-0.0001	-0.0039	-0.0025	-0.0284	-0.0307
UTI - Equity Fund-Income Option	0.0010	0.0022	0.0186	0.0283	-0.0195	-0.0304
ELSS - Private						
Birla Tax Plan 98	0.0044	0.0008	0.0049	0.0092	-0.0073	-0.0080
Escorts Tax Plan Dividend	0.0050	0.0036	0.0023	0.0050	0.0148	0.0136
Escorts Tax Plan Growth	0.0088	0.0020	0.0092	0.0185	-0.0072	-0.0096
Franklin Taxshield - Dividend	-0.0053	-0.0005	-0.0056	-0.0081	0.0156	0.0133

	Impact of Beta		Impact of Diversification		Impact of Selectivity	
	Sensex	Nifty	Sensex	Nifty	Sensex	Nifty
Franklin India Taxshield - Growth	0.0017	0.0005	0.0019	0.0047	-0.0015	-0.0031
ICICI Prudential Tax Plan-Div Option	0.0012	0.0001	0.0011	0.0004	0.0498	0.0516
ICICI Prudential Tax Plan-Gr Option	-0.0005	0.0001	-0.0006	0.0040	0.0326	0.0273
Principal Tax Saving fund	0.0000	0.0000	0.0067	0.0086	-0.0046	-0.0065
SaharaTax Gain-Growth	-0.0053	0.0210	0.0310	0.0017	-0.0236	-0.0206
Sundaram Tax Saver OE Fund	0.0066	0.0027	0.0020	0.0058	0.0835	0.0835
Sundaram Taxsaver 98	-0.0010	-0.0004	-0.0030	-0.0029	0.0648	0.0642
Tata Tax Saving	-0.0017	0.0000	-0.0051	-0.0026	0.0089	0.0048
Taurus Libra Taxshield 96	0.0056	0.0001	0.0051	0.0107	0.0145	0.0145
ELSS - Public						
Bob ELSS 96	0.0003	0.0000	0.0002	-0.0017	0.0215	0.0238
Canara Robeco Equity Tax Saver	0.0019	0.0001	0.0015	0.0014	0.0087	0.0106
LICMF Taxplan-Dividend	0.0039	0.0002	0.0106	0.0139	-0.0724	-0.0720
LICMF Taxplan-Growth	0.0025	0.0019	0.0064	0.0085	0.0099	0.0084
SBI Magnum Taxgain Sche 1993 - D	-0.0022	-0.0013	-0.0030	-0.0028	0.0133	0.0121
UTI-Master Eq Plan Unit Scheme	0.0017	0.0044	0.0067	0.0047	-0.0104	-0.0112

Source: Computed from Secondary data.

A – 11 TREYNOR AND MAZUY'S MARKET TIMING

Income - Private	*Sensex*		*Nifty*	
	Y	*t-value*	*Y*	*t-value*
Birla Sun Life Income Fund - D	3.7459	4.704**	3.8304	3.953**
Birla Sun Life Income Fund - G	2.6177	2.383*	4.0571	3.053**
DBS Chola Freedom Income -STF-Institutional	4.0973	2.426*	4.1862	2.407*
DBS Chola Freedom Income -STF-DD	3.3971	4.421**	3.4665	3.826**
FT India MIP-Growth	3.6094	4.621**	3.6546	3.921**
FT India MIP-Monthly Bonus	3.6614	4.798**	3.7283	4.067**
HDFC Income Fund - Dividend	3.5611	4.439**	3.5838	3.708**
HDFC Income Fund - Growth	3.7099	4.633**	3.7649	3.888**
ICICI Prudential Income Plan-Dividend Option	3.7382	1.749	3.6485	1.702
ICICI Prudential Income Plan-Growth Option	3.7471	4.579**	3.7446	3.790**
ICICI Prudential MIP - Cumulative	3.4668	4.569**	3.9193	4.102**
ING Income Fund- Dividend Option	3.6376	4.497**	3.4308	3.606**
ING Income Fund-Growth Option	3.6038	4.547**	3.6282	3.855**
JM Income Fund - Dividend	3.3998	3.674**	3.5749	3.430**
JM Income Fund - Growth	3.3786	4.496**	3.4553	3.932**
Kotak Income Plus - Growth	3.4329	4.555**	3.5091	3.948**
Kotak Income Plus - Monthly Dividend	3.4204	4.529**	3.4996	3.932**

	Sensex		Nifty	
	Y	t-value	Y	t-value
Reliance Income Fund - Annual Dividend	3.4832	4.361**	2.6395	2.738**
Reliance Income Fund - Growth Plan	10.7579	3.580**	12.5460	4.138**
Reliance Income Fund Retail Plan Half Yea	3.3282	4.307**	3.2456	3.627**
Sahara Income Fund-Dividend	3.6285	4.251**	3.7032	3.790**
Sahara Income Fund-Growth	3.1579	4.077**	3.3089	3.646**
Sundaram BNP Paribas Income Plus-Appre	3.2768	4.333**	3.6845	4.147**
Sundaram BNP Paribas Income Plus-D	3.4660	4.618**	3.5350	3.991**
Tata Income Fund - Monthly	4.1069	4.121**	3.6711	3.952**
Tata Income Fund - Qtrly	5.0616	6.262**	4.4599	4.789**
Tata Income Fund - Semi	3.9064	3.651**	3.4014	2.933**
Templeton India Income Fund - Dividend	9.6323	1.579	5.0933	0.853
Templeton India Income Fund - Growth	3.7429	4.583**	3.7205	3.739**
Income - Public				
BOB Income Fund - Dividend	3.4007	4.432**	3.5612	3.952**
BOB Income Fund -Growth	3.4236	4.479**	3.7942	4.273**
Canara Robeco Income - Bonus	4.2626	4.708**	3.2875	3.343**
Canara Robeco Income - Growth	3.4664	4.313**	3.4186	3.767**
Canara Robeco Income - Income	3.8637	3.417**	2.7655	2.244*

	Sensex		*Nifty*	
	Y	*t-value*	*Y*	*t-value*
LIC MF Bond Fund - Dividend	3.4482	4.371**	3.3601	3.582**
LIC MF Bond Fund - Growth	3.5982	4.621**	3.5843	3.852**
SBI Magnum Monthly Income Fund - Bonus	3.5887	4.374**	2.4510	2.601**
SBI Magnum Income Fund - Bonus	3.6378	4.318**	3.5866	3.640**
SBI Magnum Income Fund - Dividend	0.3558	0.254	-0.0717	-0.051
SBI Magnum Income Fund - Growth	3.1697	2.891**	3.3143	2.700**
UTI Mahila Unit Scheme	3.7898	1.914	3.7919	1.873
UTI Monthly Income Scheme - Growth	3.3578	2.922**	3.7053	2.853**
UTI Monthly Income Scheme - Income	0.1023	0.051	0.7383	0.365
Balance - Private				
Birla Balance (D)	4.5516	3.396**	5.9360	3.755**
Birla Balance (G)	2.6177	2.383*	4.0572	3.053**
DSP Merill Lynch Balanced Fund (D)	5.1097	2.496*	5.9143	2.953**
DSP Merill Lynch Balanced Fund (G)	4.4719	2.787**	5.2822	3.191**
Franklin India Balanced Fund (D)	3.7968	2.167*	4.2056	2.037*
Franklin India Balanced Fund (G)	4.9974	3.584**	5.7626	3.719**
HDFC Balanced Fund - Dividend	3.7617	2.225*	3.8529	2.235*
ICICI Prudential Balanced Fund (D)	2.0502	1.140	5.1682	2.516**

	Sensex		Nifty	
	Y	*t-value*	*Y*	*t-value*
ICICI Prudential Balanced Fund (G)	3.8373	3.397**	5.5295	3.941**
ING Balanced Fund (D)	3.3450	1.934	4.6359	2.500**
ING Balanced Fund (G)	3.7248	2.616**	4.7596	2.930**
J M Balanced Fund (Dividend)	2.9393	2.364*	4.3966	2.876**
J M Balanced Fund (Growth)	3.7024	2.252*	4.3647	2.425**
Kotak Balance	3.8269	3.077**	5.5492	3.944**
Principal Balanced Fund – Dividend	5.6957	2.655**	4.5225	1.997*
Principal Balanced Fund – Growth	4.7508	2.638**	3.2362	1.670
Sundaram Balanced Fund	1.2074	0.737	3.7024	2.023*
Sundaram BNP Balanced - Appreciation	4.6145	4.059**	5.3779	4.160**
Sundaram BNP Balanced - Dividend	0.9107	0.581	3.4611	1.931
Tata Balanced Fund - Dividend	3.8473	3.763**	5.0979	3.892**
Balance - Public				
Bank of Baroda Balanced - Dividend	3.8463	2.831**	4.8777	3.115**
Bank of Baroda Balanced – Growth	4.9063	3.753**	5.8592	3.804**
LIC Balanced – Plan A - Dividend	3.2246	2.703**	5.4936	3.663**
LIC Balanced – Plan C - Growth	3.6681	3.115**	4.8854	3.352**
LIC Unit Linked Insurance Scheme	3.6637	2.487*	3.7864	2.270*

	Sensex		Nifty	
	Y	*t-value*	*Y*	*t-value*
LICMF Growth Fund - Dividend Option	3.8181	1.771	6.5533	3.736**
LICMF Growth Fund - Growth Option	4.4433	2.937**	3.6358	3.802**
SBI Magnum Equity Fund - Growth	3.4831	4.359**	5.1154	2.606**
SBI Magnum Multiplier Plus Scheme - 93 -D	5.0805	3.078**	5.7970	3.338**
SBI MSFU Contra - Dividend	4.2529	2.935**	5.0201	2.712**
SBI MSFU Contra- Growth	2.5534	1.535	6.4117	4.800**
SBI MSFU IT	5.4308	3.925**	6.4340	4.532**
UTI - Equity Fund-Growth Option	2.5967	1.879	3.7125	2.254*
UTI - Equity Fund-Income Option	0.1188	0.059	0.7274	0.359
ELSS - Private				
Birla Tax Plan 98	5.5635	2.919**	9.7609	4.939**
Escorts Tax Plan Dividend	0.7713	0.322	-0.6781	-0.288
Escorts Tax Plan Growth	3.8314	2.805**	5.2527	3.192**
Franklin Taxshield - Dividend	1.9271	2.718**	5.4214	4.137**
Franklin India Taxshield - Growth	3.2956	3.288**	4.7323	3.615**
ICICI Prudential Tax Plan-Dividend Option	4.9400	2.449*	3.8566	1.742
ICICI Prudential Tax Plan-Growth Option	4.3219	2.449*	6.3713	3.184**
Principal Tax Saving fund	3.6087	2.157*	3.2304	1.884

	Sensex		Nifty	
	Y	t-value	Y	t-value
SaharaTax Gain-Growth	1.2798	0.218	0.3153	0.056
Sundaram PNB Paribas Tax Saver OE Fund	1.3043	0.768	2.8579	1.328
Sundaram Taxsaver 98	2.7409	4.526**	6.5078	4.207**
Tata Tax Saving	5.5132	2.454*	5.4757	2.347*
Taurus Libra Taxshield 96	5.5391	2.856*	8.1946	3.853**
ELSS - Public				
Bob ELSS 96	3.5669	2.036*	6.7187	3.328**
Canara Robeco Equity Tax Saver	1.8984	1.065	5.2053	2.517**
LICMF Taxplan-Dividend	3.1981	1.811	2.8086	1.487
LICMF Taxplan-Growth	0.9576	0.605	3.6339	2.154*
SBI Magnum Taxgain Scheme 1993 - D	5.2881	2.166*	6.3187	2.611**
UTI-Master Equity Plan Unit Scheme	4.5558	3.217**	2.5746	1.927

Note: * and ** indicate 5 and 1 per cent levels of significance respectively.

Source: Computed from Secondary data.

A – 12 OVERALL PERFORMANCE RANKING - I

Income - Private	*IRR*	*AR_p*	*SD_p*	*Sharpe*	*Treynor-Sensex*	*Treynor-Nifty*	*Sharpe Dif-Sensex*	*Sharp Differ-Nifty*	*Jensen Sensex*	*Jensen Sensex*
Birla Sun Life Income Fund - D	71	97	4	128	116	114	121	118	55	79
Birla Sun Life Income Fund - G	72	73	20	47	8	37	82	83	33	45
DBS Chola Freedom Income -STF-Instit	124	41	59	44	19	26	75	90	77	110
DBS Chola Freedom Income -STF-DD	116	52	7	17	2	3	90	84	64	97
FT India MIP-Growth	123	113	2	35	26	51	70	61	71	102
FT India MIP-Monthly Bonus	115	62	50	49	6	5	108	107	83	111
HDFC Income Fund - Dividend	106	114	85	123	125	127	124	123	73	103
HDFC Income Fund - Growth	99	68	60	122	123	123	128	127	60	88
ICICI Prudential Income Plan-Dividend	73	63	57	55	31	60	123	115	74	105
ICICI Prudential Income Plan-Growth	70	67	23	46	9	28	103	111	56	81
ICICI Prudential MIP - Cumulative	80	92	6	14	38	122	78	81	45	64
ING Income Fund- Dividend Option	111	120	12	99	103	19	77	93	62	95
ING Income Fund-Growth Option	105	79	10	32	124	107	100	101	59	89
JM Income Fund - Dividend	108	107	9	77	42	14	61	88	76	109
JM Income Fund - Growth	101	105	1	4	113	13	62	63	49	72
Kotak Income Plus - Growth	87	44	81	64	130	128	105	99	69	100
Kotak Income Plus - Monthly Dividend	98	56	69	82	129	118	106	85	50	76

	IRR	AR_p	SD_p	Sharpe	Treynor-Sensex	Treynor-Nifty	Sharpe Dif-Sensex	Sharp Differ-Nifty	Jensen Sensex	Jensen Sensex
Reliance Income Fund - Annual Divid	68	53	28	30	7	34	79	96	51	87
Reliance Income Fund - Growth Plan	61	45	108	56	46	9	119	64	38	41
Reliance Income Fund Retail Plan Half Yea	67	55	26	34	120	129	107	92	61	93
Sahara Income Fund-Dividend	97	103	5	20	115	105	83	80	63	96
Sahara Income Fund-Growth	103	109	3	21	4	36	63	73	52	82
Sundaram BNP Pa Income Plus-Apprec	62	54	19	102	95	93	92	103	66	98
Sundaram BNP Paribas Income Plus-Di	66	43	17	65	5	10	102	109	67	99
Tata Income Fund - Monthly	57	81	25	58	114	27	97	106	47	77
Tata Income Fund - Qtrly	76	69	8	13	14	61	85	62	72	107
Tata Income Fund - Semi	86	86	11	37	11	54	89	66	70	104
Templeton India Income Fund - Dividend	96	118	38	127	24	104	130	130	41	70
Templeton India Income Fund - Growth	92	110	62	125	128	6	109	110	53	80
INCOME - PUBLIC										
BOB Income Fund - D	125	34	18	39	3	126	65	68	57	86
BOB Income Fund -Growth	117	29	55	41	127	113	95	100	58	83
Canara Robeco Income Bonus	113	37	33	25	108	4	81	70	48	84
Canara Robeco Income – Growth	102	50	64	51	118	11	99	75	86	73
Canara Robeco Income – Income	114	42	13	5	105	99	66	71	46	69

	IRR	AR_p	SD_p	Sharpe	Treynor-Sensex	Treynor-Nifty	Sharpe Dif-Sensex	Sharp Differ-Nifty	Jensen Sensex	Jensen Sensex
LIC MF Bond Fund – Dividend	122	117	63	110	119	120	94	86	75	106
LIC MF Bond Fund – Growth	75	74	54	104	106	112	68	72	54	85
SBI Magnum Monthly Income - Bonus	119	91	44	126	117	106	117	125	65	101
SBI Magnum Income Fund – Bonus	100	84	107	117	1	15	114	119	93	92
SBI Magnum Income Fund – D	107	106	109	120	12	20	80	67	84	108
SBI Magnum Income Fund – G	74	104	76	124	122	18	104	54	94	62
UTI Mahila Unit Scheme	89	77	82	62	25	1	74	82	78	54
UTI Monthly Income Scheme – D	121	116	15	79	57	97	73	77	68	94
UTI Monthly Income Scheme – G	112	108	51	80	50	94	67	74	81	66
BALANCED - PRIVATE										
Birla Balance (D)	58	65	30	121	104	130	36	40	44	61
Birla Balance (G)	63	35	52	112	102	110	27	26	40	46
DSP M L Balanced Fund (D)	43	26	87	113	110	101	98	79	92	74
DSP M L Balanced Fund (G)	16	57	105	116	111	111	118	116	35	51
Franklin India Balanced Fund (D)	25	31	70	130	121	121	2	2	79	52
Franklin India Balanced Fund (G)	18	1	67	129	126	119	1	1	31	48
HDFC Balanced Fund	52	14	111	28	10	29	20	29	82	71
ICICI Prudential Balanced Fund (D)	82	10	110	24	32	25	14	8	80	90

	IRR	AR_p	SD_p	Sharpe	Treynor-Sensex	Treynor-Nifty	Sharpe Dif-Sensex	Sharp Differ-Nifty	Jensen Sensex	Jensen Sensex
ICICI Prudential Balanced Fund (G)	32	18	122	40	27	22	8	6	8	47
ING Balanced Portfolio (D)	34	36	41	26	15	52	32	27	128	55
ING Balanced Portfolio (G)	44	32	40	18	30	24	29	36	43	58
J M Balanced Fund (Dividend)	83	48	71	111	98	102	34	31	118	57
J M Balanced Fund (Growth)	77	20	65	68	64	7	26	19	99	63
Kotak Balance	48	23	96	27	23	2	24	23	116	53
Principal Balanced Fund – Dividend	56	90	92	118	109	117	71	87	108	123
Principal Balanced Fund – Growth	19	5	73	70	62	78	16	34	95	67
Sundaram Balanced Fund	20	40	68	114	100	109	39	49	103	28
Sundaram BNP Balanced – Appre	23	4	27	54	59	72	11	20	30	60
Sundaram BNP Balanced – Div	27	2	61	1	17	116	3	4	89	49
Tata Balanced Fund	17	82	21	76	80	77	50	59	21	21
BALANCE - PUBLIC										
B of B Balanced – D	118	61	45	53	58	49	84	44	85	43
Bank of Baroda Balanced – Growth	85	78	39	67	69	58	110	104	101	56
LIC Balanced – Plan A – Dividend	120	121	32	96	88	85	93	89	110	59
LIC Balanced – Plan C – Growth	93	76	29	57	65	45	53	105	125	78
LIC Unit Linked Insurance Scheme	104	127	42	115	101	100	126	128	122	50

	IRR	AR_p	SD_p	Sharpe	Treynor-Sensex	Treynor-Nifty	Sharpe Dif-Sensex	Sharp Differ-Nifty	Jensen Sensex	Jensen Sensex
SBI Magnum Balanced Fund – Dividend	69	59	43	52	66	63	42	37	88	112
UTI Balanced Fund – Dividend	109	122	14	101	90	91	91	97	107	27
UTI Balanced Fund – Growth	110	102	16	63	72	76	59	53	111	126
GROWTH - PRIVATE										
Birla Advant Fund – D/ Rein	39	38	91	38	53	12	35	41	126	44
Birla Index Fund – Growth	41	22	36	6	40	44	21	24	7	65
DBS Chola Growth Fund-Cumula	26	100	102	90	84	88	60	60	113	75
DBS Chola Growth Fund-Quarterly D	21	70	99	74	35	40	56	57	104	68
DSP Merrill Lynch Equity Fund	31	39	103	50	45	73	30	65	119	42
DSP Merrill Lynch Opportunities Fund	14	30	72	22	20	21	125	117	114	91
Escorts Growth Plan – Dividend	59	129	115	107	96	96	127	126	124	9
Escorts Growth Plan – Growth	45	21	112	31	36	23	18	16	27	30
HDFC Growth Fund	36	15	74	9	18	53	12	13	19	22
ICICI Pru FMCG Plan – Dividend	6	11	77	10	28	42	7	7	24	118
ICICI Prudential Growth Plan – D	11	24	113	43	51	67	25	21	112	26
ICICI Prudential Growth Plan – G	7	28	56	19	47	48	23	28	22	24
JM Equity Fund – Dividend	84	125	80	108	94	108	115	114	117	14

	IRR	AR_p	SD_p	Sharpe	Treynor-Sensex	Treynor-Nifty	Sharpe Dif-Sensex	Sharp Differ-Nifty	Jensen Sensex	Jensen Sensex
JM Equity Fund – Growth	79	94	48	78	82	70	52	48	3	6
Kotak 30 – Growth	30	6	37	3	29	17	5	12	6	128
Reliance Growth Fund – Dividend Plan	8	46	66	42	54	66	112	108	106	18
Reliance Growth Fund – Growth Plan	3	12	114	29	22	125	15	10	17	19
Reliance Vision Fund – Dividend Plan	5	19	46	7	41	39	19	15	2	129
Sahara Growth Fund-Dividend	33	111	100	94	74	87	72	78	115	3
Sahara Growth Fund-Growth	37	101	88	83	76	75	58	55	11	10
Sundaram Capex Opportun Fund-G	4	7	79	11	34	41	6	5	1	2
Sundaram Growth Fund-D	2	13	78	15	39	46	13	9	4	4
Sundaram Growth Fund-Gr	1	3	130	36	21	32	4	3	14	119
Tata Pure Equity Fund – Dividend	9	25	95	23	33	16	120	124	9	16
Tata Pure Equity Fund – Growth	12	9	35	2	13	50	10	14	130	1
Taurus Star Share	91	119	101	105	93	98	69	69	13	5
Templeton India Growth Fund-D	13	17	53	8	37	35	17	17	25	15
Templeton India Growth Fund-G	22	15	84	16	16	74	111	120	32	35
GROWTH - PUBLIC										
Baroda Diversified Fund	126	128	116	109	97	95	101	113	29	113

	IRR	AR_p	SD_p	Sharpe	Treynor-Sensex	Treynor-Nifty	Sharpe Dif-Sensex	Sharp Differ-Nifty	Jensen Sensex	Jensen Sensex
Canara Robeco Expo Growth Plan	46	71	117	86	73	64	38	33	20	23
Canara Robeco Expo Income Plan	65	96	128	95	81	86	33	25	98	120
LICMF Growth Fund – Dividend Option	55	58	124	71	60	30	41	39	12	11
LICMF Growth Fund – Growth Option	95	112	31	87	43	43	86	95	120	17
SBI Magnum Equity Fund	53	80	126	88	79	71	45	56	127	8
SBI Magnum Multiplier Plus – 93 –Di	47	47	123	69	61	57	31	30	5	130
SBI MSFU Contra – Dividend	64	66	125	84	68	33	43	43	109	122
SBI MSFU Contra- Growth	81	72	120	97	70	81	46	42	100	29
SBI MSFU IT	90	51	121	73	56	47	40	32	123	125
UTI – Equity Fund-Growth Option	94	126	118	106	99	103	122	122	15	121
UTI – Equity Fund-Income Option	127	115	127	100	89	90	113	121	90	36
ELSS - PRIVATE										
Birla Tax Plan 98	42	88	90	92	87	82	88	94	28	31
Escorts Tax Plan Dividend	50	64	104	66	71	80	48	46	96	117
Escorts Tax Plan Growth	40	95	49	72	75	68	87	98	26	32
Franklin Taxshield – Dividend	60	93	22	81	85	79	47	47	23	25
Franklin India Taxshield – Growth	51	99	24	89	86	84	64	76	16	13

	IRR	AR_p	SD_p	Sharpe	Treynor-Sensex	Treynor-Nifty	Sharpe Dif-Sensex	Sharp Differ-Nifty	Jensen Sensex	Jensen Sensex
ICICI Prudential Tax Plan-D	24	33	94	33	48	62	28	22	129	127
ICICI Prudential Tax Plan-G	29	49	83	48	55	31	37	35	34	34
Principal Tax Saving fund	54	89	34	91	112	115	76	91	37	37
SaharaTax Gain-Growth	129	123	129	98	91	89	116	112	105	114
Sundaram Tax Saver OE Fund	15	8	97	12	49	59	9	11	121	116
Sundaram Taxsaver 98	35	27	119	45	44	55	22	18	10	12
Tata Tax Saving	10	98	98	93	83	65	55	58	18	20
Taurus Libra Taxshield	38	75	93	59	63	8	49	45	42	40
ELSS - PUBLIC										
Bob ELSS 96	88	60	89	61	67	38	44	38	102	7
Canara Robeco Equity Tax Saver	78	85	86	75	77	56	57	51	97	115
LICMF Taxplan-Dividend	128	130	75	119	107	124	129	129	91	124
LICMF Taxplan-Growth	130	87	58	60	52	69	54	52	87	33
SBI Taxgain Scheme 1993 - Divi	49	83	106	85	78	83	51	50	36	38
UTI-Master Equity Plan Unit Scheme	28	124	47	103	92	92	96	102	39	39

Source: Computed from Appendix Tables.

A – 12 OVERALL PERFORMANCE RANKING - II

Income - Private	Fama beta Sensex	Fama beta Nifty	Fama Div-Sensex	Fama Div-Nifty	Fama Sel-Sensex	Fama Sel-Nifty	Timing Sensex	Timing Nifty	Total	Average
Birla Sun Life Income Fund - D	77	95	84	90	121	118	56	68	1612	**89.56**
Birla Sun Life Income Fund - G	49	35	21	28	82	83	108	62	968	**53.78**
DBS Chola Freedom Income -STF-Instit	19	28	17	15	75	90	39	60	1008	**56.00**
DBS Chola Freedom Income -STF-DD	52	65	20	29	90	84	89	97	1058	**58.78**
FT India MIP-Growth	44	49	54	70	70	61	69	84	1155	**64.17**
FT India MIP-Monthly Bonus	38	54	9	10	108	107	65	75	1162	**64.56**
HDFC Income Fund - Dividend	95	104	121	123	124	123	75	91	1803	**100.13**
HDFC Income Fund - Growth	88	105	109	114	128	127	60	72	1801	**100.06**
ICICI Prudential Income Plan-Dividend	7	6	7	8	123	115	58	85	1165	**64.72**
ICICI Prudential Income Plan-Growth	43	32	14	13	103	111	55	74	1039	**57.72**
ICICI Prudential MIP - Cumulative	13	87	33	33	78	81	79	64	1088	**60.44**
ING Income Fund- Dividend Option	64	72	49	53	77	93	67	100	1366	**75.89**
ING Income Fund-Growth Option	71	109	18	22	100	101	71	88	1386	**77.00**
JM Income Fund - Dividend	55	68	56	51	61	88	88	92	1250	**69.44**
JM Income Fund - Growth	75	56	47	61	62	63	90	99	1136	**63.11**

	Fama beta Sensex	Fama beta Nifty	Fama Div-Sensex	Fama Div-Nifty	Fama Sel-Sensex	Fama Sel-Nifty	Timing Sensex	Timing Nifty	Total	Average
Kotak Income Plus - Growth	62	76	15	20	105	99	83	95	1462	**81.22**
Kotak Income Plus - Monthly Dividend	63	78	26	43	106	85	85	96	1451	**80.61**
Reliance Income Fund - Annual Divid	39	26	11	11	79	96	76	115	986	**54.78**
Reliance Income Fund - Growth Plan	3	40	12	12	119	64	1	2	840	**46.67**
Reliance Income Fund Retail Plan Half Yea	81	79	6	14	107	92	95	109	1367	**75.94**
Sahara Income Fund-Dividend	80	103	31	38	83	80	68	80	1330	**73.89**
Sahara Income Fund-Growth	59	50	43	50	63	73	101	107	1092	**60.67**
Sundaram BNP Pa Income Plus-Apprec	57	53	38	42	92	103	97	82	1348	**74.89**
Sundaram BNP Paribas Income Plus-Di	58	59	24	24	102	109	81	94	1134	**63.00**
Tata Income Fund - Monthly	78	41	19	18	97	106	38	83	1169	**64.94**
Tata Income Fund - Qtrly	22	5	22	37	85	62	14	54	868	**48.22**
Tata Income Fund - Semi	40	16	27	36	89	66	42	103	1033	**57.39**
Templeton India Income Fund - Dividend	1	128	122	101	130	130	3	42	1535	**85.28**
Templeton India Income Fund - Growth	73	29	127	126	109	110	57	76	1582	**87.89**
INCOME - PUBLIC										
BOB Income Fund - D	56	85	23	27	65	68	87	93	1125	**62.50**
BOB Income Fund -Growth	69	107	8	5	95	100	84	69	1355	**75.28**

	Fama beta Sensex	Fama beta Nifty	Fama Div-Sensex	Fama Div-Nifty	Fama Sel-Sensex	Fama Sel-Nifty	Timing Sensex	Timing Nifty	Total	Average
Canara Robeco Income Bonus	116	55	4	7	81	70	33	108	1077	**59.83**
Canara Robeco Income – Growth	87	43	10	21	99	75	80	102	1246	**69.22**
Canara Robeco Income – Income	120	126	5	3	66	71	43	114	1178	**65.44**
LIC MF Bond Fund – Dividend	68	83	104	106	94	86	82	105	1740	**96.67**
LIC MF Bond Fund – Growth	65	73	81	82	68	72	72	90	1407	**78.17**
SBI Magnum Monthly Income - Bonus	115	127	120	115	117	125	73	118	1921	**106.72**
SBI Magnum Income Fund – Bonus	33	12	124	122	114	119	66	89	1521	**84.50**
SBI Magnum Income Fund – D	11	7	128	127	80	67	128	129	1490	**82.78**
SBI Magnum Income Fund – G	97	8	126	128	104	54	100	106	1555	**86.39**
UTI Mahila Unit Scheme	23	71	25	25	74	82	53	70	1047	**58.17**
UTI Monthly Income Scheme – D	34	102	40	46	73	77	92	79	1340	**74.44**
UTI Monthly Income Scheme – G	30	120	37	35	67	74	130	124	1400	**77.78**
BALANCED - PRIVATE										
Birla Balance (D)	125	86	125	125	36	40	28	17	1271	**70.61**
Birla Balance (G)	124	113	123	124	27	26	109	61	1320	**73.33**
DSP M L Balanced Fund (D)	104	123	108	111	98	79	12	19	1477	**82.06**
DSP M L Balanced Fund (G)	118	121	116	119	118	116	29	35	1608	**89.33**

	Fama beta Sensex	Fama beta Nifty	Fama Div-Sensex	Fama Div-Nifty	Fama Sel-Sensex	Fama Sel-Nifty	Timing Sensex	Timing Nifty	Total	Average
Franklin India Balanced Fund (D)	130	130	129	130	2	2	52	58	1266	**70.33**
Franklin India Balanced Fund (G)	129	129	130	129	1	1	17	23	1100	**61.11**
HDFC Balanced Fund	45	22	35	6	20	29	54	67	724	**40.22**
ICICI Prudential Balanced Fund (D)	42	89	66	93	14	8	116	39	942	**52.33**
ICICI Prudential Balanced Fund (G)	99	97	105	109	8	6	48	26	828	**46.00**
ING Balanced Portfolio (D)	60	48	68	67	32	27	93	52	893	**49.61**
ING Balanced Portfolio (G)	50	42	58	23	29	36	59	50	701	**38.94**
J M Balanced Fund (Dividend)	122	118	117	120	34	31	104	56	1455	**80.83**
J M Balanced Fund (Growth)	121	90	110	117	26	19	61	57	1109	**61.61**
Kotak Balance	61	69	72	40	24	23	50	25	799	**44.39**
Principal Balanced Fund – Dividend	119	112	119	121	71	87	4	53	1657	**92.06**
Principal Balanced Fund – Growth	123	119	118	105	16	34	22	110	1166	**64.78**
Sundaram Balanced Fund	128	117	114	118	39	49	123	81	1439	**79.94**
Sundaram BNP Balanced – Appre	126	125	115	110	11	20	24	32	923	**51.28**
Sundaram BNP Balanced – Div	127	17	113	116	3	4	125	98	972	**54.00**
Tata Balanced Fund	101	47	88	69	50	59	46	41	1005	**55.83**

	Fama beta Sensex	Fama beta Nifty	Fama Div-Sensex	Fama Div-Nifty	Fama Sel-Sensex	Fama Sel-Nifty	Timing Sensex	Timing Nifty	Total	Average
BALANCE - PUBLIC										
B of B Balanced – D	6	39	30	58	84	44	47	48	996	**55.33**
Bank of Baroda Balanced – Growth	10	30	28	26	110	104	20	20	1115	**61.94**
LIC Balanced – Plan A – Dividend	16	37	53	56	93	89	98	27	1362	**75.67**
LIC Balanced – Plan C – Growth	32	36	55	16	53	105	62	47	1132	**62.89**
LIC Unit Linked Insurance Scheme	21	34	45	54	126	128	64	71	1558	**86.56**
SBI Magnum Balanced Fund – Dividend	79	92	77	86	42	37	103	18	1165	**64.72**
UTI Balanced Fund – Dividend	25	14	48	55	91	97	37	119	1335	**74.17**
UTI Balanced Fund – Growth	31	44	63	72	59	53	25	34	1169	**64.94**
GROWTH - PRIVATE										
Birla Advant Fund – D/ Rein	24	46	61	30	35	41	114	49	917	**50.94**
Birla Index Fund – Growth	84	21	79	32	21	24	41	46	654	**36.33**
DBS Chola Growth Fund-Cumula	76	91	75	79	60	60	21	120	1380	**76.67**
DBS Chola Growth Fund-Quarterly D	47	51	46	49	56	57	78	73	1081	**60.06**
DSP Merrill Lynch Equity Fund	90	3	89	17	30	65	91	117	1099	**61.06**
DSP Merrill Lynch Opportunities Fund	8	13	1	2	125	117	8	29	929	**51.61**
Escorts Growth Plan – Dividend	17	31	57	68	127	126	36	31	1481	**82.28**

	Fama beta Sensex	Fama beta Nifty	Fama Div-Sensex	Fama Div-Nifty	Fama Sel-Sensex	Fama Sel-Nifty	Timing Sensex	Timing Nifty	Total	Average
Escorts Growth Plan – Growth	72	80	78	83	18	16	106	55	867	48.17
HDFC Growth Fund	67	88	76	80	12	13	105	122	834	46.33
ICICI Pru FMCG Plan – Dividend	106	111	91	99	7	7	44	16	811	45.06
ICICI Prudential Growth Plan – D	96	27	80	71	25	21	119	123	1055	58.61
ICICI Prudential Growth Plan – G	107	20	94	39	23	28	31	45	689	38.28
JM Equity Fund – Dividend	41	66	69	75	115	114	112	43	1594	88.56
JM Equity Fund – Growth	93	96	83	95	52	48	40	21	1088	60.44
Kotak 30 – Growth	108	77	103	81	5	12	45	24	728	40.44
Reliance Growth Fund – Dividend Plan	4	4	13	9	112	108	26	65	967	53.72
Reliance Growth Fund – Growth Plan	70	70	73	84	15	10	2	1	691	38.39
Reliance Vision Fund – Dividend Plan	92	99	82	97	19	15	23	15	764	42.44
Sahara Growth Fund-Dividend	48	25	52	66	72	78	35	101	1244	69.11
Sahara Growth Fund-Growth	54	67	70	77	58	55	127	121	1223	67.94
Sundaram Capex Opportun Fund-G	113	114	96	103	6	5	15	7	649	36.06
Sundaram Growth Fund-D	111	116	97	104	13	9	11	11	695	38.61
Sundaram Growth Fund-Gr	114	115	111	113	4	3	16	8	847	47.06
Tata Pure Equity Fund – Dividend	2	18	3	1	120	124	102	63	903	50.17

	Fama beta Sensex	Fama beta Nifty	Fama Div-Sensex	Fama Div-Nifty	Fama Sel-Sensex	Fama Sel-Nifty	Timing Sensex	Timing Nifty	Total	Average
Tata Pure Equity Fund – Growth	35	15	39	52	10	14	115	128	684	**38.00**
Taurus Star Share	112	106	95	102	69	69	63	36	1415	**78.61**
Templeton India Growth Fund-D	103	45	87	65	17	17	94	59	724	**40.22**
Templeton India Growth Fund-G	5	1	2	4	111	120	18	127	914	**50.78**
GROWTH - PUBLIC										
Baroda Diversified Fund	117	124	107	107	101	113	120	33	1849	**102.72**
Canara Robeco Expo Growth Plan	105	101	106	108	38	33	86	77	1225	**68.06**
Canara Robeco Expo Income Plan	100	122	112	112	33	25	110	104	1545	**85.83**
LICMF Growth Fund – Dividend Option	46	62	59	59	41	39	51	6	864	**48.00**
LICMF Growth Fund – Growth Option	53	60	34	41	86	95	30	86	1214	**67.44**
SBI Magnum Equity Fund	98	63	101	73	45	56	77	40	1286	**71.44**
SBI Magnum Multiplier Plus – 93 –Di	102	93	102	94	31	30	13	22	1087	**60.39**
SBI MSFU Contra – Dividend	89	75	99	85	43	43	34	44	1269	**70.50**
SBI MSFU Contra- Growth	85	108	92	96	46	42	113	12	1332	**74.00**
SBI MSFU IT	86	94	93	98	40	32	9	10	1220	**67.78**
UTI – Equity Fund-Growth Option	83	84	90	88	122	122	111	78	1804	**100.22**
UTI – Equity Fund-Income Option	37	19	29	19	113	121	129	125	1600	**88.89**

	Fama beta Sensex	Fama beta Nifty	Fama Div-Sensex	Fama Div-Nifty	Fama Sel-Sensex	Fama Sel-Nifty	Timing Sensex	Timing Nifty	Total	Average
ELSS - PRIVATE										
Birla Tax Plan 98	18	33	51	45	88	94	5	3	1059	**58.83**
Escorts Tax Plan Dividend	15	10	60	60	48	46	126	130	1237	**68.72**
Escorts Tax Plan Growth	9	23	36	31	87	98	49	37	1012	**56.22**
Franklin Taxshield – Dividend	109	100	100	100	47	47	117	30	1212	**67.33**
Franklin India Taxshield – Growth	28	38	64	62	64	76	96	51	1081	**60.06**
ICICI Prudential Tax Plan-D	36	58	67	78	28	22	19	66	974	**54.11**
ICICI Prudential Tax Plan-G	74	57	74	64	37	35	32	13	821	**45.61**
Principal Tax Saving fund	66	74	41	47	76	91	70	111	1312	**72.89**
SaharaTax Gain-Growth	110	2	16	74	116	112	122	126	1784	**99.11**
Sundaram Tax Saver OE Fund	12	11	62	57	9	11	121	112	892	**49.56**
Sundaram Taxsaver 98	82	98	86	92	22	18	107	9	901	**50.06**
Tata Tax Saving	91	82	98	89	55	58	7	28	1106	**61.44**
Taurus Libra Taxshield	14	61	50	44	49	45	6	4	785	**43.61**
ELSS - PUBLIC										
Bob ELSS 96	51	81	71	87	44	38	74	5	1045	**58.06**
Canara Robeco Equity Tax Saver	27	64	65	76	57	51	118	38	1273	**70.72**

	Fama beta Sensex	Fama beta Nifty	Fama Div- Sensex	Fama Div- Nifty	Fama Sel- Sensex	Fama Sel- Nifty	Timing Sensex	Timing Nifty	Total	Average
LICMF Taxplan-Dividend	20	52	32	34	129	129	99	113	1764	**98.00**
LICMF Taxplan-Growth	26	24	44	48	54	52	124	87	1141	**63.39**
SBI Taxgain Scheme 1993 - Divi	94	110	85	91	51	50	10	14	1164	**64.67**
UTI-Master Equity Plan Unit Scheme	29	9	42	63	96	102	27	116	1246	**69.22**

Source: Computed from Appendix Tables.

A – 13 KOLMOGOROV-SMIRNOV STATISTIC, 2003-2008

Income - Private	*K-S Statistic*	*p-value*
Birla Sun Life Income Fund - D	0.165	0.000
Birla Sun Life Income Fund - G	0.147	0.003
DBS Chola Freedom Income -STF-Institutional	0.511	0.000
DBS Chola Freedom Income -STF-DD	0.084	0.000
FT India MIP-Growth	0.154	0.001
FT India MIP-Monthly Bonus	0.153	0.002
HDFC Income Fund - Dividend	0.098	0.000
HDFC Income Fund - Growth	0.132	0.012
ICICI Prudential Income Plan-Dividend Option	0.389	0.000
ICICI Prudential Income Plan-Growth Option	0.148	0.002
ICICI Prudential MIP - Cumulative	0.117	0.044
ING Income Fund- Dividend Option	0.206	0.000
ING Income Fund-Growth Option	0.182	0.000
JM Income Fund - Dividend	0.485	0.000
JM Income Fund - Growth	0.142	0.005
Kotak Income Plus - Growth	0.339	0.000
Kotak Income Plus - Monthly Dividend	0.119	0.038
Reliance Income Fund - Annual Dividend Plan	0.202	0.000
Reliance Income Fund - Growth Plan	0.149	0.000
Reliance Income Fund Retail Plan Half Yearly	0.267	0.002
Sahara Income Fund-Dividend	0.234	0.000
Sahara Income Fund-Growth	0.291	0.000
Sundaram BNP Paribas Income Plus-Appreciation	0.306	0.000
Sundaram BNP Paribas Income Plus-Dividend	0.243	0.000
Tata Income Fund - Monthly	0.293	0.000
Tata Income Fund - Qtrly	0.287	0.000
Tata Income Fund - Semi	0.443	0.000
Templeton India Income Fund - Dividend	0.183	0.000
Templeton India Income Fund - Growth	0.227	0.000
Income - Public		
BOB Income Fund - Dividend	0.218	0.000
BOB Income Fund -Growth	0.312	0.000
Canara Robeco Income - Bonus	0.280	0.000

Income - Private	*K-S Statistic*	*p-value*
Canara Robeco Income - Growth	0.325	0.000
Canara Robeco Income - Income	0.155	0.000
LIC MF Bond Fund - Dividend	0.127	0.010
LIC MF Bond Fund - Growth	0.242	0.019
SBI Magnum Monthly Income Fund - Bonus	0.238	0.000
SBI Magnum Income Fund - Bonus	0.375	0.000
SBI Magnum Income Fund - Dividend	0.293	0.000
SBI Magnum Income Fund - Growth	0.297	0.000
UTI Mahila Unit Scheme	0.302	0.000
UTI Monthly Income Scheme - Growth	0.389	0.000
UTI Monthly Income Scheme - Income	0.200	0.000
Balance - Private		
Birla Balance (D)	0.147	0.000
Birla Balance (G)	0.175	0.003
DSP Merill Lynch Balanced Fund (D)	0.180	0.000
DSP Merill Lynch Balanced Fund (G)	0.236	0.000
Franklin India Balanced Fund (D)	0.204	0.000
Franklin India Balanced Fund (G)	0.185	0.000
HDFC Balanced Fund - Dividend	0.207	0.000
ICICI Prudential Balanced Fund (D)	0.152	0.000
ICICI Prudential Balanced Fund (G)	0.212	0.002
ING Balanced Fund (D)	0.219	0.000
ING Balanced Fund (G)	0.216	0.000
J M Balanced Fund (Dividend)	0.266	0.000
J M Balanced Fund (Growth)	0.151	0.000
Kotak Balance	0.259	0.002
Principal Balanced Fund – Dividend	0.235	0.000
Principal Balanced Fund – Growth	0.179	0.000
Sundaram Balanced Fund	0.136	0.000
Sundaram BNP Balanced - Appreciation	0.195	0.008
Sundaram BNP Balanced - Dividend	0.185	0.000
Tata Balanced Fund - Dividend	0.202	0.000

Income - Private	*K-S Statistic*	*p-value*
Balance - Public		
Bank of Baroda Balanced - Dividend	0.185	0.000
Bank of Baroda Balanced – Growth	0.159	0.000
LIC Balanced – Plan A - Dividend	0.173	0.010
LIC Balanced – Plan C - Growth	0.186	0.000
LIC Unit Linked Insurance Scheme	0.147	0.000
SBI Magnum Balanced Fund - Dividend	0.180	0.003
UTI Balanced Fund - Dividend	0.164	0.000
UTI Balanced Fund - Growth	0.224	0.000
Growth - Private		
Birla Advantage Fund - Dividend/ Reinvestment	0.156	0.001
Birla Index Fund – Growth	0.293	0.000
DBS Chola Growth Fund-Cumulative	0.460	0.000
DBS Chola Growth Fund-Quarterly Dividend	0.150	0.002
DSP Merrill Lynch Equity Fund - Growth	0.181	0.000
DSP Merrill Lynch Opportunities Fund - Growth	0.216	0.000
Escorts Growth Plan - Dividend	0.188	0.000
Escorts Growth Plan - Growth	0.199	0.000
HDFC Growth Fund - Growth	0.137	0.007
ICICI Pru FMCG Plan – Dividend	0.244	0.000
ICICI Prudential Growth Plan - Dividend Option	0.151	0.002
ICICI Prudential Growth Plan - Growth Option	0.223	0.000
JM Equity Fund - Dividend	0.206	0.000
JM Equity Fund - Growth	0.214	0.000
Kotak 30 - Growth	0.164	0.000
Reliance Growth Fund - Dividend Plan	0.240	0.000
Reliance Growth Fund - Growth Plan	0.161	0.001
Reliance Vision Fund - Dividend Plan	0.224	0.000
Sahara Growth Fund-Dividend	0.133	0.000
Sahara Growth Fund-Growth	0.175	0.000
Sundaram BNP Paribas Capex Opport Fund-Growth	0.171	0.000
Sundaram BNP Paribas Growth Fund-Dividend	0.172	0.000

Income - Private	K-S Statistic	p-value
Sundaram BNP Paribas Growth Fund-Growth	0.226	0.000
Tata Pure Equity Fund - Dividend	0.245	0.000
Tata Pure Equity Fund - Growth	0.164	0.000
Taurus Star Share	0.200	0.000
Templeton India Growth Fund-Dividend Plan	0.180	0.000
Templeton India Growth Fund-Growth Plan	0.154	0.001
Growth - Public		
Baroda Diversified Fund - Growth	0.115	0.050
Canara Robeco Expo Growth Plan	0.134	0.010
Canara Robeco Expo Income Plan	0.148	0.003
LICMF Growth Fund - Dividend Option	0.110	0.034
LICMF Growth Fund - Growth Option	0.167	0.000
SBI Magnum Equity Fund - Growth	0.177	0.000
SBI Magnum Multiplier Plus Scheme-93-Dividend	0.182	0.000
SBI MSFU Contra - Dividend	0.198	0.000
SBI MSFU Contra- Growth	0.198	0.000
SBI MSFU IT	0.115	0.050
UTI - Equity Fund-Growth Option	0.389	0.000
UTI - Equity Fund-Income Option	0.201	0.000
ELSS - Private		
Birla Tax Plan 98	0.242	0.000
Escorts Tax Plan Dividend	0.170	0.000
Escorts Tax Plan Growth	0.158	0.001
Franklin Taxshield - Dividend	0.141	0.005
Franklin India Taxshield - Growth	0.160	0.001
ICICI Prudential Tax Plan-Dividend Option	0.101	0.000
ICICI Prudential Tax Plan-Growth Option	0.107	0.048
Principal Tax Saving fund	0.341	0.000
SaharaTax Gain-Growth	0.103	0.006
Sundaram PNB Paribas Tax Saver OE Fund	0.138	0.007

Income - Private	*K-S Statistic*	*p-value*
Sundaram Taxsaver 98	0.209	0.000
Tata Tax Saving	0.142	0.004
Taurus Libra Taxshield 96	0.249	0.000
ELSS - Public		
Bob ELSS 96	0.150	0.002
Canara Robeco Equity Tax Saver	0.182	0.000
LICMF Taxplan-Dividend	0.127	0.019
LICMF Taxplan-Growth	0.177	0.000
SBI Magnum Taxgain Scheme 1993 - Dividend	0.139	0.006
UTI-Master Equity Plan Unit Scheme	0.331	0.003
Index		
Sensex	0.100	0.000
Nifty	0.112	0.041

Source: Computed from secondary data.

A – 14 KURTOSIS

Income - Private	*2003-04*	*2004-05*	*2005-06*	*2006-07*	*2007-08*	*2003-08*
Birla Sun Life Income Fund - D	-1.18	-0.04	-0.85	0.24	0.76	**6.50**
Birla Sun Life Income Fund - G	-0.93	4.72	0.79	3.35	1.58	**2.60**
DBS Chola Freedom Income -STF-Instit	10.98	-0.77	-0.98	0.26	10.11	**58.86**
DBS Chola Freedom Income -STF-DD	3.84	-0.36	-0.36	-0.53	1.60	**-0.11**
FT India MIP-Growth	3.04	-0.92	-0.49	-0.66	2.55	**6.04**
FT India MIP-Monthly Bonus	0.63	-1.06	1.15	-0.56	1.87	**4.85**
HDFC Income Fund - Dividend	0.32	0.25	-1.49	-0.06	4.54	**0.92**
HDFC Income Fund - Growth	-0.37	-1.24	4.85	0.42	0.49	**2.45**
ICICI Prudential Income Plan-Dividend	4.98	-0.90	1.11	-0.02	0.45	**28.23**
ICICI Prudential Income Plan-Growth	0.20	-1.09	2.43	-0.75	0.15	**3.81**
ICICI Prudential MIP - Cumulative	-0.60	2.13	2.50	5.97	-0.14	**2.45**
ING Income Fund- Dividend Option	6.87	1.52	2.10	7.64	1.74	**5.46**
ING Income Fund-Growth Option	-1.36	0.21	0.43	-0.51	2.40	**8.39**
JM Income Fund - Dividend	1.16	11.89	7.63	9.23	9.13	**58.39**
JM Income Fund - Growth	2.00	-2.05	2.53	-1.60	0.53	**1.09**
Kotak Income Plus - Growth	10.89	5.18	-0.11	-0.23	1.83	**24.24**
Kotak Income Plus - Monthly Dividend	5.95	-1.15	4.49	0.63	-0.02	**0.05**
Reliance Income Fund - Annual Divid	0.86	9.24	3.87	1.23	-1.06	**16.18**
Reliance Income Fund - Growth Plan	4.27	4.70	-1.26	2.44	1.65	**16.93**
Reliance Income Fund Retail Plan Half Yea	-0.60	3.68	5.78	0.35	2.74	**4.62**
Sahara Income Fund-Dividend	4.51	-1.16	3.46	9.82	11.67	**33.66**
Sahara Income Fund-Growth	5.87	-1.17	3.48	9.59	10.06	**19.78**
Sundaram BNP Pa Income Plus-Apprec	7.48	4.67	2.92	1.40	-0.05	**13.55**
Sundaram BNP Paribas Income Plus-Di	10.75	-1.34	1.40	1.90	2.41	**37.31**
Tata Income Fund - Monthly	-0.13	-1.01	11.14	0.37	0.78	**28.92**
Tata Income Fund - Qtrly	4.42	1.45	10.55	-0.44	-0.19	**16.77**
Tata Income Fund - Semi	5.27	1.10	8.91	2.93	0.19	**23.06**

	2003-04	2004-05	2005-06	2006-07	2007-08	2003-08
Templeton India Income Fund - Dividend	0.23	1.63	-1.54	5.50	-0.09	**28.93**
Templeton India Income Fund - Growth	-0.80	-0.14	0.27	-0.52	0.34	**5.68**
INCOME - PUBLIC						
BOB Income Fund - D	5.57	0.83	-0.93	-0.35	3.74	**21.46**
BOB Income Fund -Growth	4.97	11.07	0.96	0.07	2.02	**23.01**
Canara Robeco Income Bonus	-0.08	5.16	10.42	-1.14	-0.90	**16.33**
Canara Robeco Income – Growth	-0.48	1.05	10.47	1.88	4.99	**27.98**
Canara Robeco Income – Income	4.95	2.68	7.33	1.91	5.49	**6.91**
LIC MF Bond Fund – Dividend	-0.24	1.55	0.33	6.53	-0.40	**1.34**
LIC MF Bond Fund – Growth	-0.46	-0.86	3.51	2.46	-0.02	**0.87**
SBI Magnum Monthly Income -Bonus	1.80	10.68	10.61	3.56	-0.89	**19.25**
SBI Magnum Income Fund – Bonus	9.91	-0.86	0.09	0.20	2.33	**28.03**
SBI Magnum Income Fund – D	10.56	0.14	5.67	6.22	0.66	**54.67**
SBI Magnum Income Fund – G	4.77	1.90	-1.57	1.05	-0.61	**25.59**
UTI Mahila Unit Scheme	4.96	1.85	3.55	7.17	0.52	**24.46**
UTI Monthly Income Scheme – D	4.95	5.31	1.50	2.45	-0.68	**14.31**
UTI Monthly Income Scheme – G	10.95	5.49	1.56	2.44	-0.66	**18.03**
BALANCED - PRIVATE						
Birla Balance (D)	1.52	5.31	9.80	3.31	1.73	**5.99**
Birla Balance (G)	-0.93	4.72	0.79	3.35	1.58	**2.60**
DSP M L Balanced Fund (D)	0.57	0.53	5.01	0.60	0.12	**4.43**
DSP M L Balanced Fund (G)	-0.19	1.22	0.82	4.15	-0.13	**1.42**
Franklin India Balanced Fund (D)	-0.43	6.70	-0.64	1.98	1.15	**5.06**
Franklin India Balanced Fund (G)	-1.12	6.53	-0.67	3.94	10.85	**12.90**
HDFC Balanced Fund	0.22	2.32	-0.03	1.45	-1.26	**3.64**
ICICI Prudential Balanced Fund (D)	0.99	5.21	1.12	1.24	6.67	**6.75**
ICICI Prudential Balanced Fund (G)	-1.03	5.14	3.49	3.69	0.09	**2.31**

	2003-04	2004-05	2005-06	2006-07	2007-08	2003-08
ING Balanced Portfolio (D)	-1.14	2.43	10.00	5.72	1.40	**11.27**
ING Balanced Portfolio (G)	-1.14	6.00	9.59	3.92	0.80	**11.41**
J M Balanced Fund (Dividend)	-1.17	4.52	7.14	2.65	2.41	**5.00**
J M Balanced Fund (Growth)	2.81	4.55	-0.89	2.64	2.42	**9.65**
Kotak Balance	0.69	4.62	0.58	2.20	0.44	**1.48**
Principal Balanced Fund – Dividend	9.28	5.78	2.03	4.74	0.96	**7.75**
Principal Balanced Fund – Growth	-0.83	11.18	0.03	1.03	-0.78	**13.66**
Sundaram Balanced Fund	-0.56	1.08	2.72	3.30	-0.35	**3.06**
Sundaram BNP Balanced – Appre	-0.33	1.12	-0.41	3.30	-0.06	**0.48**
Sundaram BNP Balanced – Div	2.55	1.08	2.72	3.30	-0.35	**4.18**
Tata Balanced Fund	-1.24	6.09	0.05	4.18	1.04	**2.70**
BALANCE - PUBLIC						
B of B Balanced – D	2.17	4.03	0.97	3.61	2.12	**3.73**
Bank of Baroda Balanced – Growth	-0.33	3.89	0.95	3.63	2.09	**2.25**
LIC Balanced – Plan A – Dividend	-0.81	8.38	1.07	-1.12	0.97	**1.39**
LIC Balanced – Plan C – Growth	-0.82	8.55	0.85	3.09	1.00	**3.13**
LIC Unit Linked Insurance Scheme	0.81	7.99	3.73	0.53	0.64	**1.52**
SBI Magnum Balanced Fund–Dividend	0.84	0.30	3.64	2.54	0.70	**0.44**
UTI Balanced Fund – Dividend	-0.49	7.81	9.59	-0.31	-0.33	**7.98**
UTI Balanced Fund – Growth	0.45	0.25	2.19	2.17	0.49	**2.26**
GROWTH - PRIVATE						
Birla Advant Fund – D/ Rein	4.51	5.91	1.62	2.67	2.99	**5.73**
Birla Index Fund – Growth	-1.22	5.69	1.09	4.14	0.41	**2.11**
DBS Chola Growth Fund-Cumula	0.77	9.47	-0.17	2.13	1.14	**24.05**
DBS Chola Growth Fund-Quarterly D	4.72	-0.81	-0.93	0.30	8.91	**28.00**
DSP Merrill Lynch Equity Fund	1.45	0.21	0.63	0.66	6.15	**2.36**
DSP Merrill Lynch Opportunities Fund	-0.55	1.39	0.35	2.06	0.92	**0.77**
Escorts Growth Plan – Dividend	7.78	4.43	8.69	-0.07	0.13	**6.93**
Escorts Growth Plan – Growth	-1.17	3.41	0.54	2.43	3.06	**2.19**

	2003-04	2004-05	2005-06	2006-07	2007-08	2003-08
HDFC Growth Fund	-1.23	4.98	10.28	4.68	0.79	**4.70**
ICICI Pru FMCG Plan – Dividend	-0.80	2.64	2.91	0.41	0.66	**3.03**
ICICI Prudential Growth Plan – D	4.71	1.24	2.48	2.23	-0.32	**15.00**
ICICI Prudential Growth Plan – G	-0.27	5.49	2.93	4.82	0.09	**2.55**
JM Equity Fund – Dividend	-0.75	6.54	9.56	-1.16	2.27	**4.85**
JM Equity Fund – Growth	-0.95	5.47	-0.87	2.02	2.27	**3.24**
Kotak 30 – Growth	-1.23	5.43	-0.30	2.63	0.47	**2.42**
Reliance Growth Fund – Dividend Plan	-0.60	0.40	3.78	1.46	0.16	**0.67**
Reliance Growth Fund – Growth Plan	4.27	4.70	-1.26	2.44	1.65	**16.93**
Reliance Vision Fund – Dividend Plan	0.83	5.16	0.92	4.52	0.29	**2.65**
Sahara Growth Fund-Dividend	2.44	1.24	5.72	1.13	1.13	**2.84**
Sahara Growth Fund-Growth	8.46	1.78	0.62	5.75	0.92	**16.10**
Sundaram Capex Opportun Fund-G	-0.79	1.44	0.79	4.03	1.80	**1.71**
Sundaram Growth Fund-D	-0.79	1.52	0.79	4.03	1.93	**1.75**
Sundaram Growth Fund-Gr	-0.79	1.44	0.79	4.03	1.80	**1.71**
Tata Pure Equity Fund – Dividend	3.70	6.78	-0.40	5.23	0.96	**9.27**
Tata Pure Equity Fund – Growth	4.40	6.41	1.15	3.14	9.13	**24.47**
Taurus Star Share	-0.43	-0.20	3.57	2.49	1.38	**3.88**
Templeton India Growth Fund-D	-0.21	3.85	5.15	3.77	1.63	**2.33**
Templeton India Growth Fund-G	0.01	3.08	-0.19	3.83	0.63	**3.68**
GROWTH - PUBLIC						
Baroda Diversified Fund	0.84	3.04	1.72	4.23	1.63	**3.33**
Canara Robeco Expo Growth Plan	-1.64	0.08	0.14	2.36	0.24	**0.90**
Canara Robeco Expo Income Plan	-0.44	-0.22	1.65	2.17	2.13	**1.15**
LICMF Growth Fund–Dividend Option	-0.90	6.60	3.06	4.79	0.92	**2.98**
LICMF Growth Fund–Growth Option	-0.12	1.74	-1.16	-1.06	1.48	**2.22**
SBI Magnum Equity Fund	-0.86	5.13	2.52	0.53	-0.88	**0.87**
SBI Magnum Multiplier Plus–93–Di	4.17	4.63	0.09	2.26	2.60	**1.81**
SBI MSFU Contra–Dividend	1.27	3.51	0.57	2.48	-0.20	**1.81**

	2003-04	2004-05	2005-06	2006-07	2007-08	2003-08
SBI MSFU Contra- Growth	0.00	1.79	-0.48	2.53	5.72	**5.03**
SBI MSFU IT	0.00	1.79	-0.48	2.53	5.72	**5.03**
UTI – Equity Fund-Growth Option	-1.64	0.08	0.14	2.36	0.24	**0.90**
UTI – Equity Fund-Income Option	10.95	5.49	1.21	2.32	-0.61	**18.03**
ELSS - PRIVATE						
Birla Tax Plan 98	1.12	6.73	2.71	2.16	1.11	**3.27**
Escorts Tax Plan Dividend	-1.54	6.91	8.33	-0.04	-0.43	**9.31**
Escorts Tax Plan Growth	-1.32	5.84	0.55	6.60	3.29	**3.56**
Franklin Taxshield – Dividend	0.08	2.46	0.59	0.46	0.52	**1.36**
Franklin India Taxshield – Growth	1.01	2.70	0.13	3.69	0.29	**1.81**
ICICI Prudential Tax Plan-D	1.57	0.57	-0.02	0.91	1.74	**1.45**
ICICI Prudential Tax Plan-G	1.04	4.38	2.25	0.64	0.12	**0.74**
Principal Tax Saving fund	-1.26	-0.12	0.09	2.28	-0.80	**1.50**
SaharaTax Gain-Growth	8.25	4.61	11.85	4.00	1.96	**44.70**
Sundaram Tax Saver OE Fund	-0.66	0.10	3.24	-1.27	1.43	**1.68**
Sundaram Taxsaver 98	0.03	1.68	1.07	4.21	1.18	**1.32**
Tata Tax Saving	-0.49	6.22	7.35	4.28	1.47	**4.07**
Taurus Libra Taxshield	-0.34	1.65	-1.01	3.03	0.46	**0.41**
ELSS - PUBLIC						
Bob ELSS 96	-0.22	3.74	8.06	5.81	-0.60	**9.48**
Canara Robeco Equity Tax Saver	-0.64	1.35	3.61	-0.53	1.96	**1.83**
LICMF Taxplan-Dividend	-0.12	3.40	8.21	1.25	-0.70	**1.54**
LICMF Taxplan-Growth	-0.43	3.57	1.05	10.28	-0.10	**2.10**
SBI Taxgain Scheme 1993 - Divi	-0.26	2.05	1.29	0.34	1.31	**2.34**
UTI-Master Equity Plan Unit Scheme	0.49	1.02	-0.96	1.45	-0.81	**1.51**
Index Sensex -	**1.285**	**4.385**	**1.518**	**1.914**	**0.36**	**1.107**
Nifty	**-0.850**	**3.086**	**4.382**	**0.283**	**1.032**	**1.560**

Source: Computed.

A – 15 INVESTMENT AND NAV OF SAMPLE SCHEMES IN 2007-08

Income - Private	*Investment (Rs. Lakhs)*	*NAV(Rs.)*
Birla Sun Life Income Fund - D	1078.6	34.6618
Birla Sun Life Income Fund - G	16743.6	31.2700
DBS Chola Freedom Income -STF-Institutional	15319.5	12.8429
DBS Chola Freedom Income -STF-DD	36926.3	11.0160
FT India MIP-Growth	28696.3	10.4956
FT India MIP-Monthly Bonus	174.0	24.5659
HDFC Income Fund - Dividend	12299.1	10.6819
HDFC Income Fund - Growth	16487.0	18.3582
ICICI Prudential Income Plan-Dividend Option	4379.7	11.1137
ICICI Prudential Income Plan-Growth Option	16009.9	24.0498
ICICI Prudential MIP - Cumulative	23561.3	20.8879
ING Income Fund- Dividend Option	66.6	11.4764
ING Income Fund-Growth Option	271.7	20.1693
JM Income Fund - Dividend	807.8	10.5248
JM Income Fund - Growth	1271.2	21.9744
Kotak Income Plus - Growth	1327.5	10.0387
Kotak Income Plus - Monthly Dividend	632.4	15.8873
Reliance Income Fund - Annual Dividend Plan	652.3	13.7830
Reliance Income Fund - Growth Plan	406.5	367.0100
Reliance Income Fund Retail Plan Half Yearly	279.8	12.3375
Sahara Income Fund-Dividend	12.2	11.7268
Sahara Income Fund-Growth	140.4	14.2429
Sundaram BNP Paribas Income Plus-Appreciation	177.2	10.5416
Sundaram BNP Paribas Income Plus-Dividend	242.0	10.2456
Tata Income Fund - Monthly	331.2	27.3359
Tata Income Fund - Qtrly	1442.6	10.7730
Tata Income Fund - Semi	1469.8	11.4985
Templeton India Income Fund - Dividend	18296.6	11.0227
Templeton India Income Fund - Growth	29172.5	28.8869
Income - Public		
BOB Income Fund - Dividend	12.6	13.2524

	Investment (Rs. Lakhs)	NAV(Rs.)
BOB Income Fund -Growth	31.5	13.2524
Canara Robeco Income - Bonus	2.5	12.9360
Canara Robeco Income - Growth	61.3	14.1577
Canara Robeco Income - Income	39.4	12.8785
LIC MF Bond Fund - Dividend	1377.5	10.3051
LIC MF Bond Fund - Growth	5338.1	21.9081
SBI Magnum Monthly Income Fund - Bonus	280.3	11.4536
SBI Magnum Income Fund - Bonus	1544.4	12.9196
SBI Magnum Income Fund - Dividend	4553.2	10.4983
SBI Magnum Income Fund - Growth	5890.0	18.0197
UTI Mahila Unit Scheme	8795.3	31.6295
UTI Monthly Income Scheme - Growth	10479.1	11.3644
UTI Monthly Income Scheme - Income	3953.0	15.4025
Balance - Private		
Birla Balance (D)	6039.6	20.7900
Birla Balance (G)	4127.9	31.2700
DSP Merill Lynch Balanced Fund (D)	33547.2	22.2130
DSP Merill Lynch Balanced Fund (G)	15381.2	48.9900
Franklin India Balanced Fund (D)	19590.6	27.9200
Franklin India Balanced Fund (G)	9708.4	37.3600
HDFC Balanced Fund - Dividend	6879.9	19.2150
ICICI Prudential Balanced Fund (D)	17925.1	13.5100
ICICI Prudential Balanced Fund (G)	18186.5	40.0900
ING Balanced Fund (D)	384.7	17.0000
ING Balanced Fund (G)	313.0	15.6700
J M Balanced Fund (Dividend)	5520.0	20.4649
J M Balanced Fund (Growth)	1279.1	26.9213
Kotak Balance	7577.0	27.7650
Principal Balanced Fund – Dividend	20227.8	17.6500
Principal Balanced Fund – Growth	1106.1	22.5400
Sundaram Balanced Fund	1317.3	16.8951
Sundaram BNP Balanced - Appreciation	2997.9	39.9339
Sundaram BNP Balanced - Dividend	1312.0	16.8951
Tata Balanced Fund - Dividend	7882.3	63.4298

	Investment (Rs. Lakhs)	NAV(Rs.)
Balance - Public		
Bank of Baroda Balanced - Dividend	52.9	29.2000
Bank of Baroda Balanced – Growth	27.0	28.9000
LIC Balanced – Plan A - Dividend	1287.8	11.8340
LIC Balanced – Plan C - Growth	1202.1	55.9893
LIC Unit Linked Insurance Scheme	156.2	10.2466
SBI Magnum Balanced Fund - Dividend	20856.2	28.1800
UTI Balanced Fund - Dividend	29746.0	15.0417
UTI Balanced Fund - Growth	73159.9	64.7600
Growth - Private		
Birla Advantage Fund-Dividend/ Reinvestment	37326.0	19.5048
Birla Index Fund – Growth	1873.7	50.4115
DBS Chola Growth Fund-Cumulative	1160.8	37.1800
DBS Chola Growth Fund-Quarterly Dividend	1210.5	12.8346
DSP Merrill Lynch Equity Fund - Growth	92595.7	45.3250
DSP Merrill Lynch Opportunities Fund-Growth	1946.5	69.1330
Escorts Growth Plan - Dividend	221.1	18.1702
Escorts Growth Plan - Growth	213.5	77.6022
HDFC Growth Fund - Growth	42393.7	180.7160
ICICI Pru FMCG Plan – Dividend	2263.6	33.5400
ICICI Prudential Growth Plan-Dividend Option	10940.0	22.5700
ICICI Prudential Growth Plan-Growth Option	32783.0	108.5800
JM Equity Fund - Dividend	4800.3	19.5457
JM Equity Fund - Growth	3388.2	43.5043
Kotak 30 - Growth	28428.7	92.6290
Reliance Growth Fund - Dividend Plan	264991.1	63.3600
Reliance Growth Fund - Growth Plan	5087.4	367.0100
Reliance Vision Fund - Dividend Plan	197279.6	229.8400
Sahara Growth Fund-Dividend	216.6	24.8040
Sahara Growth Fund-Growth	399.5	66.1816
Sundaram BNP Paribas Capex Opportunities Fund-Growth	71013.7	88.7096
Sundaram BNP Paribas Growth Fund-Dividend	9706.5	88.7096
Sundaram BNP Paribas Growth Fund-Growth	6371.3	88.7096

	Investment (Rs. Lakhs)	NAV(Rs.)
Tata Pure Equity Fund - Dividend	17721.0	79.8006
Tata Pure Equity Fund - Growth	14213.6	16.3832
Taurus Star Share	19819.3	56.8200
Templeton India Growth Fund-Dividend Plan	22120.4	103.6900
Templeton India Growth Fund-Growth Plan	10314.0	123.2100
Growth - Public		
Baroda Diversified Fund - Growth	3668.0	40.5200
Canara Robeco Expo Growth Plan	157.2	54.6700
Canara Robeco Expo Income Plan	2394.1	17.3100
LICMF Growth Fund - Dividend Option	186.6	10.0446
LICMF Growth Fund - Growth Option	6514.4	20.1896
SBI Magnum Equity Fund - Growth	25938.0	30.9000
SBI Magnum Multiplier Plus Scheme-93Dividend	71896.7	56.0900
SBI MSFU Contra - Dividend	115789.6	32.2300
SBI MSFU Contra- Growth	109891.9	15.3000
SBI MSFU IT	6127.7	15.3000
UTI - Equity Fund-Growth Option	164379.4	54.6700
UTI - Equity Fund-Income Option	3015.3	15.4025
ELSS - Private		
Birla Tax Plan 98	4270.0	236.5400
Escorts Tax Plan Dividend	327.0	16.5331
Escorts Tax Plan Growth	100.6	56.8361
Franklin Taxshield - Dividend	27379.0	150.5359
Franklin India Taxshield - Growth	23395.9	74.5809
ICICI Prudential Tax Plan-Dividend Option	38374.1	20.3600
ICICI Prudential Tax Plan-Growth Option	36805.2	101.1100
Principal Tax Saving fund	27224.8	101.5400
SaharaTax Gain-Growth	143.3	27.3124
Sundaram PNB Paribas Tax Saver OE Fund	26805.0	15.0245
Sundaram Taxsaver 98	45689.2	89.8329
Tata Tax Saving	14936.2	48.7965
Taurus Libra Taxshield 96	1163.8	27.6100

	Investment (Rs. Lakhs)	*NAV(Rs.)*
ELSS - Public		
Bob ELSS 96	1129.8	25.3600
Canara Robeco Equity Tax Saver	2878.9	20.2100
LICMF Taxplan-Dividend	2125.7	10.5844
LICMF Taxplan-Growth	1858.0	29.5622
SBI Magnum Taxgain Scheme 1993 - Dividend	255401.9	45.0200
UTI-Master Equity Plan Unit Scheme	26548.3	45.7500

Source: Compiled from www.amfiindia.com

BIBLIOGRAPHY

Books

Amling, Frederic, "Investments; An Introduction to analysis and Management", Englewood Cliff, Prentice Hall Inc., 1974.

Ariff &Johnson. "Unit Trusts and their performance, securities & stock pricing", Longman Singapore publishers (Pvt) Ltd, 1990.

Bansal, L.K., "Merchant Banking and Financial Services", Unistar Books, Chandigarh, 1997.

Bansal, L.K., "Mutual Funds: Management and Working", Deep and Deep Publications, New Delhi, 1997.

Barua, Samir K., Raghnathan V. and Jayant R., "Portfolio Management", Tata McGraw Hill, New Delhi, 1991.

Bhalla, V.K. and Tuteja S.K., "Investment Management", S. Chand & Company, New Delhi, 1994.

Bhalla, V.K., "Investment Management: Security analysis and Portfolio Management", S. Chand & Company, New Delhi, 1997.

Bolten, Steven E., "Cases in Security analysis and Portfolio Management", Holt, Rinehart and Winston, Inc., New York, 1993.

Brealey Richard, An Introduction to Risk and Return, Basil Blackwell, U.K., 1983.

Bruce, Brian R., "Quantitative International Investing: A Hand Book of Analytical and Modelling Techniques and Strategies", A Probus Guide to World Markets, McGraw Hill, Inc., 1990.

Chadra Prasanna, "The Investment Game: How to win?", Tata McGraw – Hill, New Delhi, 1992, 1995.

Coales, Rober C., "Investment Strategy", McGraw – Hill, inc., 1978.

Cohen, Jerome B., Zinbarg, Edward D. and Zeikel, Arthur, "Investment analysis and portfolio Management" Irwin, Inc., 1987.

Corner, D.C. and Stafford, D.C., "Open-End Investment Funds in the EEC and Switzerland, McMillan Press, Inc., 1977.

Cottle, Sidney, Murry, Roger F. and Block, Franke E., Graham and Dodd's Security Analysis", McGraw – Hill, Inc., 1989.

Ellis, Charles D., "Investment Policy: How to win losers Game", Irwin, Hoom Wood, Illinois, 1993.

Elton, Edwin, J. and Gruber, Martin J., "Modern Portfolio Theory and Investment, Analysis, John Wiley & Sons., Inc., 1994.

Fisher, Donald E., Jordon, Ronald J., "Security analysis and portfolio Management", Prentice Hall of India, New Delhi, 1995.

Francis, Jack Clark, "Investment : Analysis and Management", McGraw – Hill, Inc., 1986.

Francis, Jack Clark, "Management of Investment", McGraw – Hill, Inc., New Delhi, 1993.

Fredman, Albert J. and Wiles, Russ, "How Mutual Funds Work", Prentice Hall of India, New Delhi, 1993.

Friend Irwin, Blame Marshall and Crockett Jean, "Mutual Funds and Other Institutional Investors: A Twentieth Century Fund Study", McGraw – Hill, Inc., New York, 1970.

Friend, Irwin and Bicksler, James L., "Risk and Return in Finance'', Ballinger, Cambridge, 1977.

Frost, A.J., and Hayer D.P., ''A General Introduction to Institutional Investment", Heinemann, London, 1986.

Fuller, Russell J. and Farrell, Jr. James L., "Modern Investment and Security Analysis'', McGraw-Hill, Inc., 1987.

Graham, Dood D.L., and Cottle C., "Security Analysis: Principles and Techniques", McGraw-Hill, Inc., New York, 1962.

Griffeth Bill, "The Mutual Fund Masters", Vision Books, New Delhi, Probus Publishing Co., Chicago, 1995.

Grinold, Richard C. and Kahn, Ronald N., "Active Portfolio Management: Quantitative. Theory and Applications", Probus, Inc., 1995.

Gujarathi, Damodar N., "Basic Econometrics", Mc Graw Hill, New York, 2003.

Gupta, L.C., "Indian Share Owners: A Survey", Society for Capital Market Research and Development, New Delhi, 1994.

Gupta L.C., "Mutual Funds and Asset Preference", Society for Capital Market Research and Development, New Delhi, 1994.

Gupta, L.C., and Choudhury, Utpal K., "How Good are Mutual funds: The Household Investors' Perceptions", Society for Capital Market Research and Development, Delhi, 2001.

Gupta, O.P., "Stock, Market Efficiency and Prince Behaviour: The Indian Experience", Ed., Anmol Publications, New Delhi, 1989.

Gupta, S.P., "Statistical Methods", Sultan Chand and sons, New Delhi, 2006.

Haslem, John A., "The Investors Guide to Mutual Funds", Prentice Hall, Englewood, Cliffs, New Jersey, 1988.

Hobert, Dougall E., "Investments", Prentice Hall, Inc., Englewood Cliff, 1973.

Hsiu – Kwang Wu, Alan Zakon J., "Elements of Investments". Ed. Holt Rinehart and Winston, Inc., New York, 1965.

Jayadev, M., "Investment Policy and Performance of Mutual Funds", Kanishka Publishers and Distributors, New Delhi, 1998.

Kuchhal S.K., (1990), "Corporation Finance: Principles and Problems", (Chaitanya Publishing House, Allahabad

Kurt, Brouwer, "Mutual Funds: How to Invest with the Pros", John Wiley and Sons, Inc., New York, 1992.

Levy, Haim and Sarnat, Marshall, "Capital Investment and Financial Decisions", Prentice Hall, Inc., 1990.

Londerman, Jaffrey M., "Business Week Guide to Mutual Funds" McGraw-Hill, Inc., 1995.

Lorie, Jame and Brealey, Richard, "Modern Developments in Investment Management", ed., Dryden Press, Illinois, 1978.

Markowitz Harry, "Portfolio Selection: Efficient Diversification of Investments, New York, 1959.

Neal, L., "The Rise of Financial Capitalism: International Capital Markets in the Age of Reason", Cambridge: Cambridge University Press, 1990.

Reilly, Frank K., "Investments", Dryden Press, New York, 1982.

Renwick, Fred B., "Introduction to Investments and Finance", McMillan, New York, 1971.

Riley, J., "International Government Finance and the Amsterdam Capital Market 1740–1815", Cambridge: Cambridge University Press, 1980.

Sadhak H., "Mutual Funds in India: Marketing Strategies and Investments Practice", Response Books, Sage Publications, Inc., 1997.

Sahadevan, K.G., and Thirupalraju M., "Mutual Funds: Data, Interpretation and Analysis", Prentice Hall of India, New Delhi, 1997.

"Security Analysis and Portfolio Management Book of Readings, AICFAI – TMH Contemporary Management Series", Tata McGraw – Hall, New York, 1996.

Verma, J.C., Mutual Funds, New Delhi: Bharat Law House Pvt. Ltd., 1992.

William, Baumol J., Stephen, Goldfeld M., Lilli, Gordan A. and Michael, Kohen, F., The Economics of Mutual Funds Markets: Competition versus regulation, Boston: Kluwer Academic Publishers, 1989.

Hsiu-Kwang Wu, Alan J. Zaskon, ed. "Element of Investments: Selected Readings", Holt, Rinehart and Winston. Inc. 1965.

Journals

Adhikari, Umesh and Meenal Bhosale, Risk – Return Analysis of Mutual Fund Growth Schemes", Indian Management, August, 1994.

Aggarwal, Navdeep and Gupta, Mohit, "Performance of Mutual Funds in India",Icfai Journal of Applied Finance, 13 (9), 2007.

Ang, James S. and Chua, Jess H, "Composite Measures for the Evaluation of Investment Performance", Journal of Financial and Qualitative Analysis, 2 1979.

Anagol, Malti, "Role of Self-regulatory Organization in Mutual Fund Industry in India" Chartered Financial Analysis, No.5, 1992.

Ankrim, Ernest M., "Risk Adjusted Performance Attribution", Financial Analysis Journal, No.2, 1992.

Ansari M.N.A., "Mutual Funds in India, Emerging Trends" Chartered Accountants, No.2, 1993.

Arditti, Fred D, "Another look at Mutual Fund Performance", Journal of Financial and Quantitative Analysis, No.3, 1971.

Badrinath, Radha, "Contra Fund in India: A Quick Look", Portfolio Organiser, January, 2008.

Barras, Laurent, Scaillet , O. and Wermers, Russ R., "False Discoveries in Mutual Fund Performance: Measuring Luck in Estimated Alphas", Robert H. Smith School Research Paper No. RHS 06-043, Available at http://ssrn.com/abstract=869748, September, 2008.

Barua, SK., and Verma, JR., "Master Share: A Bonanza for Large Investors", Vikalpa, Jan-March, 1991.

Bauer, Rob, Otten, Roger and Koedijk, Kess C.G., "International Evidence on Ethical Mutual Fund Performance an Investment Style" Journal Banking and Finance, Vol.29, 2005.

Blake, Christopher R., Elton. Edwin J, and Gruber, martin J., "The Performance of Bond Mutual Funds", Journal of Business, No.3, 1993.

Bodla, B.S., and Garg, Ashish, "Performance of Mutual Funds in India – Empirical Study of Growth Schemes", GITAM Journa lf Management 5 (4), October-December, 2007.

Busse, - Jeffrey. A., "Volatility Timing in Mutual Funds; Evidence from Daily Returns" Review of Financial Studies: 12(5), Winter, 1999.

Cai, Jun and Yamada, K.C.Chan Takeshi, "The Performance of Japanese Mutual Funds", The Review of Financial Studies, Vol.10, No. 2, 1997.

Carhart, Mark M., "On Persistence in Mutual Fund Performance", The Journal of Finance, March, 1997.

Carlson, Robert S., "Aggregate Performance of Mutual Funds, 1960-69", Journal of Financial and Quantitative Analysis, 5 (1970), pp. 1-32.

Chander, Ramesh, "Performance appraisal of Mutual Funds in India", Finance India, 14 (4), December, 2002.

Chang, Eric C. and Lewellen, Wilbur G., "Market – Timing and Mutual Fund Investment Performance", Journal of Business, No.1, 1984.

Choi, Yoon K., "Relative Performance Evaluation and Incentive Structure", Journal of Business, Vol.79, No. 2, 2006.

Chordia Tarun, "The Structure of Mutual Fund Changes". Journal of Financial Economics, No.1, 1996.

Coggin, Daniel T., Fabozzi, Frank J. and Rahman Shafiqur, "The Investment Performance of U.S. Equity Pension Fund Managers". An Empirical Investigation", Journal of Business, No. 3, 1993.

Connor, Gregory and Korajczyk, Robert A., "Performance Measurement with the Arbitrage Pricing Theory: A new Framework for Analysis", Journal of Financial Economics No. 3, 1986.

Cornell, Bradford, "Asymmetric Information and Portfolio Performance Measurement", Journal of Financial Economics, No.3, 1979.

Cover Story, Mutual Fund Insight, "Low Gain but Low Risk", February 15- March 14, 2008.

Cumby, Robert E. and Glen, Jack D., "Evaluating the Performance of International Mutual Funds", Journal of Finance, No.2, 1990.

Dahlquist, Magnus, Engstorm, Stefan and Soderhind, Paul, "Performance and Characteristics of Swedish Mutual Funds", Journal of Financial and Quantitative Analysis, 35 (3), September, 2000.

Davanzo, Lawrence E., and Nesbit, Stephen L., "Performance Fees for Investment Management"' Financial Analysts Journal, 1987.

Detzler, Miranda – Lam, "The Performance of Global Bond Mutual Funds", Journal of Banking and Finance; 123(8), August, 1999.

Elton, Edwin, J., Gruber, Martin J. and Blake, Christopher R., "The Persistence of Risk-Adjusted Mutual Fund Performance", Journal of Business, No.2 1996.

Fabozzi, Frank J., Francis, Jack C. and Lee, Chang F., "Generalized Functional Form for Mutual Fund Returns", Journal of Financial and Qualitative Analysis, No.2, 1980.

Fama, Euegen F., "Components of investment Performance", Journal of Finance, No.27, 1972.

Ferron, Wayne E, and Warther, Vincent A., "Evaluating Funds Performance in a Dynamic Market", Financial Analysts Journal, Vol. 52, No.6, 1996.

Friend I., Brown F., Herman E. and Vickers D., "A study of Mutual Funds", The American Economic Review, 54 (2), March, 1964.

Friend, Irwin, Brown, E. Herman Edward, C., and Vickers Douglas, "A Study of Mutual Funds: Investment Policy and Investment Company Performance" in Hsiu-Kwang Wu, Alan J. Zaskon, ed. "Element of Investments: Selected Readings", Holt, Rinehart and Winston. Inc. 1965.

''Fundamentals", Reliance Mutual Fund, March, 2008.

Gangadhar, V., "The changing Pattern of Mutual Funds in India", Management Accountant, No.12, 1992.

Grinblatt, Mark and Titman Sheridan, "Mutual Fund Performance: An Analysis of Quarterly Portfolio Holdings" Journal of Business, No.3, 1989.

Grinblatt, Mark and Titman Sheridan, "A Study of Mutual Fund Return and Performance Evaluation Techniques", Journal of Financial and Quantitative Analysis, No.3, 1994.

Gruber, Martin, J., "Another Puzzle: The Growth of Activity Managed Mutual Funds", Journal of Financial Review, No.3, 1996.

Guha Deb, Soumya, "Performance of Indian Equity Mutual Funds vis-a-vis their Style Benchmarks", The Icfai Journal of Applied Finance, Vol. 14, No. 1, January, 2008.

Gupta, Amitabh, "Investment Performance of Indian Mutual Funds: An Empirical Study", Finance India, Vol.XIV No.3, Sept. 2002.

Gupta, Manak C., "The Mutual Fund Industry and its Comparative Performance", Journal of Financial and Quantitative Analysis, No.6, 1974.

Gupta O.P., and Sehgal, Sanjay, "Investment Performances of Mutual Funds", Journal of Financial Review, No.39, 1998.

Gupta O.P., Gupta, Amitabh, "Performance Evaluation of Selected Indian Mutual Fund Schemes: Empirical Study", The Icfai Journal of Applied Finance, 10 (3), 2004.

Guy, James R F., "The Performance of British Investment Trust Industry", Journal of Finance, No.33, 1978.

Hendricks Darryll, Patel Jeyendu, Zeekhauser Richard, "Hot Hands in Mutual funds: Short-Run Persistent of Relative Performance" Journal of Finance, No.1, 1993.

Hendrickson, Roy D., "Market Timing and Mutual Fund Performance: An Empirical Investigation: Journal of Business, No.1, 1984.

Hendrickson, Roy D and Merton, Robert C., "On Market Timing and Investment Performance II: Statistical Procedures for Evaluating Forecasting Skills", Journal of Business, No.4, 1981.

Huang, Jennifer, Wei, Kelsey D., and Yan, Hong, "Participation costs and the Sensitivity of Fund flows to Past performance", Journal of Finance, May, 62, (3), 2007.

"Investmap", Fund Fact Sheet, Sundaram BNP Paribas, March, 2008.

Ippolito, Richard a., "Efficiency with Costly Information: A Study of Mutual Fund Performance, 1965-1984", The Quarterly Journal of Economics, February, 1989.

Jaideep Sarkar, and Majumdar, Sudipata, "Performance Evaluation of Mutual Funds in India", NMIS Management Review Vol. VI No. 2, (July – Dec, 1994.

Jensen, Michael C., "The Performance of Mutual Funds, 1948-67", Journal of Finance, No.23, 1968.

Jobson, J.D. and Korkie, Bob M. "Performance Hypothesis Testing With the Sharpe and Treynor Measure", Journal of Finance, No.4, 1981.

Kane, Alex and Marks Gray, "Performance Evaluation of Market-Timers: Theory and Evidence", Journal of Financial and Quantitative Analysis, No.4 1988.

Kaura, Mohinder N. and Jayadev, M., "Performance of Growth Oriented Mutual Funds: An Evaluation". The ICFAI Journal of Applied Finance, I (1), January, 1995.

Keswan I Abnel and Stolin, David, "Which money is Smart? Mutual Fund Buys and Sells of Individual and Institutional Investors", Journal of Finance, February, 63, (1), 2008.

Khorana Ajay, "Top Management Turnover – An Empirical Investigation of Mutual Fund Mangers", Journal of Financial Economics, No.3, 1996.

Khorana, Ajay, "Performance Changes Following Top Management Turnover: Evidence from Open-end Mutual Funds", Journal of Financial Quantitative Analysis, 36 (3), September, 2001.

Khorana, Ajay, Henri Servaes, B.C., Peter Tufanod, E., "Explaining the size of the mutual fund industry around the world", Journal of Financial Economics, October, 2005.

Klemosky, Robert C., "he Bias in Composite Performance Measures", Journal of Financial and Quantitative Analysis, No.8, 1973.

Kon, Stanley J., "The Market-Timing Performance of Mutual Funds Mangers" Journal of Business, No.3, 1983.

Kon, Stanley J., and Jen, Frank C., "Estimation of Time-Varying Systematic Risk and Performance of Mutual Fund Portfolios: An application of Switching Regression", The Journal of Finance, No.3, 1978.

Lee, Cheng – Few and Rahman Shafiqur, "Market Timing, Selectivity and Mutual Fund Performance: An Empirical Investigation" Journal of Business, No.21, 1990.

Levy, Robert A., "Measurement of Investment Performance", The Journal of Financial and Quantitative Analysis, No. 3, 1968.

Lo, Andrew W., "Where Do Alphas Come From?: A New Measure of the Value of Active Investment Management', Available at http://ssrn.com/abstract=985127, May, 2008.

Malkiel, Burton G., "The Valuation of Closed – end Investment Company Shares", Journal of Finance, No. 3 1977.

Malkiel, Burton G., "Returns from Investing in Equity Mutual Funds. 1971 to 1991", Journal of Finance, No. 2, 1995.

Markowitz, Harry, "Portfolio Selection", Journal of Finance, 7 (1), March, 1952.

McDonald, John G., "Objectives and Performance of Mutual Funds, 1960- 69", Journal of Financial and Quantitative Analysis, No. 9 1974.

Meyer Jack, "Further Applications oaf Stochastic Dominance to Mutual Fund Performance", Journal of Financial of Quantitative Analysis, No.12, 1977.

Mohinder N. Kaura, M. Jayadev, "Performance of Growth Oriented Mutual Funds: An Evaluation". The ICFAI Journal of Applied Finance Vol. I. No. 1, January, 1995.

Muralidhar, S, "MFs match FII's financial night in stock markets" The Financial Express, February 4, 2000.

Muthappan, P.K., and Damodharan E., "Risk-adjusted Performance Evaluation of Indian Mutual Fund Schemes", Finance India, 20, (3), September, 2006.

Obaidullah, M., and Ganesan, Sridhar, "Do Mutual Funds in India provide abnormal returns: Chartered Financial Analysts, No.5, 1991.

Panwar, Sharad and Madhumathi, R., "Characteristics and Performance Evaluation of Selected Mutual Funds in India", accessed from http://papers.ssrn.com/sol3/papers.cfm, on 11.03.2008.

Pastor, Lubos and Stambaugh, Robert F., "Investing in Equity Mutual Funds", Journal of Financial Economics, 63 (3), 2002.

Prther, Laurie, Bewrtin, William J., and Henker, Thomas, ''Mutual Funds characteristics, Managerial Attributes and Fund Performance", review of Financial; Economics, 13 (4), 2004.

Ravindran M., and Rao, Narayan S., "Performance Evaluation of Indian Mutual Funds", SSRN.com Article No.107, 2003.

Rouwenhorst, K. Geert, "The Origins of Mutual Funds", Yale International Centre for Finance Working Paper No. 04-48, December, 2004, Accessed at www.ssrn.com

Saha, Ashish and Murthy, Y. Shree Rama, "Managing Mutual Funds: Some Critical Issues", Pranjan, No.1, 1994.

Santini, Donald N. and Aber Jack W., "Investor Response to Mutual Fund Policy variables", Financial Review, No.4, 1996.

Sarkar, A.K., "Performance Evaluation of Mutual Funds" Management Accountant, No.9, 1991.

Sarkar, A.K. "Should We Invest In Mutual Funds", Management Accountant, No.10, 1992.

Shah Ajay, Thomas, Susan, "Performance Evaluation of Professional Portfolio Management in India". A paper prepared by CMIE, 10, April, 1994.

Sharpe, William F. "Mutual Fund Performance". Journal of Business, 39, 1966, Supplement.

Sharpe, William F., "Adjusting for Risk in Portfolio Performance Measurement," *Journal of Portfolio Management*, Winter, 1975.

Shashikant Uma, "Money Market Mutual Funds: Scope and Opportunities", Chartered Financial Analyst, No.4, 1993.

Shukla, Ravi and Singh, Sandeep, "Are CFA Charter – holders Better Equity Fund Mangers", Financial Analysts Journal, No.2, 199€4.

Simonson, Donald G., "The Speculative Behaviour of Mutual Funds," Journal of Finance, No.2, 1972.

Smith, Keith V. and Tito, Dennis A., "Risk-return Measures of Post-Portfolio Performance", Journal of Financial and Qualitative Analysis, No.4, 1969.

Sodhi H.J., and Jain P.K., "Financial Performance of Equity Mutual Funds: Empirical Evidence from India", Dias Technology Review, 1 (2), 2004.

Thomson, Rex, "The Information Contents of Discounts Manage and Premiums on Closed – End Funds Shares", Journal of Financial Economics, No.2-3, 1978.

Treynor, Jack l., and Mazuy, Kay K., "Can Mutual Funds Outguess the Markets". Harvard Business Review, No. 44, 1966.

Treynor, Jack L., "How to Rate Management of Investment funds", Harvard Business Review, No. 43, 1965.

Tripathy, Nalini Prava, "Market Timing Abilities and Mutual Fund Performance- An Empirical Investigation into Equity Linked Saving Schemes", Vilakshan, XIMB Journal of Management, 2007.

Tripathy, Nalini Prava, "An Empirical Analysis of Performance Evaluation of Mutual Funds in India-A Study on Equity Linked Schemes" The ICFAI Journal of Applied Finance, July, 2004.

Warther, Vincent A., "Aggregate Mutual Fund Flows and Security Returns", Journal of Financial Economics, No.39, 1995.

Wermers, Rus, "Mutual Fund Performance: An Empirical Decomposition into Stock-picking Talent, Style, Transaction Costs and Expenses", The Journal of Finance, August, 2000.

Williamson, Peter J., "Measurement and Forecasting of Mutual Fund Performance: Choosing an Investment Strategy", Financial Analysis Journal, No.28, 1972.

Ph.D. THESES

Gali, Kanti Kumar, "Mutual Funds' Performance Appraisal ad Organizational Factors: an Analysis Based on Risk-Adjusted Returns", unpublished PhD. Thesis, IIM – Bangalore, 1995.

Govindrajan K., "Performance of Public Sector and Private Sector Mutual Funds in India, Unpublished Ph.D. Thesis, Annamalai University, Annamalai Nagar, 2001.

Shome, Sujan, "A Study of the Performance of Indian Mutual Funds", Unpublished Ph.D. Thesis, Study, Jhansi University, 1994.

REPORTS

- Annual Reports and Offer Documents of Various Mutual Funds.
- Currency and Finance, Reserve Bank of India, 1987-88 to 1999-2000.
- Reserve Bank of India Guidelines for Mutual Funds, July' 1989.
- Securities and Exchange Board of India, Annual Report, 1994-95.
- Economic Survey, Ministry of Finance, Govt. of India, various years.

WEB SITES

www.amfiindia.com

www.finmin.nic.in

www.econstats.com

www.icmrindia.org

www.mutualfundsinindia.com

www.rbi.org.in

www.sebi.gov.in

www.ssrn.com

www.valueresearchonline.com

INDEX